MW00461264

MARK

MARK

A Commentary for Bible Students

DAVID SMITH

Copyright © 2007 by Wesleyan Publishing House
Published by Wesleyan Publishing House
Indianapolis, Indiana 46250
Printed in the United States of America

ISBN: 978–0–89827–344–1

WESLEYAN BIBLE COMMENTARY SERIES

GENERAL PUBLISHER
Donald D. Cady

EXECUTIVE EDITOR
David W. Holdren, D.D., S.T.D.

EDITORIAL ADVISORY COMMITTEE

Joseph D. Allison, M.Div.
Coordinator of Communications and
Publishing
Church of God Ministries

Ray E. Barnwell
Illinois District Superintendent
The Wesleyan Church

Barry L. Callen, M.Div., M.Th., D.Rel., Ed. D.
University Professor of Christian Studies
Emeritus, Anderson University
Special Assistant to General Director, Church
of God Ministries

Ray Easley, M.Div., Ed.D.
Vice President of Academic Affairs
Wesley Biblical Seminary

Maj. Dorothy Hitzka
National Consultant for Christian Education
The Salvation Army

Arthur Kelly
Coordinator of Christian Education and
Congregational Life
Church of God Ministries

Stephen J. Lennox, Ph.D.
Dean of the Chapel; Professor of Bible
Indiana Wesleyan University

Bonnie J. Perry
Director
Beacon Hill Press of Kansas City

Dan Tipton, D.Min.
General Superintendent (retired)
Churches of Christ in Christian Union

John Van Valin
Free Methodist Pastor
Indianapolis, Indiana

EDITORS
Lawrence W. Wilson, M.Div.
Managing Editor

Stephen J. Lennox, Ph.D.
Theological Editor

Darlene Teague, M.Div.
Senior Editor

To Angie: the woman who introduced me to the fullness of life in Christ
and each day teaches me what it means to "follow Him."

ευθυ.φ αϖνε,βλεψεν και. ηϖκολου,θει αυϖτω/| εϖν τη/| ο δω/|ᶺ
(Mark 10:52b)

CONTENTS

EXECUTIVE EDITOR'S PREFACE

L ife change. That, we believe, is the goal of God's written revelation. God has given His written Word so that we might know Him and become like Him—holy, as He is holy.

Life change is also the goal of this book, a volume in the Wesleyan Bible Commentary Series. This series has been created with the primary aim of promoting life change in believers by applying God's authoritative truth in relevant, practical ways. This commentary will impact Bible students with fresh insight into God's unchanging Word. Read it with your Bible in hand.

A second purpose of this series is to assist laypersons and pastors in their teaching ministries. Anyone called to assist others in Christian growth and service will appreciate the practical nature of these commentaries. Writers were selected based on their ability to soundly interpret God's Word and apply that unchanging truth in fresh, practical ways. Each biblical book is explained paragraph by paragraph, giving the reader both the big picture and sufficient detail to understand the meaning of significant words and phrases. Their results of scholarly research are presented in enough detail to clarify, for example, the meaning of important Greek or Hebrew words, but not in such a way that readers are overwhelmed. This series will be an invaluable tool for preaching, lesson preparation, and personal or group Bible study.

The third aim of this series is to present a Wesleyan-Arminian interpretation of Scripture in a clear and compelling fashion. Toward that end, the series has been developed with the cooperative effort of scholars, pastors, and church leaders in the Wesleyan, Nazarene, Free Methodist, Salvation Army, Church of God (Anderson), Churches of Christ in Christian Union, Brethren in Christ, and United Methodist denominations. These volumes present reliable interpretation of biblical texts in the tradition of John Wesley, Adam Clarke, and other renowned interpreters.

Throughout the production of this series, authors and editors have approached each Bible passage with this question in mind: How will my life change when I fully understand and apply this scripture?

Let that question be foremost in your mind also, as God speaks again through His Word.

DAVID W. HOLDREN

INTRODUCTION TO MARK

Welcome to the "Gospel Story of Mark." This commentary will take that opening line seriously. Mark is "good news" housed in a story. Life in Christ as described in Mark is a process whereby one is asked to ponder seriously the words and the works of Jesus. The lessons are often cloaked in parabolic form (4:2, 33–34), which demands careful interpretation. One must listen intently, and even then Jesus' truth may escape those closest to Him (8:17–21). Readers must look carefully and examine each of Jesus' miracles for their revelatory quality. Yet, in the end, we still may only see partially what is transpiring as Jesus ushers in the kingdom of God in our midst (8:22–26). Though Jesus stops to explain His words to the disciples, His answers leave them (and us) just as much in the dark (4:10–12; 8:4–41). People's confusion leads to Jesus' words and deeds being rejected outright, not just by His opponents (2:6–7; 3:22–30; 14:61–64), but also by His family (3:20–21, 31–35) and His disciples (8:31–33; 14:10–11, 50). Employing the words of the fourth Gospel, "On hearing it [His teaching], many of his disciples said, 'This is a hard teaching. Who can accept it?'" (John 6:60). The answer to this dilemma of how to hear and understand Jesus is not found exclusively in the content of the book of Mark. It is in the process of walking and following Jesus throughout the entirety of His journey, beginning in the rural villages of Galilee down to His final hours in the religious center of Jerusalem. One does not "know Mark" by selecting a few of its key verses and committing them to memory. No, "knowing Mark" is a wonderful yet slow discipleship process whereby day after day we are shaped and transformed to think less like men and women and more like God (8:33). But in the end, that will not take place through mere human intellect or an act of the will. Mark's story climaxes on the outskirts of Jerusalem, as countless onlookers mock the very words and work of Jesus, as His life mission is summed up on the cross. Humanity reviles what He stands for and seemingly would choose any alternative to following a suffering Messiah. Yet in the end, one man, a Gentile centurion who was personally responsible for placing Jesus on the cross, cries out, "Surely this man was the Son of God!" (15:39). All the angels in heaven must have rejoiced that someone has finally seen through the blindness of human vision and heard His words for what they truly represent. But wait, they have killed Him. What hope is there for a civilization that has spurned the very ambassador of their salvation and mocked Him in both life and death? Come, let me invite you to enter the story of Mark; to listen, to watch, and to process the way God, through His Son, Jesus, will speak words of life into you. This is not a story for the faint of heart, for it paints humanity for who we are: rebels. But come both to discover ourselves and the wondrous man called Jesus.

HOW IS MARK DIFFERENT FROM PAUL?

The story of Mark is written differently than other genres of the New Testament. For example, in the first letter to the Corinthians, Paul states the core of the gospel this way:

> For Christ did not send me to baptize, but to preach the gospel—not with words of human wisdom, lest the cross of Christ be emptied of its power. For the message of the cross is foolishness to those who are perishing, but to us who are being saved it is the power of God. (1 Cor. 1:17–18)

Pauline letters such as 1 Corinthians, Romans, and Galatians proclaim truth in propositional form, directly and succinctly. The outline is clear; in most of Paul's letters, the first half is comprised of theology and the second half is ethics. Simply put, the assumption is that right thinking about Christ will lead to right living for Christ. For example, Romans 1–11 is a lengthy discussion about the righteousness of God as displayed in His Son, Jesus Christ, (theology—right thinking). Chapters 12–16 are a lengthy propositional commitment to Christ (ethics—right living). The right living section begins with these well-known words:

Therefore, I urge you, brothers, in view of God's mercy, to offer your bodies as living sacrifices, holy and pleasing to God—this is your spiritual act of worship. Do not conform any longer to the pattern of this world, but be transformed by the renewing of your mind. Then you will be able to test and approve what God's will is—his good, pleasing and perfect will. (Rom. 12:1–2, italics added)

This makes application of Paul's expectations for a Christian quite straightforward. Read and unpack chapters 1–11, and then when you reach the "therefore" in 12:1, simply do what it says. All we must do is to follow the propositions that are often found in imperatives or commands. Moreover, though the New Testament letters are written to ancients who are separated from us by two thousand years of linguistic and cultural history, they still seem to be written to each of us. When we encounter the text of 1 Corinthians or Romans devotionally, we interject ourselves into each admonition of Paul that begins with the pronoun "you." "Bless those who persecute you; bless and do not curse" (Rom. 12:14). These are words to us, right here and right now. Application seems so simple.

If the application of Paul's writings seems straightforward, a commentary on the gospel of Mark will at times take a bit more work. One reason is that many Wesleyan-Arminians (and most Protestants for that matter) were brought into the faith, weaned if you will, as "Pauline people." Maybe another way to express it is that modern western evangelical Christians are propositional people at the core. Our lives are oriented around the Word and we are warm-hearted, obedient folk. We often say in daily prayer, "God, simply tell me what your expectations of me are and I will wholly submit." To test this theory, simply reflect on what passages you have memorized. Are they the lengthy passages from the gospel narratives or are they predominantly commands and promises from Paul's letters?[1] For the most part, at the center we are Pauline disciples. In our homes and in our churches we certainly teach the Bible stories of Abraham, Moses, Elijah, Daniel, and Jesus. But often when it comes to issues of Christian ethics and personal holiness, we turn to the clarity of principles and precepts, often arguing that precepts trump story.

In our fast-paced, results-oriented world, we are often looking for a biblical shortcut to a lifetime of discipleship. The classic disciplines of the church that look to practicing spiritual formation over time are out.[2] The Christian Church has become a casualty of the instant-gratification society we wish to evangelize.

Please, do not hear the wrong message. I love Paul. What I am sketching for you is a picture that we, as evangelicals, may actually be disconnecting Paul (and his call to the life of scriptural holiness) from the story that grounds it in the life and times of Jesus. Behind all of Paul's preaching lies the *story* of God's faithful walk with Israel,[3] specifically the climax of this story in the death and resurrection of Jesus. In the background of every propositional truth in Paul, or in life for that matter, lies a story that cries to be heard.

The real problem with the propositional or formulaic system of belief is that by nature, we are people of story. We may claim to live in a world of propositions; we may testify to being principle centered. But in actuality, propositions are simply a shorthand way to tell our story. So, I welcome you to the story of Jesus, as told by Mark.

THREE PRELIMINARY ISSUES FOR A WESLEYAN COMMENTARY

MARK IS ABOUT WHOLENESS, NOT JUST FORGIVENESS OF SIN

If we are to read Mark as story and appropriate it for a life of faith in a Wesleyan tradition, we must consider three preliminary issues. First, let me correct this fallacy: *the Gospels are principally about salvation and forgiveness, but to find any discussion of sanctification and personal holiness we must look to the letters of Paul.* Nothing could be further from the truth. As a matter of fact, salvation and forgiveness were already available via the old covenant. Sacrifices could be made daily at the Temple to eliminate ritual uncleanness, and the Day of Atonement made available forgiveness to the entire nation of Israel. Moreover, the book of Leviticus, often quoted by Jesus, is quite simply a manual for the pursuit of personal and corporate holiness within the Jewish community. However, the Gospels in general and Mark in particular portray salvation and holiness housed in a story. They are not *something* to be pursued but rather *someone* to be followed. Salvation and holiness are not duties to be performed in a prescribed manner but a life to be lived in a purposeful direction. They are a call to utter abandonment of self (8:34–38) and to service of others (9:35; 10:42–45).

Additionally, in Mark the disciples (and we) gain a firsthand understanding of the nature of sin. It is not a commodity that can be remedied by the ritual washing of hands (7:1–4). Rather, sin so corrupts and permeates a person's body and mind that it becomes a part of every action and thought. For example, Jesus carefully instructs that "nothing outside a man can make him 'unclean'" (7:14–16). In another place, following Peter's rejection of Jesus' mission of suffering and death (8:31–32), Jesus squarely identifies that source of those rebellious thoughts: "'Get behind me, Satan!' he said. 'You do not have in mind the things of God, but the things of men'" (8:33). The blackness of people's hearts (often labeled as "hardness" in Mark, 6:52; 8:17) is the source of our blindness to what Jesus does and our deafness to what He says. The cure He offers is both radical and at times nonsensical. He must suffer and die "as a ransom for many" (meaning "for all" in ancient Jewish thought, 10:45).

Though how the atonement actually works to carry out such a radical transformation in the human heart is "fleshed out" in story as a whole; specifically in the climactic passion narrative (chapters 14–16). The closer Jesus comes to the cross, faithful followers as predicted fall away (14:27) one by one, until in the final moments on the cross, all have abandoned Him. Utterly alone, Jesus' last moments seem to show He has failed in His mission to usher in the kingdom of God (1:14–15). No repentant people are seen anywhere. There is even a perception that God himself has turned a deaf ear (only a perception; see commentary for full discussion on Jesus' cry from the cross, 15:34). Then Jesus dies. The wording is simple and seemingly ineffective: "Jesus breathed his last" (15:37). However, two quite different results are reported. First, "the curtain in the temple was torn in two from top to bottom" (15:38). Access to God has now been made fully available (see Heb. 9:11–12; 10:19–23). One might imagine that this imagery means that we can now approach God. True, but it also carries the connotation that a holy God now has full access to His created world. Just as in the "tearing of the heavens" and the descent of the Holy Spirit upon Jesus at His baptism (1:11), at this strategic moment another "tearing"[4] has taken place, and God is loose on the world to empower us with the same newness of life that directed Jesus' life.

The second result of Jesus' ignominious death is found in the confession of the centurion: "Surely this man was the Son of God!" (15:39). As will be argued later in the commentary, this confession has been the goal of the gospel of Mark from the outset: to have humanity recognize what all of creation has already known—Jesus is God's Son.

It was what the centurion "heard" and "saw" that generated his confession. Throughout the gospel of Mark, the human dilemma of sin has been described using the key words "deafness" (4:11–12; 8:17–18) and "blindness." The great discipleship training that takes place in chapters 8–10 is bracketed by the two healings of blind men (8:22–26 and 10:46–52). Ironically, the first to proclaim Jesus as God's Son is not a disciple who walked, ate, and listened to countless hours of instruction. No, it was a centurion whose only real background was to *hear* Jesus' cry and to *see* how He suffered and died (15:39). The transforming message of Mark's gospel story is that no one can find a cure for the human heart dilemma without going through the Cross of Jesus. It is not our heritage that will bring us to salvation. It is not our intellectual prowess that will cause us to recognize the greatness of Jesus. Rather, we find our sole hope for the complete transformation of our lives and loves in the death of Jesus.

MARK IS ABOUT A LIFETIME OF FOLLOWING, NOT JUST ONE-TIME REPENTANCE

Second, if we are to read and live the gospel story, we may need to adopt a new vocabulary. It may be familiar, but not under the heading of salvation and personal holiness. Paul employs the common terms "sanctified," "filled with the Spirit," and "live by the Spirit." In addition, throughout the last century the primary agenda of the evangelical church could be summed up in a three-word definition: "repent and believe." Though these are Jesus' words, He almost never uses them in the same sort of formulaic structure as we have done. In the gospel of Mark, the verb "repent" only occurs twice. First, in Jesus' opening remarks: "The time has come. . . . The kingdom of God is near. Repent and believe the good news!" (1:14–15). The second time is when the disciples go out in similar fashion two by two proclaiming "that people should repent" (6:12).

What terms best define the call of Jesus upon the lives of individuals in the Gospels? What language do Jesus and Mark use to call individuals to salvation and holiness? Two texts will be our lexical starting point. First, Mark 1:17–18. "'Come, *follow* me,' Jesus said, 'and I will make you fishers of men.' At once they left their nets and *followed* him" (italics added).

Literally, Jesus says, "Come, behind Me." This initial call is simply one of location. "Place yourself right in line with me," Jesus says, "and walk." Their response was immediate, and they followed Him. The language of the New Testament, Greek, is a highly inflected language with subtle nuances that reveal profound insights. Most verbs in Greek take a direct object in the accusative case. The word "followed," however, takes a direct object in the dative case. For among other things, the dative case describes a noun not as an entity but with reference to its location. Thus, the response of the disciples is in obedience to both the person and the place of Jesus. He says, "Come *behind* Me." The disciples "follow *to* Him."

This initial call of Jesus also carries with it theological content. Jesus says that if you follow, "I will make you fishers of men." In our contemporary world, that certainly is heard as a call to evangelism. Yet Jesus' original disciples may have interpreted it slightly differently. For the imagery of "fishing for men" in the Old Testament is not grace-oriented, but resounds with divine judgment. Jeremiah 16:10–18 contains an ominous warning for those who disobey the Lord. The same is true with the "fishing" metaphors in Amos 4:2 and Habakkuk 1:14–17. It is no blessing to be caught as a fish by God. It is highly likely that the disciples viewed their role as assisting God in passing judgment on the unrepentant Jews and the Gentile defilers of the land.

The second text worth benchmarking for a new gospel vocabulary of salvation and holiness is 8:34, for it radically reorients the disciples with a new meaning to their call; not one as purveyors of judgment but recipients of self-denial. "If anyone would *come after me*, he must deny himself and take up his cross and *follow me*" (italics added). In the verses immediately preceding this passage, Jesus has just taught, for the first time in Mark, that suffering and death will become a major element in His ministry (8:31). Peter, as is his nature, has reacted impulsively, and he rebuked Jesus (8:32), obviously hearing the teaching of Jesus through a distorted (unredeemed) mind. Jesus then counter rebukes Peter with these notorious words: "Get behind me, Satan! . . . You do not have in mind the things of God, but the things of men" (8:33). Immediately after that Jesus gives His ultimate call of discipleship (note: in the Greek, the words are identical to the former rebuke). If anyone will "get behind Me," self-denial and personal cross bearing must join forces with the action of following (8:34). No longer is discipleship determined by mere location as it might have been assumed in the call of Jesus in 1:14–15. Now, Jesus has made it clear that discipleship content (a correct Christological understanding of who Jesus is) must be integrated into the journey. Disciples are being taken in a clearly predetermined direction, to Jerusalem and specifically to the Cross. The vocabulary of "repent and believe" is now being recast in what might be called more accurately "follower-ship." This is a call of full commitment to a person (Jesus) and a direction (Jerusalem, self-denial, suffering). Simply, it is a call to that which is "other than us." Everything logically points us to run in the opposite direction while Jesus stands facing Jerusalem (Luke 9:51). The gospel of Mark is saying that salvation and holiness are defined by our following Him on a journey filled with elements that most humans flee in fear. And in this Gospel they often do.

KEY IDEAS

SALVATION AND HOLINESS

Justification (He brought us out)	Sanctification (He brought us in)
What Christ does for us	What the Spirit does in us
Removes the guilt of sin	Breaks the power of sin
A judicial act in the mind of God	An inward change in the heart of man
Forgives our sin	Cleanses our sin
Positionally holy	Actually holy

Yet if we will risk life to fulfill this call to commitment, the promise is for a transformation so complete that we will actually take on the mind of God and see things from His perspective (8:33).

MARK IS ABOUT READING THE WHOLE STORY, NOT JUST PART

The third and final issue that will assist us in experiencing the gospel as story is that we must discuss the entire story of Mark. It is best understood if it is read and interpreted as a whole. However, our modern devotional approach of reading a few verses and asking, "How does this apply to me?" may actually work against this. Let me use a love letter as an example. No one receiving a letter from a loved one would only read one paragraph a day just to savor the moment and make it last. No! We read it in one sitting and then possibly go back to reread it later.

With that in mind, this commentary will attempt to integrate the parts of Mark's story into the scripted whole. Most sections will begin with a brief discussion of the overall themes and how carefully Mark is crafting a story that is moving toward a climax at the cross. Moreover, it will be the position of this commentary that if you read only a selected few passages, you may actually come to a very different conclusion than the intention of the Gospel writer. Thus, if Mark is indeed the inspired author, having his finger on the pulse of Christ, we ought to strive with all our body, soul, mind, and strength to discover what is on his mind regarding the life, teaching, and death of Jesus.

HOW TO READ MARK AS A WHOLE

OPTION I: TWO HALVES, TWO STORIES

First, let me take you through the entire book of Mark in a few paragraphs. There are two equally fine ways of breaking down the sixteen chapters of Mark into thematic units. The first way of reading Mark is to break it in half, chapters 1–8 and 9–16. In the first half, Jesus' popularity escalates primarily because of the miracles He performs. The passages that describe His compassionate healing ministry regularly raise the question, "Who is this man?" (4:41; 6:2–3, 14–16; 8:27–29).

Almost in an apocalyptic fashion, Mark depicts another perspective on reality that comes not from the natural world but from behind the scenes in what might be called the "cosmic" world. Mark removes the veil from our limited time-and-space-bound physical world, which is based upon what we can see, feel, touch, smell, and taste, and gives us a glimpse of something that nonetheless is just as real. This is first reported by Mark in 1:10–11, at Jesus' baptism. At that moment the heavens are torn open, the Spirit like a dove descends upon Him, and a heavenly voice calls Jesus His beloved Son. Mark is telling his readers that God's Spirit is loose on earth, and He is found in the man Christ Jesus. As the story further develops in the opening chapters, unclean spirits are confronted with the power of Jesus, and they also recognize Jesus as the Son of God (1:23, 32–34; 3:11; 5:7), yet humanity sees nothing more than a miracle-working man and struggles to comprehend, "Who is this man?"

If the search in the first half of Mark is for Jesus' identity, a parallel question that drives the first half of Mark is "Why are people following Jesus?" The answer is textually straightforward; they come to Him because of the things He does for them, primarily exorcisms and healings. The answer that most people in the Gospel conclude is that Jesus is a miracle worker. Problematically, this is because they are viewing Jesus and His mighty deeds predominantly from a materialistic, earthly perspective. For the most part, people become His faithful followers because Jesus will provide them with ample food, restored health, and all of life's necessities. This is no less true in the twenty-first century than it was in the days of Jesus. Follower-ship should never be based principally upon what Jesus does for us but rather upon a biblical answer to "Who is this man?"

The first miracle in Mark is an exorcism (1:21–28), with the result that "news about him spread quickly over the whole region of Galilee" (1:28). Mark reports that people flocked to Jesus from all over both the Jewish (Judea and Jerusalem) and Gentile areas of Palestine (regions across the Jordan, Tyre, and Sidon). Specifically, the people came because they knew Him to be a miracle worker and He could take care of their physical needs. If one only had the first half of Mark, the answer to Jesus' identity question would be "Jesus is a miracle worker." We as readers of the text must not superimpose our understanding of the end of the story upon the people in these early chapters of the gospel of Mark. As of yet, the concept of Messiah, Redeemer, Lord, or Savior with all of our modern divine overtones is nowhere on the people's radar. Humanity is hungry, and they are blind to any reality other than to see Jesus as a man who can feed them.

The first half of the Gospel ends with Peter's confession, "You are the Christ," immediately followed by Jesus' stern warning that the disciples should not tell anyone about this newfound revelation (8:29–30). The last eight chapters of Mark try to unpack the meaning of "Christ" as it answers its own question: "What kind of Messiah are you?" The second half begins with the first of Jesus' three Passion predictions (8:31).

For the disciples, and most likely all others in Jesus' day, this was an enormous shock. For them, the term "Christ" meant something completely different from what is heard in our modern world. The "Christ/Messiah" was certainly a representative of God on earth, but that one was essentially devoid of any divine manifestations. Rather, the Christ was a man appointed by God to serve as Israel's deliverer from her pagan oppressors, in this case, Rome. The Messiah was thought of as a composite of a warrior like David and a priest like Aaron. He would purge the land of pagan influence (i.e., Romans) and cleanse the Temple (i.e., the priestly

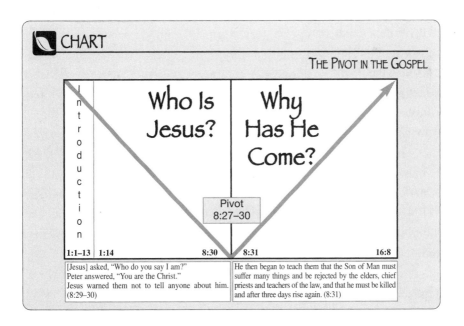

CHART

THE PIVOT IN THE GOSPEL

Introduction	Who Is Jesus?	Why Has He Come?
1:1–13	1:14 — 8:30	8:31 — 16:8

Pivot 8:27–30

| [Jesus] asked, "Who do you say I am?" Peter answered, "You are the Christ." Jesus warned them not to tell anyone about him. (8:29–30) | He then began to teach them that the Son of Man must suffer many things and be rejected by the elders, chief priests and teachers of the law, and that he must be killed and after three days rise again. (8:31) |

leadership) of her collusion with Rome during the time of occupation. In the end, the Messiah would triumphantly reestablish the throne of David and return God's people to their glory days. For the Jews in Jesus' day, suffering and death played no part of this scenario. As a matter of fact, death by its very definition described failure. Chapters 9–16 are Jesus' definition of what a suffering, dying Messiah looked like and how that image consistently clashed with the mind-set of the Jewish leaders and with the disciples.

OPTION 2: THEMES AND PLACES

A second and equally accurate way of looking at the book of Mark in its entirety is to see the progression as both thematic ("Who is this man?") and geographic ("Where is He going?"). The book can be broken down into an introduction (1:1–13) and three major sections:

1:14–8:21	Jesus in Galilee: The Land of Miracles
8:22–10:52	Jesus on the Way to Jerusalem: Discipleship Training
11:1–16:8	Jesus in Jerusalem: The Place of Suffering and Death

One major advantage of this approach is that it allows for dual themes to drive the narrative. A good story is much like modern situation comedy on television. There are multiple story lines being woven together simultaneously with a resolution only coming in the end. Mark functions in much the same manner. The first question, "Who is Jesus?" can be alternately pursued by asking the second question, "Who are His followers?" The disciples' character development profoundly affects the reader, since most of us want to be known as one of His followers. Problematically, the twelve initial disciples consistently are shown to be deaf and blind (see 8:17–21) and unable to comprehend the nature of His kingdom (see 8:17–21). A third theme that carries this book to its climax is "How can God relate and communicate to humanity if we continually move at cross purposes with His will?" Moreover, if humanity is inherently deaf and blind, how can we ever truly know Him? This will occur in both a place, Jerusalem, and with a transforming event, the Cross.

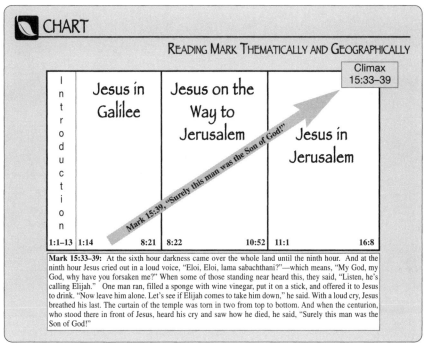

CHART

READING MARK THEMATICALLY AND GEOGRAPHICALLY

Climax
15:33–39

| I n t r o d u c t i o n | Jesus in Galilee | Jesus on the Way to Jerusalem | Jesus in Jerusalem |

Mark 15:39, "Surely this man was the Son of God!"

1:1–13 | 1:14 | 8:21 | 8:22 | 10:52 | 11:1 | 16:8

Mark 15:33–39: At the sixth hour darkness came over the whole land until the ninth hour. And at the ninth hour Jesus cried out in a loud voice, "Eloi, Eloi, lama sabachthani?"—which means, "My God, my God, why have you forsaken me?" When some of those standing near heard this, they said, "Listen, he's calling Elijah." One man ran, filled a sponge with wine vinegar, put it on a stick, and offered it to Jesus to drink. "Now leave him alone. Let's see if Elijah comes to take him down," he said. With a loud cry, Jesus breathed his last. The curtain of the temple was torn in two from top to bottom. And when the centurion, who stood there in front of Jesus, heard his cry and saw how he died, he said, "Surely this man was the Son of God!"

Climactically in the story, the death of Jesus may even be eclipsed by the confession of the centurion. Now, for the first time in the Gospel, a human has confessed what the larger cosmic realm has already known: "Surely, this man was the Son of God!" (15:39).

Tying together a few of the more subtle story lines might be helpful before a detailed work through the text itself. The best place to start is in the first verse, in which Mark provides introductory information regarding Jesus' identity: **the beginning of the gospel about Jesus Christ, the Son of God.** This is closely linked with the prediction of the Isaianic witness (1:2–3)[5] and its almost instantaneous fulfillment in the person of John (1:4–8). Next the reader hears of the pleasure of God the Father by means of the confirming voice from heaven (1:11). Thus, in a few short verses, Mark has established his agenda: (1) it is good news; (2) it is in direct continuity with the Old Testament prophetic tradition; and (3) Jesus,[6] the central character, is in harmony with God the Father.

As a powerful precursor to the Gospel, the opening words (1:1–13) establish this gospel story and the man Jesus as the new authoritative norm, against which Mark's readers will be required to evaluate all other opinions of Jesus. Simply put, if you differ with Jesus, you reject the Father's agenda. It is also worth noting that Mark has shared all the opening words as insider information with his readers, seemingly unknown to the characters in the story. Even the words of the Father appear to be given in secret. "You are my Son, whom I love; with you I am well pleased" (1:11) is a private conversation between Jesus and His Heavenly Father, with only the reading audience privileged to overhear this most intimate discussion. From the outset, we as the readers know more than the characters in the story. Mark has crafted these words and deeds into a community-shaping gospel story.

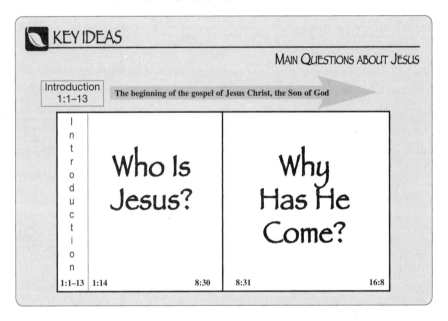

It is important to recognize that the story functions on yet a deeper level. With the introduction of Satan in 1:13 and the ongoing battle with demons in the first half of the book, the controversies between Jesus and His human counterparts are being pushed beyond the categories of mere religious and political power. Mark is attempting to convey to his readers that Jesus' ultimate conflict is of cosmic proportions and that any opinion regarding Jesus' person and mission that differs from the Jesus-norm is Satanic in origin (compare with Mark 8:33).[7]

Mark's overall literary structure accentuates this two-level story by designating people as being in one of two categories, "insiders" or "outsiders" (4:10–12). Mark's duality is first introduced with the initial confrontation of Jesus (good) and Satan (evil) in 1:12–13. The insider versus outsider continuum is continually reinforced as Mark's readers hear voices from heaven (1:11; 9:7) and from the netherworld (1:24, 34; 5:7) who both fully comprehend the identity and mission of Jesus. Ironically, those closest to Jesus, such as in family gatherings (3:31–35), in hometown reunions (6:1–6), or in the midst of miraculous events (4:35–41; 8:14–21) most often misunderstand Him. It seems as though the disciples and other participants inside the story have their knowledge about Jesus confined to the physical world, while Mark provides his Gospel readers with insider information from the larger cosmic realm.[8] These irreconcilable worldviews are later clarified in Jesus' words to Peter, "Get behind me, Satan! . . . You do not have in mind the things of God, but the things of men" (8:33). The point is clear: Thinking like men is not reality, but only the appearance of reality. The reader is called to look for truth beyond the empirical world and to find it in Jesus' words and actions as told through Mark's omniscient knowledge of the events.

A FIRST-CENTURY ORAL STORY

There is nothing like a well-told story. Modern readers may not be able to understand the effect that a story has. For in ancient times, the illiteracy rate was over 90 percent. This means that if someone was to receive the good news, it had to be told. Reading as we know it was a skill limited to a privileged few. So in the ancient world, the gospel of Mark was primarily heard and not read. This means that the reading event of the second Gospel was most certainly in a public venue, further heightening the community-shaping affect.

There were three main ingredients to an ancient person's experience with Mark: a reader, a text, and an audience. All three come together simultaneously to create much more of a sensory event than any modern Bible readers might experience in the privacy of their own study. A helpful analogy comes from music. Symphonies were originally composed to be heard, even though the compositions are written and can be studied as documents. "Our present pattern of experiencing biblical traditions is as if we were primarily to study Mozart's *Requiem* or *The Magic Flute* by only reading the scores and talking about them without ever performing or listening to his music."[9] James D. G. Dunn further refines the discussion as he says it is not just the difference between reading silently and hearing.

> For anyone who has experienced a first performance of a great musical work, like Beethoven's Ninth or Verdi's Requiem, the difference between hearing in the electric atmosphere of the live performance and hearing the recorded version played later at home (let alone simply reading the score) is unmistakable.[10]

Thus, if folk would like to experience the gospel of Mark as the original audience did, they might want to watch or listen to the Gospel performed. Moreover, I would suggest that everyone develop the practice of reading the stories of the Bible aloud as a form of *lectio divina* (spiritual readings).

Another problem in our modern reading of the Bible may come from the very form in which we encounter it: the printed page with chapters and verses. Most readers may not be aware that the chapter divisions that we have today were set by Stephen Langton, the Archbishop of Canterbury in 1527, one-and-a-half millennia after Christ! The versification of the Bible was not incorporated until Robert Estienne (also known as Stephanus) included it for his printed edition of the Greek text in 1555. The verses have survived in printed editions ever since, but they were never a part of Mark's ancient manuscript. Thus, maybe a wonderful beginning point is to go back and simply read the book of Mark as one piece of sacred literature, rather than as sixteen bite-sized morsels. For the average reader it will only take ninety minutes to read. Or maybe even closer to the original audience's experience, purchase a copy of the gospel of Mark on tape or CD and listen to it.[11] Maybe the best first-time experience of the gospel of Mark might be to find a professionally made video of the Gospel being performed.[12]

If one takes this oral encounter seriously, it will dramatically affect the way one comprehends the text. Throughout the Gospel, an abundance of verses refer to the way someone in the Gospel story (mis)understands Jesus, and it is usually due to their lack of sight or hearing. This is most prominently displayed in the parabolic instruction in chapter 4. The parable of the sower (or sometimes called the parable of the four soils) begins with the one and only command in the entire chapter, "Listen!" (4:3). It concludes with the common New Testament axiom, "He who has ears to hear, let him hear" (4:9). Jesus' interpretation of the parable elaborates upon this hearing dilemma that seems to debilitate most if not all of all humanity. "The farmer sows the word. . . . As soon as they hear it, Satan comes and takes away the word that was sown in them" (4:14–15). The verb "hear" is the theme that unifies this parable as well as defines the human auditory (or even total sensory) problem. Humankind is not able to hear (comprehend) Jesus. This theme continues throughout the Gospel as a whole. This is emphasized in the first half of the Gospel by the disciples' inability to grasp the meaning that Jesus was emphasizing in two feeding narratives in chapter 6 and chapter 8. This is brought to the forefront following the feeding of the five thousand, when Mark told his readers that the disciples "had not understood about the loaves; their hearts were hardened" (6:52). Then, following the feeding of the four thousand, the disciples once again were discussing the bread. Jesus firmly rebuked them with words reminiscent of the earlier parable in chapter 4: "Why are you talking about having no bread? Do you still not see or understand? Are your hearts hardened? Do you have eyes but fail to see, and ears but fail to hear? And don't you remember?" (8:17–18).

This hearing dilemma escalates in the second half of the Gospel. The dullness of the disciples progresses from a mere hearing disorder to outright rebellion. Following Peter's confession that Jesus is the Christ (8:29), for the first time in the Gospel, Jesus taught them "that the Son of Man must suffer many things and be rejected by the elders, chief priests and teachers of the law, and that he must be killed and after three days rise again" (8:31). Peter's response was one of open rebuke. He rejected any concept that integrated suffering and the messianic hope of Israel. Jesus properly diagnosed the problem: "You do not have in mind the things of

God, but the things of men" (8:33). Peter's and the entire group of disciples' inability to attend to the heart of the gospel was not that they could not hear, but that the kingdom of God looked entirely different than they expected. Rather than adopting Jesus' agenda, they continued to interpret Jesus and understand their religious commitment through their own humanly conceived life lens that prohibited them from perceiving the truth. Humans, across all generations, will remain in the same hopeless predicament unless they encounter the Cross of Jesus in a life-transforming manner. This means that they must discard the social and religious agenda of comfort and come face to face with a suffering and dying Messiah. Mark urged his listening audience to commit themselves to Jesus, on His terms, or pass judgment on themselves as faithless followers.

THE AUTHOR

WRITTEN BY MARK, THE SCRIBE

The authorship of each of the four gospels is anonymous. The subtitle that is affixed to the Gospel narrative, in this case, *the Gospel According to Mark*, was added in early church history by later copyists, most likely not original with the Gospel author. However, other New Testament references alert a careful student to the person of Mark. The name Mark is first mentioned as John Mark in Acts 12:12, whose house the disciples were praying in after James' martyrdom and following Peter's arrest by Herod. While this episode was going on in Acts 12, Barnabas and Paul were in Antioch for a whole year as they "met with the church and taught great numbers of people" (Acts 11:26). At the close of chapter 12, John Mark becomes the traveling companion of Paul and Barnabas on their first missionary journey (12:25; 13:5). The text of Acts subtly reveals that a serious problem occurred during the trip as John (Mark) returns to Jerusalem (13:13). Paul's displeasure with Mark's early departure is later chronicled in a well-known disagreement between Paul and Barnabas in Acts 15. Here, the argument is clearly centered on whether to replace John Mark as a part of their missionary team on their second missionary journey, especially since "Paul did not think it wise to take him, because he had deserted them in Pamphylia and had not continued with them in the work" (15:38). Paul is so opposed to reinstating John Mark that he chooses another traveling companion, Silas. Barnabas in turn takes Mark to Cyprus as he embarks on his own second journey.

What makes this so interesting is that the man ascribed as being the author of the second Gospel is biblically depicted as a missionary failure. Though his action is somewhat cryptic as Luke says "he had deserted them" (Acts 15:38), yet this act was enough to break up Paul and Barnabas. The redemptive nature of the Bible is that God does not abandon us over one's initial failure. Paul, at the very end of his life when writing 2 Timothy says, "Only Luke is with me. Get Mark and bring him with you, because he is helpful to me in my ministry" (2 Tim. 4:11; see also Col. 4:10; Philem. 24). Somewhere between John Mark's original desertion of Paul on his first missionary journey and these closing words of the apostle Paul to his own disciple Timothy, Paul and John Mark must have reconciled. Two men who were embittered over ministry issues now find themselves looking forward to a warm embrace.

TOLD BY PETER, THE APOSTLE

Another early source describing the authorship of Mark's gospel comes from Papias, the Bishop of Hierapolis in Asia Minor (modern Turkey). In the *Interpretation of the Lord's Oracles* (circa A.D. 110–130), he writes,

> This also the presbyter said: *Mark, having become the interpreter of Peter*, wrote down accurately, though not indeed in order, whatsoever he remembered of the things said or done by Christ. For he neither heard the Lord nor followed him, but afterward, as I said, he followed Peter, who adapted his teaching to the needs of his hearers, but with no intention of giving a connected account of the Lord's discourses, so that Mark committed no error while he thus wrote some things as he remembered them. For he was careful of one thing, not to omit any of the things which he had heard, and not to state any of them falsely.[13]

A Gospel was not placed in the New Testament canon simply because it is about Jesus, for there were many spurious "gospels" written in the centuries after Jesus.[14] A book was canonized, at least in part, because its contents can be clearly traced back to apostolic origins. Thus, Papias's comments tell us that Mark received his Gospel directly from Peter himself. Here we find the earliest evidence of apostolic authority accredited to the gospel of Mark.

This raises another interesting distinction, which the second Gospel contributes to the fourfold tradition. None of the other gospels present the disciples in such a pervasive negative manner. Rather than saying they have "little faith" (Matt. 8:26), Mark's words accused them of having "no faith" (Mark 4:40). In another parallel account, Luke presented the disciples in a most favorable light as he removed altogether Jesus' rebuke of Peter, "Get behind me, Satan!" (Mark 8:33). It is true that the disciples initially left everything and followed Jesus (1:18, 20; 2:14; 10:28–30). But their motives never seem to have been in sync with the Kingdom principles Jesus repeatedly championed. The more He healed, the blinder they became to His person. The more He taught, the more deaf they became to the truth. Not even the privileged insight bestowed to them (4:11) seem to have enlightened them. They seem to be the poster children for bad disciples. They are constantly described as fearful (4:40; 6:49–50), they pursued selfish ambition (9:34; 10:35–45), and they publicly displayed spiritual failure (9:14–29). Their climactic act as a group was their corporate flight at the moment of Jesus' arrest (14:5–52). A summary statement about the disciples could be put this way: They gave all they had and tried to the best of their human ability, but in the end they were sinners at heart in need of transformation (6:52). The answer to this discipleship dilemma is found in the Cross, which will change them from the inside out. To their shame, the disciples constantly ignored or completely rejected this solution when it was predicted by Jesus (8:31–33; 9:30–37; 10:32–45). Nevertheless, all present and future disciples can be thankful that Jesus fully embraced this as the Father's perfect plan for redeeming a deaf and blind humanity.

Not only are the disciples as a whole presented critically by Mark, but Peter's behavior as an individual is strikingly suspect. He appears self-absorbed and utterly blind to the words and agenda of Jesus from beginning to end. In his last fateful appearance in the Gospel, Mark utilized Peter's own first-person account to portray the last of his threefold denial: "I don't know this man you're talking about." The irony of this fact is that Mark received this material from the lips of Peter himself. This speaks to the veracity of the second Gospel. If Peter had not been personally transformed by the forgiveness of Jesus Christ, what would have been his rationale for sharing this dishonorable story? It seems as if the credibility of Jesus stands on the premise that Peter was wrong on both his perception of Jesus and his rejection of Jesus' conception of the Kingdom. Peter's journey does not end when the gospel of Mark ends. For Peter, the end of chapter 16 is only the beginning.

THE AUDIENCE AND DATING: ROMAN CHRISTIANS

In Justin Martyr's *Dialogue with Trypho* (written in A.D. 150), "It is said that he [Jesus] changed the name of one of the apostles to Peter; and it is written in his memoirs [Mark] that he changed the names of others, two brothers, the sons of Zebedee, to Boanerges, which means 'sons of thunder'"(106.3). But additional sources not only link Peter to the gospel of Mark, but they also discuss the place where this writing relationship flourished. Irenaeus, who lived from A.D. 130–200, says that Mark was written "When Peter and Paul were preaching the gospel in Rome and founding the church there." He adds, "After their departure, Mark, Peter's disciple, has himself delivered to us in writing the substance of Peter's preaching."[15] An ancient source by Eusebius reports that Clement of Alexandria (A.D. 150–215), citing an ancient tradition of the elders, described how the gospel of Mark came into being as follows:

> When Peter had preached the gospel publicly in Rome . . . those who were present . . . besought Mark, since he had followed him (Peter) for a long time and remembered the things that had been spoken, to write out the things that had been said; and when he had done this he gave the gospel to those who asked him. When Peter learned of it later, he neither obstructed nor commended.[16]

Thus, there is extensive external evidence that points to Rome as the place for the composition of the gospel of Mark.[17]

If the traditional place was indeed Rome, the dating for the Gospel can be determined accordingly. Mark must have received his material from Peter during his closing days in Rome. Irenaeus, as quoted above, says that it was after Peter's death that Mark produced his gospel: "And after the death of these (Peter and Paul) Mark, the disciple and interpreter of Peter, also handed down to us in writing the things preached by Peter." This traditionally took place during the reign of Emperor Nero (A.D. 54–68). The best ancient source for the persecutions that took place under Nero was written by the Roman historian Tacitus, who was a young boy in Rome during this time.

> Therefore, to stop the rumor [that he had set Rome on fire], he [Emperor Nero] falsely charged with guilt, and punished with the most fearful tortures, the persons commonly called Christians, who were [generally] hated for their enormities. Christus, the founder of that name, was put to death as a criminal by Pontius Pilate, procurator of Judea, in the reign of Tiberius, but the pernicious superstition—repressed for a time—broke out yet again, not only through Judea, where the mischief originated, but through the city of Rome also, whither all things horrible and disgraceful flow from all quarters, as to a common receptacle, and where they are encouraged. Accordingly first those were arrested who confessed they were Christians; next on their information, a vast multitude were convicted, not so much on the charge of burning the city, as of hating the human race. In their very deaths they were made the subjects of sport: for they were covered with the hides of wild beasts, and worried to death by dogs, or nailed to crosses, or set fire to, and when the day waned, burned to serve for the evening lights. Nero offered his own garden players for the spectacle, and exhibited a Circensian game, indiscriminately mingling with the common people in the dress of a charioteer, or else standing in his chariot. For this cause a feeling of compassion arose toward the sufferers, though guilty and deserving of exemplary capital punishment, because they seemed not to be cut off for the public good, but were victims of the ferocity of one man.[18]

One can easily see how the second Gospel is speaking powerfully to people in just such dire situations. The dominative theme of fear portrayed in the second Gospel not only resonates in the life of the original disciples of Jesus, but also in the daily life of followers of Jesus in a subsequent generation under Nero in Rome. Jesus spoke openly about His own persecution and death (3:6; 8:31; 9:31; 10:33, 45) and promised the same for anyone who followed after Him (8:34–9:1; 4:17; 10:30; 13:1–13). This truth is unfolding before the eyes of these second-generation Christians in Rome. They were being asked to acknowledge who was Lord, Caesar or Jesus. Christians were liable to suffer penalties imposed by Roman law just because they were Christians. Ancient Christian writers document that they were innocent of any crime, but their protests went unheeded. "Those who voiced such protests were told that they might easily prove their loyalty to the empire by worshipping the state gods, and in particular by burning incense to the emperor's image or swearing by his divinity. A Christian's refusal to countenance such claims, and the language in which they ascribed divine honor to Jesus, could easily be given the appearance of sedition."[19]

Thus, early Christians in Rome were being asked to deny their Lord to save their own lives or those of their families. The primary question circulating among the church must have been, "Could there be forgiveness for such a heinous crime?" And who holds the keys to the answer? It was the first bishop of Rome, Peter himself, who stood before them proclaiming the power of Christ's salvation. The leader of the church in Rome is the very same man who thirty-five years earlier denied Jesus. And he was not standing before a Roman tribunal with the fear of a sentence of death. Rather, at the time of his threefold denial he stood before a powerless maidservant of the high priest (14:66). Yet now, at the end of his life, Peter willingly faces suffering at the hands of his all-powerful Roman adversaries. The power of Christ's forgiveness is the message of the second Gospel for the early Christians and for us as well in this contemporary world; a Gospel of second chances. For you see, Mark was penned by a missionary failure, John Mark, and the message was dictated to him by an apostate follower, Peter. Mark's message of forgiveness for any and all sinners cannot be hidden. Full and free salvation is found for even the worst sinners among us all.

ENDNOTES

1. For many folks, the words of Jesus have a special reverential place in their private devotions and public, ethical, decision-making process. But often, Jesus' words are memorized without their larger narrative framework, which might lead to a partial distortion of their meaning and application. For example, many have memorized short sections of the Sermon on the Mount, such as the Beatitudes (Matt. 5:3–10), which is an extremely healthy spiritual exercise. However, in the larger Matthean context, they serve primarily as an introduction to the rest of the sermon. They are a preface rather than stand-alone words. The same might be true for one to memorize Jesus' red-letter words to the neglect of the surrounding narrative context, as if Jesus' words are *more* inspired than the rest of the Gospel.

2. A great starting place would be to choose any of these books that introduce the reader to the classic spiritual disciplines: Richard Foster, *Celebration of Discipline: The Path to Spiritual Growth*; Dallas Willard, *The Spirit of the Disciplines: Understanding How God Changes Lives;* Keith Drury, *With Unveiled Faces: Experience Intimacy with God through Spiritual Disciplines.*

3. See Richard Hays, *Echoes of Scripture in the Letters of Paul* (New Haven, Conn.: Yale University Press, 1993).

4. The verb in Greek is the same in both 1:11 and 15:38, "tearing," from which we derive our English word "schism."

5. There is solid evidence that 1:1 is connected with 1:2–8 and does not stand alone as a book level title or superscription. First, the Greek word *kathōs* never introduces a sentence in Mark or the rest of the New Testament (V. Taylor, *The Gospel According to St. Mark* [London: Macmillan, 1959], p. 153). Second, when *kathōs* is used in conjunction with "it is written" it always refers to the preceding not the following material (compare 9:13; 14:21).

6. Jesus is present in every scene in the Gospel except two: John the Baptist's death (6:14–29) and, of course, the empty tomb (16:1–8).

7. It must be emphasized that Jesus' conflict with Satan and with his human adversaries is not unrelated. As Rhodes and Michie (*Mark as Story: An Introduction to the Narrative of a Gospel* [Philadelphia: Fortress Press, 1982], pp. 78–79) have pointed out, "Jesus' conflict with Satan indirectly comes in focus in the conflict with people. Because of the limitations on Jesus' authority in relation to people, his conflicts with people are more difficult and more evenly matched than those waged directly with demonic forces or with nature."

8. This is first put forth when the heavens are "torn open" (1:10) and the listeners are shown that there is action taking places beyond the physical world. The one who stands behind the torn heaven is the sending and blessing agent of

Jesus. This vital information is withheld from the participants of the story world of Mark (not so in Matthew). Mark utilizes the second-person singular ("You are my Son, whom I love," 1:11) rather than Matthew's third-person singular ("This is my Son, whom I love," Matt. 3:17).

9. Thomas Boomershine, "Peter's Denial as Polemic or Confession: The Implications of Media Criticism for Biblical Hermeneutics." *Semeia* 39 (1987), p. 54.

10. J. D. G. Dunn, "Jesus in Oral Memory: The Initial Stages of the Jesus Tradition," in *Jesus: A Colloquium in the Holy Land*, ed. D. Donnelly (New York & London: Continuum, 2001), p. xx.

11. One of the best is Max McLean, http://www.listenersbible.com/ or the plethora of online sites, such as http://www.biblegateway.com/resources/audio/ where full downloads of audio versions of the Bible in numerous translations are available.

12. Max McLean, *Mark: Live Onstage with Max McLean* (DVD).

13. The words of Papias are preserved in Eusebuis, *Ecclesiastical History*, 3.39.15. Found online at http://www.newadvent.org/fathers/250103.htm.

14. Gospel of Thomas and other works written under pseudonymous authorship, gospel of Peter, gospel of James, gospel of Philip, gospel of Judas.

15. *Adversus Haereses* (Against Heresies) 3.1.1; *Historia Ecclesiastica* (Ecclesiastical History) 5.8. pp. 2–4.

16. *Historia Ecclesiastica* 6.14. pp. 6–7. Another ancient document, the fragment of the Anti-Marcionite prologue says, "Mark declared, who is called 'stump-fingered,' because he had rather small fingers in comparison with the stature of the rest of his body. He was the interpreter of Peter. After the death of Peter himself he wrote down this same gospel in the regions of Italy."

17. There is some internal evidence that Mark was intended for a Roman audience. First, various Aramaic phrases are translated in the Gospel (for example, Mark 3:17; 5:41; 7:11, 34; 10:46; 15:22). Second, numerous Latin loan-words appear throughout: in 4:27—a measure; 5:9, 15—legion; 6:27—guard; 6:37—denarius (a Roman coin); 15:15—to whip; 15:39, 44–45—centurion (Matthew and Luke use a different Greek term).

18. Tacitus, *Annals* 15.44.

19. F. F. Bruce, *The Defense of the Gospel* (London: Intervarsity Press, 1982), p. 67.

OUTLINE OF MARK

I. **Jesus in Galilee—The Land of Miracles (1:1–8:21)**
   A. Prologue (1:1–13)
   B. Jesus' Words and Works (1:14–45)
      1. Jesus' First Words (1:14–15)
      2. Jesus' First Disciples (1:16–20)
      3. A Day in Jesus' Life (1:21–39)
      4. Making the Unclean Clean (1:40–45)
   C. Early Controversies (2:1–3:6)
      1. Authority to Forgive Sins (2:1–12)
      2. A Dinner and the Call of Levi (2:13–17)
      3. The Fasting Question (2:18–22)
      4. The Sabbath Question (2:23–27)
      5. Second Sabbath Controversy (3:1–6)
   D. The Crowds Gather (3:7–35)
      1. Summary of Success (3:7–12)
      2. Appointment of the Twelve (3:13–19)
      3. Transference of Demonic Role to Opponents (3:20–35)
   E. The Kingdom in Parables (4:1–34)
      1. Parable Introduction (4:1–2)
      2. Parable of the Sower (4:3–9)
      3. Parabolic (Mis)Information (4:10–12)
      4. The Parable Explained (4:13–20)
      5. Parables about Hiddenness (4:21–25)
      6. Two Seed Parables (4:26–32)
      7. Conclusion (4:33–34)
   F. Lord over All (4:35–5:43)
      1. Who Is this Man? (4:35–41)
      2. Lord over Demons (5:1–20)
      3. Lord over Disease; Lord over Death (5:21–43)
   G. Valleys and Peaks in Ministry (6:1–56)
      1. A Prophet without Honor (6:1–6)
      2. Mission of the Twelve (6:7–13, 30)
      3. Death of John the Baptist (6:14–29)
      4. Feeding of the Five Thousand (6:31–44)

III. Jesus in Jerusalem—the Place of Suffering and Death (11:1–16:8)

A. Arriving in Jerusalem (11:1–33)
   1. The Royal Entrance (11:1–10)
   2. The Fig Tree and the Temple (11:11–25)
   3. Reaction by the Jewish Leaders (11:27–33)
B. The Parable of the Vineyard (12:1–12)
C. Confrontations, Questions, and Commandments (12:13–44)
   1. To Pay or Not to Pay (12:13–17)
   2. Sadducees and Resurrection (12:18–27)
   3. The Greatest Commandment (12:28–34)
   4. The Question of David's Son (12:35–37)
   5. The Scribes and the Widows (12:38–44)
D. Prophets and Prophecies (13:1–37)
   1. Jesus' Prediction and the Disciples' Question (13:1–4)
   2. False Prophets and Wars (13:5–8)
   3. The Promise of Persecution (13:9–13)
   4. A "Sign"? (13:14–20)
   5. More about False Prophets (13:21–23)
   6. The End of the World? (13:24–37)
E. Anointing for Burial (14:1–31)
   1. Anointing for Burial (14:1–11)
   2. The Preparation of the Lord's (Last) Supper (14:12–16)
   3. The Prediction of Betrayal (14:17–21)
   4. The Institution of the Last Supper (14:22–25)
   5. The Prediction of Denial (14:26–31)
F. In the Garden (14:32–52)
   1. Gethsemane (14:32–42)
   2. Jesus' Arrest (14:43–52)
G. On Trial (14:53–15:15)
   1. Jesus' Trial before the High Priest (14:53–65)
   2. Peter's Trial before the Servant Girl (14:66–72)
   3. Jesus' Trial before Pilate (15:1–15)
H. From the Cross to the Grave (15:16–47)
   1. Soldiers Mocking Jesus (15:16–20)
   2. Crucifixion of Jesus (15:21–32)
   3. Death of Jesus (15:33–39)

Part One

Jesus in Galilee—The Land of Miracles

MARK 1:1–8:21

PROLOGUE

Mark 1:1–13

S cholars agree that 1:1–13 forms an introduction to the book of Mark. If this is true, then the themes the reader is prepared to find in the rest of the narrative should be initially presented. The opening lines of the Gospel (1:1–8) introduce the reader to the idea that God's plan, which had been asserted in the Old Testament writings, was on the verge of breaking forth into human history. The baptismal scene (1:9–11), though short, reveals the author's intention for the remainder of the book. This condensed baptismal scene can be viewed as a calling or commissioning of Jesus, as the heavenly voice speaks directly to Jesus (and the readers) and declared what His role would be: "My beloved Son." We find Jesus as God's ambassador on earth to announce God's rule. This theme of being God's authority figure is quickly picked up in the opening healing stories (1:21–28; 2:1–12). First the people recognized Jesus as having authority that was different from the scribes'; Jesus had a self-authenticating authority, which was unheard of in the first century. The theme is reinforced in 2:1–12 as Jesus proclaimed to possess the very authority of God by forgiving sins. The implication of the opening passage is that human authorities "have been ruling themselves rather than God"[1] and that Satan has been the strong man in charge of the house (3:27).

In the temptation narrative (1:12–13), rather than "lording over" the world and its inhabitants through this authoritative position, Jesus was thrust by the Spirit into the midst of wilderness to be tempted by Satan. Mark 1:24 tells the reader that Jesus' mission is further qualified as destroying the demons, and 9:22 informs the readers that the demons are intent on destroying their victims.

The insertion of 1:14–15 as a new beginning[2] to the narrative allows the reader to sense that the baptism-temptation episode is not simply the first in a series of cosmic confrontations, but it is the foundation of the series. The struggle introduced in the temptation would continue until it comes to a climactic solution.

The next issue is to address the overall purpose of the opening line: **The beginning of the gospel about Jesus Christ, the Son of God** (1:1). Is this a title for the entire Gospel, or does it merely serve as an introduction to the first thirteen verses? What did Mark mean by using the term "beginning"? Was he referring to the prophetic announcement by Isaiah (1:2–3), to John the Baptist (1:4–8), and the baptism and temptation of Jesus (1:9–13) as the beginning of the gospel? Or should Mark's readers prepare themselves for a beginning that will not even be fully completed by chapter 16? This truncated beginning that contains no annunciation to Mary and has no nativity scene is a perfect match for Mark's abrupt ending in 16:8, where the witnesses ran from the tomb in fright and remained silent. But that cannot be the "end," for what about the resurrection? Thus, in the gospel of Mark, the end is not really the end; it is only the end of the beginning. The story of the resurrection will be told and retold by countless disciples, in all nations, in every generation. Thus, the first line, **the beginning of the gospel**, prepares the reader for an amazing ride as God invades the world in the form of His Son, Jesus. Furthermore, the story ends with a call to all readers from all times, regardless of their fears, to rally around the truth that has been revealed in the intervening chapters and to go and tell the message that the women seemed momentarily to keep to themselves. Thus, Mark begins and ends with ambiguity, which would be fleshed out as one walked and listened to the Master teach.

Mark introduced three precise terms that will shape the rest of the story: gospel, Christ, and Son of God. Modern readers should be cautious not to read into the term "gospel" any bookish conations, for in Mark's time, the genre of gospel was only beginning. Nevertheless the word "gospel" was rich in ancient tradition. In the Greek translation of the Old Testament, the verb form of the word (*euangelizo*) was utilized in a sacred manner, declaring the establishment of the reign of God and the good news of salvation (Isa. 40:9; 52:7; Ps. 40:9; 96:2).

Yet there was a second use of *euangelizo* linked directly to the emperor worship of the first century. The emperor's birthday or accession to power was labeled as a *euangelizo*. Mark's use of the word seems to link up both of these uses, declaring the arrival of Jesus on earth as a "royal visit" of the King's Son. But Mark's readers cannot understand the term *gospel* in a safe and sterile kind of way. Salvation entered the world at a bloody cost, not only for Jesus, but for all. The call of all future disciples is to abandon everything of value that they have (10:17–31) and to follow Him, carrying their own cross (8:34–38).

The second term Mark employed in his gospel's title line is "Christ." The term "Christ" most literally means "the anointed one." It was a common term in the Old Testament, but it did not hold the divine imagery that most modern Christians might expect. For the most part, it was ascribed to a man who would carry out specific tasks to free the nation of Israel from her oppressors. Even one as pagan as King Cyrus of Persia was called an "anointed" one (Isa. 45:1), for he allowed the return of the Jews from exile. The apocryphal book, the Psalms of Solomon, may best sum up the first-century expectation of the Messiah of God:

BACKGROUND

SEPTUAGINT

The Septuagint (sometimes abbreviated LXX) was translated about 250 B.C. in Alexandria, Egypt. This Greek translation of the Hebrew Scriptures was produced because many Jews had ceased being fluent in Hebrew and needed a Greek translation. According to tradition, approximately seventy Jewish scholars were commissioned to translate the Hebrew Scriptures. Septuagint ("seventy" in Latin) is named to honor the seventy scholars.

A majority of Old Testament quotes cited in the New Testament are quoted directly from the Septuagint.

MANNERS AND CUSTOMS

EMPEROR WORSHIP

The Greeks, Romans, and other peoples in the Roman Empire worshipped multiple deities (polytheism). Beginning in 29 B.C., the "Imperial cult" was the worship of the Roman emperor as a god. Cities built temples to the emperors in order to show their loyalty. In return for their loyalty, these cities received help and prestige from the Roman authorities. Christians agreed to pray for the well-being of the emperor, but refused to worship the emperor as a god. Their refusal sometimes led to persecution.

Behold, O Lord, and raise up unto them their king, the son of David,

At the time in which Thou sees, O God, that he may reign over Israel Thy servant. And gird him with strength, that he may shatter unrighteous rulers,

And that he may purge Jerusalem from nations that trample (her) down to destruction. Wisely, righteously he shall thrust out sinners from (the) inheritance;

He shall destroy the pride of the sinner as a potter's vessel.

With a rod of iron he shall break in pieces all their substance,

He shall destroy the godless nations with the word of his mouth;

At his rebuke nations shall flee before him,

And he shall reprove sinners for the thoughts of their heart. (Psalm of Solomon 17:21–25)

The predominant first-century Jewish messianic expectation was that he would be a warrior-king-like figure, wielding a sword in one hand and a royal scepter in the other. Thus, a gospel whose core truth proclaims a dying Messiah was an enigma to some, to others an utter absurdity (1 Cor. 1:23). The most pressing task for the early church was to reconcile the prophetic words of the Old Testament with the life and teachings of Jesus, which may be the reason why Mark began with Isaiah's prophecy in 1:2–3.

Many commentators wrestle with how to understand the grammatical construction, "gospel of Jesus Christ." It hinges upon how one is to understand the modifying phrase "of Jesus Christ." Is it the gospel concerning Jesus or the gospel proclaimed by Jesus? The only other place in the gospel where a similar construction occurs is in 1:14, "gospel of God," which has a similar elusiveness to its meaning. The remaining uses of the noun *gospel* refer to a concrete message to be proclaimed or believed (1:15; 13:10; 14:9). This is also the more natural way to understand the use of the noun throughout the rest of the New Testament (though exceptions arise in Rom. 2:16 and 16:25). On the other side of the grammatical argument, early on in the second Gospel, "Jesus went into Galilee, proclaiming the good news of God" (1:14). Thus, within the introduction itself, Jesus is depicted as the object of the gospel as well as the proclaimer. Knowing the intrigue and mystery of Mark, it should not surprise any reader that Mark was playing for both meanings, for throughout the Gospel, Jesus is both the subject matter under discussion and the teacher in every scene.

The final phrase in Mark's opening line attributes to Jesus the title **Son of God.** Though some of the early manuscripts omit this last phrase, it certainly plays a key role in the remainder of the gospel story. Initially, at Jesus' baptism, the Father from heaven declared Jesus' Sonship: **And a voice came from heaven: "You are my Son, whom I love; with you I am well pleased"** (1:11). This divine designation was reiterated in the Father's words to the disciples as they witnessed the Transfiguration: "This is my Son, whom I love. Listen to him!" (9:7).

Throughout several of the opening miracle scenes, as Jesus confronted the evil spirits, they clearly recognized His role on earth: "Whenever the evil spirits saw him, they fell down before him and cried out, 'You are the Son of God'" (Mark 3:11; see also 1:24; 5:7). With Jesus on trial, the question posed to Him by the chief priest again centered on this title: "Are you the Christ, the Son of the Blessed One?" (14:61). To this question Jesus abruptly answered, "I am" and was condemned to death. Finally, the first time a human proclaimed Jesus to be the Son of God was at the cross, when the centurion said, "Surely this

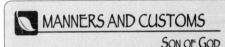

MANNERS AND CUSTOMS
SON OF GOD

The "son of god" in the ancient world had three presumptions: (1) it spoke of a devoted servant of the gods, (2) it referred to someone with gifts that surpassed normal expectations, and (3) it referenced political rulers. According to Mark, Jesus was the Son of God because He (1) accepted the ministry that God prepared for Him, (2) possesses supernatural abilities (expelled demons, healed the sick, and forgave sins), and (3) will rule at the right hand of God. However, Mark's specific understanding of Jesus as Son of God cannot be divorced from the Jewish "son of man" concept. (See "Manners and Customs" on p. 48.)

man was the Son of God!" (15:39). This most certainly is the climactic confession by anyone in the gospel. Humankind had finally comprehended what the Heavenly Father had twice declared and the truth that caused the demons to shake in terror: Jesus is the Son of God. Ironically, no one on earth seemed to comprehend this until after His death.[3] The first person who made the confession, the centurion, was both a Roman and the man most directly responsible for killing Jesus, the leader of the execution squad. Thus, the goal of the gospel of Mark is clearly illuminated for the readers. Jesus is the Christ, the Son of God. And the next sixteen chapters will attempt to see how these two titles, which essentially have warrior and royal connotations, climax on a cross. Until humankind confesses Jesus as a dying Messiah, all is lost.

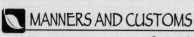

MANNERS AND CUSTOMS

SON OF MAN

The "son of man" concept is rooted in the Old Testament as an emphasis on one's humanity (Num. 23:19; Job 25:6; Ps. 8:4; 80:17; 144:3; and multiple references in Ezekiel). In Daniel (7:13), the prophet saw a person that resembled a "son of man" arriving to institute His divinely ordained authority; Jesus seemed to base His understanding of the term here. In the wisdom literature, this concept was linked to persecution and righteousness. As a result, the "son of man" concept developed from emphasizing humanity to emphasizing a messianic figure ordained by God to carry out divine intentions.

The first verse of Mark opens with the reader being informed of Jesus' identity: **Jesus Christ, the Son of God.** This is closely linked with the prediction of the Isaianic witness (1:2–3) and its fulfillment in the person of John the Baptist (1:4–8). Thus, the true beginning of the good news of Mark began in Isaiah. Consider these three preliminary comments regarding this Old Testament quotation. First, this is the only quotation in the second Gospel directly ascribed to an Old Testament author, in this case Isaiah. Scripture and its fulfillment in Jesus plays an enormous role in the gospel of Mark (see 9:12; 11:17; 14:21, 27, 49), but at no other juncture in the remainder of the book did Mark name the source of his quotations. Second, the words of Isaiah are in actuality a composition of Isaiah, Exodus, and Malachi. **It is written in Isaiah the prophet:**

- **"I will send my messenger ahead of you** (Exod. 23:20)
- **who will prepare your way"**— (Mal. 3:1)
- **"a voice of one calling in the desert, 'Prepare the way for the Lord, make straight paths for him.'"** (Isa. 40:3)

The theological importance of these scriptural choices should not be overlooked. Exodus marks Israel's first exodus as a key for understanding God's unique relationship with His people. Malachi warns that God will send "my messenger" to prepare for the coming judgment day. The third reference comes for the last half of the book of Isaiah, which speaks of a second exodus through the desert for a final deliverance. Interestingly, Mark attributed all the material to Isaiah. This is not a historical inaccuracy, but Mark's way of saying the themes that will unfold in the ensuing chapters will remind one of Isaiah's promises of a new exodus.

Finally, this prophecy is not directly about Jesus, but His forerunner, John, who played an instrumental role in this story. John prepared the world for the coming of the Lord through his preaching and baptism. Additionally, he prepared Jesus for His ministry to the world in His baptism and Spirit filling. But finally, John is reintroduced in chapter 6 as one who prepared Mark's readers for the perception that prophets who stand for God will suffer the ultimate sacrifice. John was Jesus' forerunner in faithful ministry even unto death.

And so John came, baptizing in the desert region and preaching a baptism of repentance for the forgiveness of sins (1:4). The announcement of the ministry of John appears in the form of the simple words **John came**. Easily lost in the English text is the succession of the next two key players in the story introduced in exactly the same fashion: (1) **Jesus came** (1:9); (2) **a voice came** (1:11). All three converged at the baptismal site of Jesus. Furthermore, Mark informed his readers little about John other than his role.[4] His clothing (**John wore clothing made of camel's hair, with a leather belt around his waist**) and his diet (**he ate locusts and wild honey**, 1:6) preempt other human interest details. The gospel of Luke reports his priestly lineage and his miraculous birth. But for Mark, John was exclusively a forerunner, and an odd one at that.

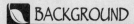

BACKGROUND

QUMRAN AND DEAD SEA SCROLLS

The Qumran community was located on the northwestern shore of the Dead Sea. Some scholars have associated Qumran with the Essenes. The inhabitants of Qumran adhered to a strict, almost ascetic, lifestyle. From 1947–56, numerous valued manuscripts that dated to the mid third century B.C. were found in eleven caves. Copies of every Old Testament book except Esther were discovered. Findings from the Qumran community have provided a much-needed window into the textual history of what became canonical Scripture.

The real focal point for Mark is John's place of ministry and his preaching. The location seems surprising as he was **baptizing in the desert region** (1:4). The note about the desert connects John with the prophetic words of Isaiah in 1:3, but also with a long-standing prophetic tradition that describes the desert as the beginning of a new exodus and a place looked upon with fond memories (Jer. 2:2; 31:2; Hos. 2:14; Amos 5:25). The Qumran community, whom many scholars attribute as part of John's upbringing, supported just such a reading of Isaiah 40:3 when they instructed that those who join them "will separate from the habitation of ungodly men and shall go into the wilderness to prepare the way of Him [Messiah]" (1QS 8:12–16). But it is the content of the preaching that set the stage for the coming of Jesus: **preaching a baptism of repentance for the forgiveness of sins** (1:4). The grammar of the passage is not helpful in determining the direct relationship of baptism, repentance, and forgiveness. Some have read baptismal regeneration into this passage while others believe that Mark is referring to the forgiveness that will become manifest to humanity through the ultimate sacrifice in Jesus' death. As Wesleyan-Arminians, we would hold to this latter interpretation; John the Baptist called people to repentance, and baptism was offered with or following their repentance. It seems from all the accounts we have of John's ministry (four Gospels and the ancient Jewish historian Josephus) that practicing the rite of baptism was not his dominant emphasis. Rather, his preaching was centered upon a declaration of repentance in the face of an impending divine judgment. Moreover, his goal was not merely to initiate individuals into new life through baptism, but it was to call the people of Israel to repentance and restore them to their covenant faithfulness before God. Thus, it might be more accurate to understand John the Baptist's ministry as calling people to repentance, with baptism offered following or in conjunction with their repentance.

Mark seemed less concerned with John the Baptist's theology and more focused on his practice. Baptism (*baptisma*) is a uniquely Christian word. It may have first come into existence in Paul's writing (Rom. 6:4) and from a historical perspective, this rite was new. The Jews of the first century had ceremonial washings (7:3–4), and the Qumran community themselves practiced ritual immersion baths. But these are both with reference to being ceremonially impure, and modern research into John's culture says, "There is nothing morally sinful about being impure. One cannot avoid it. Becoming impure happens quite naturally all the time."[5] The model for Christian baptism most likely was the immersion of Gentile converts upon becoming proselytes.

If that is true, John seemed to be calling his people *out* to a completely new place in preparation for a completely new order, of which his baptism is only preliminary. For **this was his message: "After me will come one more powerful than I, the thongs of whose sandals I am not worthy to stoop down and untie. I baptize you with water, but he will baptize you with the Holy Spirit"** (1:7–8). It seems that the combination of the place, the proclamation, and the people is the key. For a first-century Jew, forgiveness was found exclusively in the Temple practices through the Levitical sacrifices. Yet Mark reported that **the whole Judean countryside and all the people of Jerusalem went out to him. Confessing their sins, they were baptized by him in the Jordan River** (1:5). This may be an expression of hyperbole, for it seems unlikely that Jerusalem turned into a ghost town for the people to be repatriated in the desert. But it does express the people's hopes and expectations for more than the current condition of the Jewish cult can offer them. Mark was certainly depicting its impotence at dealing with personal sin and sin's inherent manifestations (illness, disease, evil spirits). Everyone Jewish was streaming out of Jerusalem. For them, this city, and specifically, the Temple, was the very location where, in the end, all nations would ultimately stream to find God. Yet, all were journeying to the desert to find a wild man in strange garb who was calling them to begin their new journey like a common Gentile.

These opening verses depict a land with long-term, great spiritual hunger, going back to the days of Isaiah. Mark succinctly identified it to the audience as sin: **Confessing their sins, they were baptized by him in the Jordan River** (1:5). It was a pervasive problem, as all Judea and Jerusalem sought out John to receive what he had to offer. John's own words then indicated his work was merely preparatory for the more efficacious baptism of Jesus. Thus, even with water baptism and sincere repentance, there was something more that needed to be done for *all* the people. John's time was transitioning with the coming of Jesus and the hope of the one who **will baptize . . . with the Holy Spirit** (1:8).

Jesus arrived on the stage set by John. **At that time Jesus came from Nazareth in Galilee** (1:9). The readers know nothing about Him as He descends from the north without pomp and circumstance, coming from one rural district (Galilee) to a deserted region along the Jordan; hardly the expectation of one coming who has just been described as being "more powerful" than John. In an understated manner, he **was baptized by John in the Jordan** (1:9). But this unassuming demeanor would become Jesus' watchword. In Mark, it is less what He says and more who He is. No trumpets will blare at Jesus' first arrival. Jesus seems more to blend in with the crowd than to stand out. Then, **as Jesus was coming up out of the water, he saw heaven being torn open and the Spirit descending on him like a dove** (1:10). Mark provided an interesting perspective to this passage. It is told exclusively in the third person, with Mark as the omniscient narrator. The others being baptized by John at the Jordan seemed oblivious to this heaven-splitting event. Mark's telling of this event is exclusively for his readers, giving them insider information seemingly unknown by the participants in the remainder of the story. One only needs to compare Mark with the other Gospels to sense the subtle nuance. Matthew reported not that Jesus saw the heavens opened but that "heaven was opened." Moreover, the divine voice that follows is recorded in third person, not the second person of Mark. Luke concurred with Matthew, but added the unique phrase "in bodily form" (Luke 3:22), implying that the Spirit was perceived by others witnessing the event. In the fourth Gospel, John explicitly stated that he indeed "saw the Spirit come down from heaven as a dove and remain on him" (John 1:32). Mark told his readers that humanity was oblivious to the implications of this event. Only Jesus **saw heaven being torn open** (1:10). This term, "torn open," appears at only one other time in the Gospel, at Jesus' death when the same word is employed to describe the tearing of the curtain in the Temple (15:38). Thus, Mark was conveying to his readers that heaven was torn open at the onset of Jesus' ministry, and the world will never be the same. The readers have a glimpse into the heart of heaven as Jesus walked, talked, and lived before them. Moreover, God, through His Son, has access to the world in a new, tangible way. This dovetails into Mark's overall theme of fear; God is loose on the world.

The insider information was not only limited to the tearing of heaven, but also to the overhearing of the voice. **And a voice came from heaven: "You are my Son, whom I love; with you I am well pleased"** (1:11). The readers of Mark are given the opportunity to overhear the most personal conversation between Jesus and His Heavenly Father. Throughout the rest of the Gospel narrative, people wrestle with the various pieces of information about Jesus as they seek an answer to the question, "Who is this man?" The disciples struggled with this identity issue on the Sea of Galilee (4:41); Jesus' family friends from Nazareth pondered the origin of His wisdom (6:2–3); Herod in similar fashion wondered if He is John the Baptist back from the dead (6:16); the people believed He must be a prophet like Elijah. But from the very outset of the story, Mark's readers know Jesus is the divinely appointed Son. This calls to mind Old Testament passages such as the royal enthronement language (1 Sam. 7:12–16; Ps. 2:7; Isa. 42:1). Yet how and when will people recognize Jesus as the king that He is? The next time the divine voice is heard is on the Mount of Transfiguration (9:7). This is on the heels of the confession of Peter that Jesus is the Christ (8:29). Yet as the disciples were descending the mountain, Jesus commanded them "not to tell anyone what they had seen until the Son of Man had risen from the dead" (9:9). Jesus is indeed the royal Son of God, but His throne would be seen first as the cross, His crown as one of thorns, and His royal robe placed upon Him surrounded by mockers. The obedient Son, who has the favor and pleasure of God, was linked intimately with humanity in baptism, suffering, and death.

There are simply not enough textual details to interpret fully Jesus' personal preconceptions regarding this baptismal rite, yet the text implicitly gives the readers a few insights. At the very least, He was linking himself intimately with all humans though He did not need cleansing from sin. Moreover, as He was baptized, He was filled with the very Spirit John had just finished talking about. Thus, He was being depicted as the ideal man, the perfect Son whom Israel has failed to produce. It would be easy to overplay one's hand with what this scene of Jesus' entrance into the Gospel depicts. However, with the exception of the Transfiguration scene in chapter 9, the arrival of Jesus for the human rite of baptism is unsurpassed in its exalted view of Jesus.

The final scene of the book's introduction is Jesus' temptation in the wilderness (1:12–13). The passage begins with a seemingly innocent word for Mark, "immediately" (*euthus*), translated as "at once" in the NIV. The word occurs forty-two times in Mark's gospel, usually during a transitional point in the story. When one scene ended, and metaphorically Jesus might have caught His breath, another event was engaged *immediately*. More than just a throwaway term, this word drives the story forward from one scene to the next at an exhausting pace. And if alert readers read the story (book) as it would have been encountered in the first century—in its entirety—at the same frantic tempo, they will get to the end and be equally fatigued. Thus, Mark would be encountered not simply intellectually but also physically. **At once the Spirit sent him out into the desert** (1:12). The NIV's translation of the word "sent" is just a bit tame. It's a forceful word used eighteen times, almost exclusively associated by Mark with Jesus casting out demons (1:34, 39) and most certainly sets the tone for future cosmic resistance. Possibly the better translation of the word might be the Spirit "drove"[6] Jesus into the desert. This is alarming since Jesus so willingly submitted to the baptism of John, and the readers just heard the words of the Father's divine commendation. Now a word denoting violence and force leaps from the page.

A true difficulty at this point is to read Matthew and Luke's more extensive temptation narrative into this scene to address Mark's more sketchy account. Its brevity cries out for more details. There are no details of the temptations themselves, no reference to the "Son of God" title (which is central to Mark's gospel), no reported conversation between Jesus and Satan, and finally no quotation of Scripture. But just as Mark's baptism sets a theological trajectory of identification with human ills, so does the temptation (1 Cor. 10:13; Heb. 2:17–18). Moreover, adding non-Markan words to the event will certainly deafen his account. For example, the main verb in these two verses is the Spirit "driving" Jesus, not the temptation itself. And the only other active verb is associated with the **angels** who **attended him** (1:13). The one common ingredient with the other accounts is not the presence of Satan, but the place where the event transpires: **in the desert**. Mark described Jesus in passive terms: **he was in the desert . . . He was with the wild animals** (1:13). The juxtaposition of this scene with the previous one demonstrates to Mark's readers that Jesus' role as the "beloved Son" anticipated the ensuing cosmic struggle. One might understand Mark to be arguing that Jesus the ideal Son of God would be doing forty days of battle in the very place where Israel the son wandered faithlessly for forty years. Additionally, Mark established a suspenseful story line for the remainder of the book as he did not elaborate upon the outcome of the wilderness temptations. Though the other synoptic traditions portray at least a temporary victory in the wilderness, in Mark, we are informed only of the existence of the conflict, not the victor. This leaves the reader with the understanding that this occurrence is not a one-time good-evil encounter but will be ongoing until one is destroyed by the other.

ENDNOTES

1. D. Rhodes and D. Michie, *Mark as Story: An Introduction to the Narrative of a Gospel* (Philadelphia: Fortress Press, 1982), p.74.

2. The announcement of the new rule of God is officially proclaimed to the story's participants as Jesus says, "The time has come, . . . The kingdom of God is near." The first opening (1:1–13) is for the reader, the second (1:14–15) in summary fashion reveals the new rule of God to the participants inside the story of Mark.

3. To be precise, Mark reports that the confession arose directly from the centurion's viewing *how* Jesus died. "And when the centurion, who stood there in front of Jesus, heard his cry and saw how he died . . ." (15:39).

4. Readers do not hear this role officially ascribed until 6:14, 24–25. One may wonder if the title was given to him after death, as his name or role was shaped by the tradition that preserved this story. His name is not John the Baptist but John, the one who baptizes.

5. See J. Taylor, *The Immerser: John the Baptist Within Second Temple Judaism* (Grand Rapids, Mich.: William B. Eerdmans, 1997), pp. 58–64 for detailed discussion of impurity.

6. This is the first of more than 150 historic presents in the gospel of Mark. By definition, a historic present occurs when an author uses a present-tense verb referring to a past event. This adds to the vividness of the scene, for it sounds as if it is actually happening right before the reader's eyes. Literally the verse should be translated "Immediately the Spirit is driving Him into the wilderness."

2

JESUS' WORDS AND WORKS

Mark 1:14-45

1. JESUS' FIRST WORDS 1:14-15

There is major shift in the story as Jesus began His speaking ministry. Furthermore, 1:14–15 may serve as a heading or new beginning to the narrative as the announcement of the new rule of God is officially proclaimed as Jesus said, **"The time has come, . . . The kingdom of God is near."** The first opening (1:1–13) provides insider information to the reader. None of the participants seemed to be aware of these facts. If they were, it would be hard to understand how they missed the Christological point of Jesus' words throughout the Gospel. However, this second introduction (1:14–15) summarizes Jesus' ministry in Galilee: declaring the new rule of God.

For the first time in the Gospel, Jesus spoke, and He proclaimed an almost identical message (repent and believe the good news) as that of John the Baptist. Moreover, there is a parallel drawn between the ministry of John and that of Jesus: They both preached (1:7, 14), and they both baptized (1:5, 8). So, it might be fair to assume that if all Judea and Jerusalem responded obediently to John's message, how much more should people respond to this one who is stronger? In these opening words, Mark set the stage for God to reclaim His dominion through His agent, the Son of God. Yet, sadly, Jesus' call to repentance and belief in the gospel only seemed to be superficially fulfilled. There was only minimal response to Jesus' words. Certainly people responded, but nothing comparable to the "all of Judea" response received by the weaker John. Why?

These two verses serve to introduce the Galilean ministry of Jesus, speaking in general terms as if this proclamation may summarize the essential nature of His message. Immediately, there was a location change from the wilderness of Jordan to Galilee. There, Jesus was at the seashore calling disciples (1:16–20) and teaching in the synagogue (1:21–27) so powerfully that His fame spread to all the region of Galilee (1:28). Jesus' renown heightened as He healed (1:29–31), cast out demons (1:32–34), and preached (1:35–39) with such force that He could not enter a town publicly (1:45). Ironically, His only option was to return to the wilderness (1:45), where people from all directions came to Him (1:45). The place where John lived (in the wilderness, 1:4) and preached, the place where the people came out see and hear him (1:5), the place where they repented and were baptized was the place where Jesus' ministry returned because of His outward success. Sadly, the further Mark takes his readers on the journey with Jesus, the more His call fell upon deaf ears (4:10–12; 8:17–21) and hard hearts (6:51; 7:6–7). The more Jesus taught about the gospel and the Kingdom, the more people resisted.

Thus, the repentance described by the opening words of Jesus is not to be understood as an act of the will, as if a character in the story merely needed to correct a false notion of religion (like understanding of Sabbath in chapters 2–3 and purity laws in chapter 7) or revise a cultural norm (family or wealth). Rather, repentance is linked to the battle waged in the wilderness on a cosmic scale.

2. JESUS' FIRST DISCIPLES 1:16–20

Jesus' first foray into the world to bring His kingdom message was the gathering of His first disciples. These men would play a vital role in the ensuing chapters and would be with Him day and night for the next three years, until the arrest in Gethsemane. These men would fail, misunderstand, and desert Jesus. Yet for Mark, they were front and center with the entrance of the kingdom of God. Mark's readers will follow their development and ask all future disciples, if even by contrast, to likewise abandon all and follow Jesus.

As Jesus walked beside the Sea of Galilee, he saw Simon and his brother Andrew casting a net into the lake, for they were fishermen (1:16). The first four disciples were two sets of brothers: Peter and Andrew plus James and John. They would become the inner circle of the Twelve (see 1:29; 13:3; minus Andrew 5:37; 9:2; 14:33). Jesus appeared by the lake with no announcement, and He surprisingly chose fishermen from a rural fishing village to lead this new movement. Peter and Andrew might have been poorer than the rest, for they did not even have a fishing boat like the one the next two disciples possessed. But initially Jesus did not call out leaders but followers: **"Come, follow me"** (1:17). A literal translation of the phrase is "Here, behind Me." Thus, the person of Jesus must have been the deciding factor, not just His persuasive words. He called them to locate themselves directly in line with Jesus, the teacher. It is best not to hear this in the framework of a rabbi in relation to his students, for rabbis did not call their students; students chose their teachers. The relationship Mark was depicting is similar to a charismatic leader in the line of Elijah-Elisha (1 Kings 19:19–21) and may explain why most people misunderstood Jesus to be only an Elijah-like prophet (6:15; 8:28).

Their role was not to be merely passive followers, but Jesus said, **"I will make you fishers of men"** (1:17). This can be heard one of two ways. First, possibly Jesus asked His followers to offer to Him all they had personally and financially, and Jesus would multiply it. Second, this call to be "fishers of men" echoes profoundly the words of Old Testament prophets who used fishing metaphors with reference to drawing people back to God (Jer. 16:14–16; Ezek. 29:4; 47:10; Amos 4:2). Jesus may have been aligning His own followers with the covenant promises of God. He was not moving them in a radically new direction, but rather making a mid-course correction, bringing them back to a scriptural position. There is a striking dissimilarity between this call of Jesus and an Old Testament prophetic call. Jesus called His disciples to follow Him. Prophets, such as Elijah, called people to follow God (1 Kings 19). Rabbis called people to learn and follow the Torah. Jesus was calling them to himself. He expected them to hold nothing back as they followed Him.

The brothers immediately broke their family ties and means of livelihood: **At once they left their nets and followed him** (1:18). Mark gave no clear explanation for the disciples' response. One implication is the authority of Jesus, which will become a major theme in the rest of the book. However, the gospel of John provides other background information; these men had previously been associated with the followers of John the Baptist (John 1:35–42). Additionally, though their decision to follow was abrupt, they remained near Galilee from their call until the end of chapter 8, when they began the final journey to Jerusalem for Jesus' crucifixion. Mark may have been emphasizing the reestablishment of authority; a disciple answered to his teacher, not to the patriarchal authority, in first-century society. Disciples had to reorient their priorities. Jesus was fashioning a new community, even a new family. He said, "Whoever does God's will is my brother and sister and mother" (see 3:31–35).

The second set of brothers whom Jesus called was James and John. They were **in a boat, preparing their nets. Without delay he called them, and they left their father Zebedee in the boat with the hired men and followed him** (1:19–20). Once again we see the reorientation of Jesus' disciples around a new head of household, a new authority. Moreover, the second brothers had a boat and hired men, indicating some sort of business offerings beyond a subsistence family network. This point enhances the level of their sacrifice and undergirds Peter's later claim: "We have left everything to follow you!" (10:28).

3. A DAY IN JESUS' LIFE 1:21–39

Mark 1:21–39 is a series of exorcisms (1:23–26, 32, 34), healings (30–31, 32–34), and teachings (21–22, 27) that are temporally set in the same twenty-four-hour period (see 1:29, 32, 35). This unit seems to climax with Jesus at prayer early the next morning when the disciples declared, **"Everyone is looking for you!"** (1:37). Jesus responded with an early glimpse at His overall mission: **"Let us go . . . to the nearby villages—so I can preach there also. That is why I have come"** (1:38). Thus, this first day in Capernaum is a concise summary of Jesus' work during His Galilean ministry (1:14–8:21).

TEACHING WITH AUTHORITY

They went to Capernaum, and when the Sabbath came, Jesus went into the synagogue and began to teach (1:21). This is an ideal place for a short aside on Jesus as a teacher. There is a close connection between the Markan concept of preaching and teaching. Whatever differentiates them, it is not their content.[1] Though Mark contains more references to Jesus as teacher than any other Gospel, it contains far fewer of Jesus' actual words, with only a few extended examples of His teaching (1:21–27; 2:13; 4:1–9; 6:2, 6, 30, 34; 7:7; 8:31; 9:31; 10:1; 11:17; 12:14, 35; 14:49). The title "teacher," or "rabbi," is the most common one used for Jesus in Mark. Moreover, the major blocks of teaching found in Mark do not contain straightforward instruction, but rather consist of the parabolic material of chapters 4 and 12 and the enigmatic discourse of chapter 13.

This first synagogue scene in 1:22–28 is one of the prime examples. Here the passage opens with Jesus teaching and the people's astonishment at His teaching, yet there is no direct account of the actual content of His teaching. It might well be argued that Mark's Jesus teaches not primarily by word but by action. Specifically in this passage, Mark linked teaching with the divine power of exorcism.

Finally, as will be demonstrated through this commentary, each of Jesus' most revealing teaching moments, such as the parabolic instruction, the feeding narratives, and especially His passion predictions, escaped the grasp of the disciples. He was the teacher sent by God and anointed by His Spirit, yet humanity refused or resisted His instruction at every juncture.

BACKGROUND

SCRIBES

Scribes in antiquity can be likened to the modern secretary as they offered their record-keeping abilities for hire. However, scribes were often associated with political officials or other members of high society. The New Testament links the scribes with the chief priests and the Jewish religious establishment, and it even seems to suggest some authority in their teaching. The New Testament also portrays scribes as a unified group, but this apparent unity was due to their common opposition regarding Jesus.

The people were amazed at his teaching . . . he taught them as one who had authority (1:22). There is something undeveloped in this observation made by Mark that he slowly and subtly unveiled throughout the remainder of the book: an explicit contrast between Jesus and the teachers of the law (traditionally translated as scribes).

Synagogue worship in Jesus' day most likely included prayers, blessings, readings from the Law and the Prophets, translations of the material into Aramaic, and finally an interpretation of the readings. This last element was not based on a scribe's personal exposition of the text, but consisted of a series of interpretations of the passage known as the Oral Tradition (or Tradition of the Elders; see Mark 7:5, 13). Thus, what the scribes taught was essentially a series of legal precedents surrounding the text from previous rabbis, securing their authority from tradition while holding back any personal renderings.[2] Jesus, on the other hand, consistently taught with what Mark called "authority." His source of authority originated from the baptism of the Holy Spirit. Thus, while the scribes quoted other rabbis, Jesus' authority was self-authenticating. **The people were amazed**. A careful exegete of the texts where this word "amazed" (1:22; 6:2; 7:37; 10:26; 11:18) and its synonym (1:27; 10:24, 32) occurs should be cautious not to over-read its meaning. This specific occurrence of the word "amaze" does not denote a faith-creating event, nor for that matter do any others in Mark. Rather, the words "amazed" or "astonished" indicate that the crowds or onlookers had been impacted by Jesus' teaching or by their witness of His miracles. But it does not explicitly mean that they came to faith nor that they adopted Jesus' worldview as their own.

A man . . . who was possessed by an evil spirit cried out (1:23). Literally, the Greek term is "unclean spirit." This is a common way for Mark to refer to a demonic possession.[3] It may be that this was to be contrasted with the designation given to Jesus by the unclean spirit: **"I know who you are—the Holy One of God!"** (1:24). Moreover, for Jesus, this man was not a distraction from His teaching, but Jesus' teaching included bringing mercy and deliverance to the suffering. The words of the man sound more like a confession than a cry, for they contain both Jesus' earthly designation—Jesus of Nazareth—and His divine origin—Holy One of God. In Mark, the residents of the heavenly realm knew and trembled at the name of Jesus; it was humanity who was oblivious to His majesty. Additionally, the unclean spirit sought information relating to

Jesus' mission. **"Have you come to destroy us?"** (1:24). Jesus' response was not to be heard as conversation with the demons, but to silence them. It was to announce once again His mission to the listening crowds as He cast out the demons[4] with a firm rebuke. This act rhetorically answered the unclean spirit's question. Indeed the Holy One of God had come to destroy the works of the evil one.

One should not overlook this first command to silence in the Gospel of Mark (1:25, the same word as to the wind and waves in 4:39). The unclean spirits in this and other passages knew Jesus to be the all-powerful Son of God. However, from Mark's perspective, that message is only partially right. Jesus was not to be proclaimed until He was understood to be the one who had come to suffer and die. Thus, the words of the demons are only partially right, and half a gospel message can be just as dangerous as none. Thus, this is the beginning of what scholars have called the Messianic Secret that runs throughout the first half of the Gospel. It refers to those places where Jesus commands the demons to silence (1:24, 34; 3:11), preventing people from receiving a distorted view of Christ. Surprisingly, Jesus also ordered His disciples to remain silent (8:30; 9:9) until after His death and resurrection.

The closing words of this passage again make note of the people's amazement on the Sabbath day teaching: **The people were all so amazed that they asked each other, "What is this?"** (1:27). This passage is difficult since it is hard to determine with which clause to equate the phrase "and with authority." Should it read as the RSV renders it: "What is this? A new teaching! With authority He commands even the unclean spirits, and they obey him"? Or is the NIV closer to Mark's intent when it associates the authority more directly to the teaching? The best answer is the ambiguous *both*. Earlier in the passage, the authority of Jesus was shown to exceed that of the scribes' (1:22). Moreover, the amazement of the synagogue listeners was squarely based on Jesus' teaching, which could be understood as purely based on Jesus' physical presence and verbal presentation. But here, the crowd's astonishment arose not only from His authoritative teaching, but also His ability to command of the unclean spirits.[5]

News about him spread quickly over the whole region of Galilee (1:28). Ironically, Jesus' command to secrecy did not stop the spread of

His popularity throughout Galilee. Thus, the first miracle in the Gospel, this synagogue power-encounter, was the basis of Jesus' fame. He has authority, much more than the scribes, and He commands demons. The real question that is just beneath the surface will become the driving force in the rest of Mark: "Who is Jesus?" The rest of Mark enumerates the answer, and every word should be heard as a Jesus "teaching moment" for the sole purpose of discovering the nature and purpose of Jesus.

Finally, this initial synagogue event should be seen as a synopsis of Jesus' plan in dealing with both the human and cosmic realms. Humans are whole persons, in need of a holistic salvation. The answer is never to be trivialized into a "going to heaven" answer. Yet people will flock to the spectacular and fixate upon the instant spiritual gratification. Jesus will never cease to offer miracles of mercy, but He will not allow himself to be defined solely by those events. It is full freedom and release from what holds men and women captive that Jesus will proclaim with His teaching and with His suffering and death. In the end, Jesus will not allow a partial gospel to be proclaimed. He will silence any and all people who speak only of the miracles without the cross.

A FEVER HEALED

As soon as they left the synagogue, they went with James and John to the home of Simon and Andrew (1:29). The men took Jesus to their home for what most certainly would be the Sabbath meal. Upon arrival, they discovered Simon's mother-in-law had a fever. For most contemporary readers, this may be the least impressive of Jesus' miracles. But for Torah-centered Jews, a fever was not simply a symptom of an illness. The Law (Lev. 26:16; Deut. 28:22) often gave the impression that fever was a penalty sent by God.[6] **So he went to her, took her hand and helped her up** (1:31). The translation is quite understated with the choice of the word "helped." The original literally says "raised up," which is cloaked in radical healing (2:9, 11–12; 3:3; 5:41; 9:27) and resurrection language (6:14, 16; 14:28; 16:6). This was no less a miracle than the synagogue exorcism; it is simply narrated differently. The first miracle was public; this one is private. The first had Jesus speaking; this time He remained silent. The first He commanded from a distance; He performed this one with a touch. One focused on demon possession, the other with physical illness. The first was dramatic and created amazement; this one is told in tranquil tones.

The scenario closes with words of full healing: **The fever left her and she began to wait on them** (1:31). The domestic qualities of Simon's mother-in-law go beyond first-century hospitality, for the word "wait" is the same word used to describe the angels' ministry to Jesus after His wilderness experience in 1:13. It is the same word Jesus used to describe His overall life-call in 10:45: "For even the Son of Man did not come to be *served*, but to *serve*, and to give his life as a ransom for many" (italics added). It also reflects the discipleship language of the faithful women who followed Jesus to the crucifixion after the disciples themselves deserted Him (15:41). Thus, Jesus' healing readied this woman to follow Him.

A HEALING SUMMARIZED

In the two previous episodes, there was a single exorcism and an individual healed by Jesus. Still, **that evening after sunset the people brought to Jesus all the sick and demon-possessed** (1:32). This intimately linked this event to the other two. In typical summary fashion (see also 1:39; 3:10–12; 6:53–56), Mark reminded his readers that the events reported in this gospel were only a sampling of Jesus' work. Moreover, it was evening, and the Sabbath that began in 1:21 was officially over. The people were carefully adhering to Sabbath practices, while this record may hint that Jesus was demonstrating more mercy to the afflicted than observance to the Jewish Law. This turned to conflict with the Pharisees over Sabbath regulations in 2:23–3:6. One wonders if Mark meant that the whole town was physically gathered at His door, or was this an idiomatic way of saying Jesus was the talk of the town? Either way, once Jesus came to town, it was never the same.

Jesus healed many who had various diseases. He also drove out many demons (1:34). It is quite interesting to note that in this summary statement Jesus distinguishes illness from demonic possession. The second Gospel will always maintain this distinction between healing and exorcism.[7] Jesus almost always touched the sick to cure them, but He vocally commanded the demons to come out.[8] Thus, it would be unfair to say that ancients could not comprehend or communicate the difference between demon-possession and illness. Though they were not inhabitants of a modern scientific age, they were far from naive.[9] An observant reader will notice that **all** the town was at Jesus' doorstep, yet He only healed **many** of the sick and cast out **many** demons. Mark may have been hinting that healing is not some sort of magical or automatic process. Faith will be brought front and center in the Gospel, and this may be preparing for it. By the time Jesus returned home to Nazareth, miracles were restricted by the people's lack of faith. Additionally, in the following episode, the people were still searching for Jesus, meaning all of the needs were yet to be met.

A SOLITARY PRAYER

This next passage begins with Mark's typical dual-faceted introduction—**very early in the morning, while it was still dark** (1:35)—in which he used two expressions where one would seem adequate. Yet the phrase "while it was still dark" temporally links this event to the same Sabbath day as 1:21–34. Thus, in a typical Galilean day, Jesus confronted demons, illness, and exhausting demands on His private time. How do solitude and prayer fit in? **Jesus got up, left the house and went off to a solitary place, where he prayed** (1:35). Possibly for the first time in the Gospel, Mark illuminated that there was an overt difference between Jesus' agenda and the pressing needs of humans. If the primary issue was making Jesus known to the masses, then healing services and public exorcism would accomplish that better than anything. Yet in the Gospel, Jesus never initiated a healing or pursued a demon-possessed person; He responded to human initiative. Thus, it may be fair to say that Jesus' ministry was not a healing ministry as such, but it seemed to arise from the enormity of human suffering combined with Jesus' unique power to meet the need.

Jesus left the house and sought out a solitary place for prayer. The word "solitary" is the same word used in 1:1–13 for "desert." One should not over play the meaning of desert since Jesus was just outside of

Capernaum and since the disciples easily found Him. This must have been a place that Jesus frequented; it is worth noting that Jesus often withdrew from the public forum (1:45; 3:13; 6:31–32, 46; 7:24; 8:27; 9:2, 30–31). **Simon and his companions went to look for him** (1:36). The construction of the phrase "Simon and his companions" may seem strange, since presumably at this point there were only four disciples, but it may indicate that at this early point Simon Peter had assumed the role of leader. Their exclamation that everyone was looking for Jesus gives the readers a feel for the human expectation for Jesus' ministry: "More healings like yesterday, please."

More healings and more exorcisms in the same place was not Jesus' agenda for the new day. **Jesus replied, "Let us go somewhere else—to the nearby villages—so I can preach there also"** (1:38). Jesus called for a move of ministry that had centered itself in Capernaum to smaller, out-of-the-way villages. The core of ministry would not be healing as such but preaching.[10] And it is further described with a clause to substantiate this specific mission: **"That [for this reason] is why I have come"** (1:38). This phrase is pregnant with meaning. It could simply mean that Jesus had come out from Capernaum to the villages. Yet Mark may have had in mind much more. The word "come" is a compound word more literally read "come out." Thus, it may rightly be read "why I have come (out)" at this time to this place (that is, from the thirty-year preparation in Nazareth for this moment). Luke's gospel may take it just a bit further since he worded it, "I must preach the good news of the kingdom of God to the other towns also, because that is why *I was sent*" (Luke 4:43, italics added). It is easy to make the next step to link this concept with the gospel of John's "coming into the world" feature. Is this Mark's way of cloaking the incarnational language of Matthew, Luke, and John?

4. MAKING THE UNCLEAN CLEAN 1:40–45

This final scene in chapter 1 may best be described as transitional. First, it closes Mark's discussions about the healings and exorcisms by directly interjecting Jesus' personal reaction to the despair of others: He was **filled with compassion** (1:41). Thus, His healings in the previous passages are not to be seen as raw power, but divine authority over demons and illness clothed in empathy. Second, it connects Jesus' healing ministry directly to what has been traditionally discussed as the controversy narratives of 2:1–3:6 as Jesus and His disciples engaged the Jewish leaders on a number of religious issues. Thus far, Jesus' actions were universally welcomed, albeit the demons were somewhat distraught. But soon Jesus' perspective will confront the worldview of the Pharisees and the scribes. In this passage, Jesus commanded the now-healed leper, **"go, show yourself to the priest and offer the sacrifices that Moses commanded for your cleansing, as a testimony to them"** (1:44). It is the closing phrase that attracts attention and serves to prepare Mark's readers for the impending confrontation. This was not just Jesus confronting the illness of leprosy, but He was contrasting His compassion with what might be labeled as the normal, callous application of the Levitical laws, seen in His willingness to touch the unclean. This will not go unnoticed by the scribes and Pharisees in Mark 2.

The setting of 1:40–45 appears to be essentially the same as the previous section. Jesus and His disciples were in and around Capernaum, though their sphere of influence had expanded to include more of Galilee (1:39). During their preaching and healing ministry, **a man with leprosy . . . begged . . . , "If you are willing, you can make me clean"** (1:40).

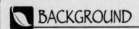

BACKGROUND

LEPROSY

The concept of leprosy is incredibly difficult to understand completely. The problem stems from the symptoms described in Leviticus, from which no specific medical condition can be derived. Through the text of Leviticus, several types of skin lesions that exfoliate the skin are suggested, in which the medical condition leprosy finds its place. The New Testament seems to carry forth these ideas established in the Old Testament.

The Law of Leviticus 13–14 legislates that a priest must declare a person as ceremonially clean or unclean with reference to leprosy. This was one of the most feared diseases and demanded a supernatural cure (Exod. 4:6–8; Num. 12:9–15; 2 Kings 5:1–27). Due to the fear of communal contamination, lepers were excluded from society (Lev. 13:45–46). Jesus was, therefore, probably outside the town during this conversation. The unclean man takes the initiative and comes within close proximity of Jesus. Breaking the taboo was only one issue for Mark; the real question was not one of Jesus' power but of His nature and character. The leper inquired, "I know you have the power, but do you care?"

Filled with compassion, Jesus reached out his hand and touched the man (1:41). There is an interesting debate among scholars as to exactly what word expresses the emotion of Jesus in this encounter. The majority of the ancient manuscripts have the word "compassion," but some of the most ancient documents have instead the word "angry." Both words fit well with Mark's description of Jesus. Throughout the gospel, when Jesus encountered human need, the word "compassion" is often used (see 6:34; 8:2; 9:22). But at the same time, it would be unfair to exclude "anger" from depicting Jesus' response to situations (3:5; 10:14). Either word would be accurate as long as we carefully consider the object of Jesus' compassion or anger. The compassion of Jesus was directed to the leper, while the anger would be intended toward the disease or even toward the social customs that forced the leper to live as an outcast.

Then Jesus broke the legal customs of the day and touched the man (Lev. 11:24–40; 14:46–47). With Jesus, the need of the man superseded the Law. **Immediately the leprosy left him and he was cured** (1:42). The result was instant and apparent to onlookers. But the word "cured" does not have a medical connation as much as a legal or ceremonial one, since it literally reads "clean." He had not just been restored to health, but with a priest's approval, he could reenter the community and return to the Temple to worship and offer sacrifices. Jesus sent him away with a firm warning to silence, with a single exception: **"But go, show yourself to the priest and offer the sacrifices that Moses commanded for your cleansing, as a testimony to them"** (1:44). One could argue that Jesus had discarded the Law for a need, but that is far too simplistic a reading of Jesus. He demanded that the "clean" man adhere to what was a lengthy, eight-day cleansing process for the restoration of a healed leper to society (Lev. 14:1–32).

Instead he went out and began to talk freely, spreading the news (1:45). The term "spreading the news" is the formal term for preaching. This testimony of what Jesus did might have been seen by the Pharisees and scribes as Jesus condoning lawbreaking. Thus, the man's disobedience of Jesus' command to silence and His call to follow the law in fact initiated Jesus' confrontation with the religions leaders.

Jesus could no longer enter a town openly. . . . Yet the people still came to him from everywhere (1:45). This final verse points in two directions. Initially, Jesus' intense popularity demonstrated the caution He had to take in exercising His power and authority, for it begs the question, "Why are they coming?" Simply, they came for a touch from Jesus, the miracle worker. Little else was known by the general public about Jesus; there had been minimal teaching but countless miracles. It will take the remainder of the book of Mark to fill out a deeper, more nuanced understanding of Jesus—not just Messiah but suffering Messiah. The second issue this passage reveals is that when Jesus encounters the Pharisees in the next section, we know that the religious leaders possess the minority opinion. At this point, Jesus' popularity was unparalleled.

ENDNOTES

1. Christopher D. Marshall, *Faith as a Theme in Mark's Narrative* (Cambridge: Cambridge University Press, 1989), pp. 38–39 goes on to argue that in 6:12, 30, both words are used to depict the same event, and the phrase "speaking the word" serves as an equivalent for both preaching (1:15, 45; 14:9) and teaching (4:33; 8:32; 9:31). Furthermore, faith is the desired response to both preaching (1:15) and teaching (2:2, 5; 6:2, 6).

2. This is the oral tradition, often from memory, that would be later codified in the Talmud.

3. Mark uses the term "unclean spirits" eleven times (1:23, 26; 3:11, 30; 5:2, 8, 13; 6:7; 7:25; 9:25) and "demon" or "demon-possessed" fifteen times (1:32, 34, 39; 3:15, 22; 5:15, 18; 6:13; 7:26, 29; 9:38), an almost equal distribution.

4. The NIV reads, "'Be quiet!' said Jesus sternly." The NASB follows the Greek more literally: "Jesus rebuked him, saying, 'Be quiet and come out of him.'" This is typical exorcism language for the gospel of Mark. Jesus commands the demons, and they must comply.

5. The NIV correctly adds the seemingly insignificant word "even" that logically links the two clauses together and places an increasing emphasis upon the exorcism as the source of the amazement. Literally, "What is this? A new teaching . . . with authority . . . and *even* (or also) the unclean spirits he commands and they obey!"

6. David Garland, *Mark: The NIV Application Commentary* (Grand Rapids, Mich.: Zondervan, 1996), p. 72, enumerates places in rabbinic tradition and in Philo where they regarded fever as demonic and as divine punishment.

7. This parallel concept is mentioned again in 3:10–11 and 6:13.

8. Thanks to R. T. France, *The Gospel of Mark: New International Commentary on the Greek Testament* (Grand Rapids, Mich.: William B. Eerdmans, 2002), p. 109, for this insightful observation.

9. Gerd Theissen, *The Miracle Stories of the Early Christian Tradition* (Minneapolis: Fortress Press, 1983), pp. 85–94.

10. This is the last time Jesus is said to preach in the gospel. He is only the subject of the verb in 1:14 and 1:38–39. From here on out, His disciples will do the preaching, as well as a few other followers. His ministry is defined by the term "teach."

EARLY CONTROVERSIES

Mark 2:1—3:6

1. AUTHORITY TO FORGIVE SINS 2:1–12

If one assumes that the issue of controversy is subtly introduced in the previous story about the healing of the leper, Mark brought it front and center in Jesus' confrontation with the scribes. This miracle on the surface is much like an extension of the previous ones in chapter 1. It is a demonstration of Jesus' authority over illness, described in summary form in 1:32–34. Yet by means of His declaration "Son, your sins are forgiven" and His self-authenticating Son of Man statement, Jesus extended the scope of His authority exponentially. "Miracle worker" is no longer a title that explains Jesus. Christological titles must be employed to speak properly about Him. This may be summarized well by the people's response to the entire incident: **This amazed everyone and they praised God, saying, "We have never seen anything like this!"** (2:12).

The setting of this passage is somewhat linked to the previous by location (**Capernaum**), by time (**a few days later**), and by the repetition of the word **home** (2:1). The latter likely refers to the home of Simon and Andrew (1:29). Moreover, all this is in response to the people "hearing." Though this term may have a commonplace feel about it, this theme of "hearing" occurs for the first time and will keep rising up at strategic points throughout the gospel. In Jesus' parabolic instruction in chapter 4, the only command given to the disciples was "Listen!" During Jesus' most pressing teaching moments, He asked for listening ears (7:14; 8:18). The conflict with the Jewish leaders in the Temple (chapters 11–12) centered in their refusal to listen. Most importantly, the words of the Father's voice from heaven at the Transfiguration were clear: "This is my Son whom I love. Listen to him!" (9:7). The gospel of Mark from start to finish is a call to discipleship, which begins with auditory obedience.

Mark set the scene in the first four verses of the chapter, and the crowd that had gathered is reminiscent of 1:33, when the whole town came together. **So many gathered that there was no room left . . . and he preached the word to them. Some men came, bringing to him a paralytic** (2:2–3). Though the NIV reads "some men," the original is a bit less clear, simply reading an unidentified "they." Again Mark set a healing in the context of preaching (see 1:21–28; 1:45; literally, "speaking the word"). **They made an opening in the roof above Jesus and, after digging through it, lowered the mat the paralyzed man was lying on** (2:4). The crowd prevented the men from getting their friend to Jesus, so they must have taken an outside staircase to the roof and torn away the mud and twig roof. Debris must have showered the crowd below. Their behavior must have been tremendously disruptive to Jesus and the listeners, but Jesus' first response was warmly affirming. **When Jesus saw their faith, he said to the paralytic, "Son, your sins are forgiven"** (2:5). The surprises kept coming; Jesus did not comment on the man's illness, but declared his sins forgiven. This must have silenced the crowd since to a Jew, sin and illness were intimately linked (Isa. 40:2; John 9:1–3; 1 Cor. 11:30), and Jesus had connected His authoritative word with the offering of forgiveness. Jesus was certainly taking this beyond what the Law has prescribed. In the previous story, when He healed the leper, He instructed him to fulfill the Law's legal requirements, to go to a priest and have himself declared ceremonially clean. Moreover, a priest could pronounce forgiveness based upon a number of criteria: repentance, restitution, and sacrifice (Lev. 4, 5, 16, 17). But here, Jesus' bold words seem to be above the Law, and onlookers easily could have assumed He was taking sin lightly if forgiveness is free. There were only two possibilities that could be drawn from this declaration by Jesus: the kingdom of God had come or Jesus was a blasphemer.

Interestingly, Mark did not report the reaction of the friends, but the angst of the scribes. This initial conflict with the scribes set the tone of the relationship for the rest of the gospel. But in this episode, it is important to note that nothing was said directly to Jesus. **Now some teachers of the law were sitting there, thinking to themselves** (2:6). Elsewhere in Mark (8:16; 9:33), this phrase implies private conversation meant to exclude Jesus because His teachings were too difficult to integrate. The content of their private discussion is revealed: **"Why does this fellow talk like that? He's blaspheming! Who can forgive sins but God alone?"**[1] (2:7). God alone can forgive sins (Exod. 34:7; Isa. 43:25; 44:22), and the scribes knew this too well. But they missed what the prologue to the Gospel had declared to the readers: the "more powerful one" announcement of John the Baptist and the Sonship language of the Father at Jesus' baptism. Jesus spoke for God.

Immediately Jesus knew in his spirit that this was what they were thinking in their hearts (2:8). It would be minimizing the text to conclude that Jesus was simply reading the scribes' body language. Mark tried to covey that Jesus was not pronouncing forgiveness flippantly, but He knew (and knows) the hearts of people, good and evil.[2] Thus, the true contrast in the story is not between Jesus and the scribes, but between the paralytic (pronounced forgiven) and the scribes (pronounced hardhearted). To their lack of faith, Jesus retorted, **"Why are you thinking these things? Which is easier: to say to the paralytic, 'Your sins are forgiven,' or to say, 'Get up, take your mat and walk'?"** (2:8–9). Jesus followed scriptural guidelines for determining a faithful prophet.

I will raise up for them a prophet like you from among their brothers; I will put my words in his mouth, and he will tell them everything I command him. . . . You may say to yourselves, "How can we know when a message has not been spoken by the LORD?" If what a prophet proclaims in the name of the LORD does not take place or come true, that is a message the LORD has not spoken. That prophet has spoken presumptuously. Do not be afraid of him. (Deut. 18:18, 21–22)

Thus, to convince the scribes that He indeed had the authority to declare the paralytic forgiven, **He said to the paralytic, "I tell you, get up, take your mat and go home." He got up, took his mat and walked out in full view of them all** (2:10–12). The paralytic's healing thus authenticated Jesus' declaration of the man's forgiveness.

This amazed everyone and they praised God, saying, "We have never seen anything like this!" (2:12). The crowd had already witnessed numerous miracles of Jesus, so their amazement could not be solely based on that fact. Rather, Jesus' ordering of the events is most revealing. For according to the Law, one is healed and then declared clean by the priests. But in this episode, Jesus first declares who is clean, and then healed based upon faith. The world seemed no longer to be functioning under Law, but under the grace of the one who knew what was in one's heart.

2. A DINNER AND THE CALL OF LEVI 2:13–17

This passage and the earlier call narrative of 1:16–20 have many similarities, yet the striking difference is quite illustrative. Levi was not a fisherman, but a tax collector. For Jesus to call a "sinner" (2:15) to be a part of His inner circle was highly inappropriate from a Jewish perspective. Not only would this further the animosity between Jesus and the scribes, but His choice of dinner companions most certainly would have offended the sensibilities of the common person.

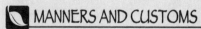 **MANNERS AND CUSTOMS**

TABLE FELLOWSHIP

Table fellowship was the quintessential social event and public act of acceptance. It also was the event that separated Jews from non-Jews. Jews, by tradition, were not to eat with Gentiles (Acts 10:27–28; Gal. 2:11–13). Therefore, when Jesus ate with the sinners, it was a sign that He accepted them, to the abhorrence of the Jewish leaders. It served as one of the defining characterizations of the kingdom of God.

In each of the next four scenes, Jesus' actions raised a question by His opponents, which in turn Jesus directly answered. In this case the question was **"Why does he eat with tax collectors and 'sinners'?"** (2:16). The answer was the core of His very mission: **"It is not the healthy who need a doctor, but the**

sick. I have not come to call the righteous, but sinners" (2:17). This question-answer repartee continued until the conclusion of the larger section (2:1–3:6), when finally the Pharisees and the Herodians conspired together to kill Jesus (3:6). Jesus was that offensive.

Once again Jesus went out beside the lake. A large crowd came to him, and he began to teach them (2:13). Jesus had not moved far from home, His popularity had not waned, and His customs of ministry had not varied. **As he walked along, he saw Levi son of Alphaeus sitting at the tax collector's booth** (2:14). This person called Levi by Mark and Luke may be the tax collector named Matthew in the first Gospel. An individual having two names was not unusual in the first century. Peter had two Hebrew names, Simon and Peter (Cephas); another disciple was known primarily by his Hebrew name, Thomas, but sometimes by his Greek title, Didymus (John 11:16).

Is this Levi (Matthew?) one of the twelve disciples? For the name Levi does not occur in any of the four lists of the disciples (Matt. 10:2–4; Mark 3:16–18; Luke 6:13–16; Acts 1:13). But Matthew does appear in all of the lists, as does James the son of Alphaeus (Mark 3:18). It is possible that Matthew/Levi and James had different fathers by the same name. But more probable, Jesus named three sets of brothers in the Twelve: Andrew-Peter, James-John, and Matthew-James.

However, if one fixates upon the Levi-Matthew debate, there is a potential to be distracted from another keen twist that is a part of Mark's story. Maybe a reader will wonder if the summons of a tax collector (or a factory worker, truck driver, teacher, homemaker) is just the same as those of Jesus' inside core. Then a profound truth arises: Jesus' words **"Follow me"** (2:14) were in no way limited to the Twelve. The bidding of Jesus is open to all, regardless of their stature in society or their religiosity. This would be brought to the forefront in just a few verses when Mark described the people eating with Him in Levi's house: **While Jesus was having dinner at Levi's house, many tax collectors and "sinners" were eating with him and his disciples, for there were many who followed him** (2:15). On one hand, Mark may have been making a distinction between the Twelve and all others. But on the other hand, he was not saying that the "average" call was any less profound, nor that "following Jesus" was to be seen as optional to people other than the disciples.

The voice of God beckons all men and all women to repentance, and the appropriate response of all humanity is to follow Him.

Mark highlighted both the immediacy and the permanence of obedience as **Levi got up and followed him** (2:14). Levi was abandoning his post, which would have been under the control of Herod Antipas rather than the Romans. The other disciples were fishermen and easily could return to their lifelong trade—and they indeed did (see John 21:3)—but not so with Levi.

One can hear the inflammatory language that paints the picture of the ensuing dinner party. **While Jesus was having dinner at Levi's house, many tax collectors and "sinners" were eating with him and his disciples** (2:15). Around the table sat Jesus, the disciples, and "many" tax collectors and sinners.[3] The scribes were strict law keepers, and the law clearly stated who was clean and unclean, who was welcome company at a meal and who was not. In the previous episode Jesus forgave sinners; here He ate with them, ratcheting up the level of conflict.

This is the first time in the gospel that Mark employed the term "disciples." It is not used exclusively of the Twelve, but it does denote a closer association since it is often used in parallel with the phrase "with him" (3:14, 34). With the interjection of the explanatory clause, **for there were many who followed him** (2:15), a reader may wonder if Jesus was considering the many tax collectors and sinners among His disciples. Three times in succession, Mark used the phrase "tax collectors and sinners,"[4] bringing the issue to the table, so to speak. Since the conflict had taken on a public nature, the scribes saw the necessity to ask the disciples, **"Why does he eat with tax collectors and 'sinners'?"**[5] (2:16). Each of the questions raised by Jesus' opponents in this extended controversy unit (2:7, 16, 18, 24) begins with the word "why." They are seeking the rationale for His counter-religious behavior. At this point in the story it is unclear if they sincerely are seeking for the truth or for evidence to discredit Him.

Jesus' reply is housed in the form of a mission statement: **"It is not the healthy who need a doctor, but the sick. I have not come to call the righteous, but sinners"** (2:17). A careful reader will remember that in 1:38, Jesus stated His reason for coming was to preach the good news and drive out demons. He further refined the reasons for His coming to include another group that would have been excluded in a wholesale manner by the religious leaders: the sinners. Additionally, the object of Jesus' mission was seen as parallel with that of John the Baptist: for "repentance for the forgiveness of sins" (1:4). This also lined up with Jesus' first words in the Gospel: "Repent and believe the good news" (1:15). Jesus' proverb-turned-to-mission-statement defended the company with whom He ate, since any doctor must attend to sick patients. Thus any effective healer must be allowed to get his hands dirty.

3. THE FASTING QUESTION 2:18–22

The previous story was an exuberant dinner party, and this next one centers around fasting. Thus, the story linkage is not temporal but topical. **"How is it that John's disciples and the disciples of the Pharisees are fasting, but yours are not?"** (2:18). For the first time, a question was directed to Jesus, but ironically it was in reference to His disciples, not to His words or behavior. It is worthy to note that this was a clash of three sets of disciples: Jesus', John's, and the Pharisees'. The question set the disciples into camps of the old order or the new order. The practice of fasting was not seen as obedience to laws in the Old Testament but was more ascetic.[6] Thus, this may have been a clash of competing "renewal" movements in first-century Judaism. Moreover, the conviction of the two fasting groups was that self-denial is certainly more spiritual than celebration.

First, Jesus did not dismiss fasting, as the continuation of fasting in the future Christian community demonstrates. Rather, He asserted that the time was not best served by fasting, which He illustrated with three parabolic statements. The first involved **the guests of the bridegroom**. They would fast **when the bridegroom will be taken from them** (2:19–20). Jesus portrayed himself as the bridegroom, and entrance into the Kingdom was analogous with a wedding feast. This assertion may be viewed as overtly messianic, since God himself is portrayed as the bridegroom of Israel and the wedding metaphor is scattered throughout the Old Testament (Isa. 61:10; 62:4–5; Hos. 2:14–20). Whether the two opposing fasting groups caught this messianic claim is unknown. But at the lowest level, Jesus was asserting that a wedding is a time of joy and feasting, not one of fasting and sorrow. The exuberance of the people toward Jesus thus far in His ministry affirmed Jesus' declaration of the Kingdom. Jesus' harsh, contrasting remarks, **but the time will come . . . and on that day,** asserted that a time of mourning and fasting would be more appropriate when the bridegroom was taken away, perhaps a subtle reference to His impending death. However, another interpretation that is equally fitting in the Gospel is that there would come a time when the enthusiasm of following Jesus would dissipate and a more stoic or even more disciplined form of discipleship may be called for. This would come about once the participants in the Kingdom realized that a party atmosphere was not always in vogue, but the call to follow would soon be coupled with a call to sacrifice and death (8:31–38).

"No one sews a patch of unshrunk cloth on an old garment. . . . And no one pours new wine into old wineskins" (2:21–22). These two parables, taken from everyday life, further supported Jesus' argument that His "new" was incompatible with the "old." The old was represented by a system of disapproval and rejection of sinners that arose in the immediately previous two passages. The new was displayed by Jesus' declaration of forgiveness and healing. He was not a reformer but a transformer. And if one adopted the position merely to "patch" the old system by means of compromises or concessions, the outcome would be bankrupt.

4. THE SABBATH QUESTION 2:23–27

In this incident in the larger controversy section (2:1–3:6), the Pharisees were not accusing Jesus' disciples of neglecting marginal Jewish matters (fasting) but of breaking the legal core: Sabbath regulations. The next episode is linked thematically by another Sabbath day challenge (3:1–6), but that took place inside a synagogue rather than out in a grain field. What may have begun back in 2:6 as a private, scribal conversation expressing reservations toward the words and actions of Jesus became a full-fledged plan to eliminate Jesus (3:6). This passage plays a central role in demonstrating that Jesus and His disciples were a threat that had to be purged from society.

One Sabbath Jesus was going through the grainfields, and as his disciples walked along, they began to pick some heads of grain (2:23). Mark's temporal marker, **one Sabbath**, does not situate this episode with precision, but in Palestine, grain harvests take place in April or May. But the issue of **Sabbath**, which is a core value in Judaism, became the primary dividing point of this debate as **the Pharisees said to him, "Look, why are they doing what is unlawful on the Sabbath?"** (2:24). Sabbath keeping was one of the values that set Jews apart from all other people (circumcision was another). However, the definition of how to keep the Sabbath properly was not universally agreed upon by all Jews. The Old Testament contains two

MANNERS AND CUSTOMS
PROPERLY OBSERVING THE SABBATH

One of the chief characteristics of the Sabbath was the abstinence from work. However, the natural progression would be to define "work" properly. Hoping to prevent even the most unintentional violation, preventative decrees were installed in order to deter such a possibility. These laws were later defined by Jesus as the "tradition of the elders" (Mark 7:5) or the "traditions of men" (7:8). These laws were designed with inherently good motives, but Jesus clashed with them when they hindered God's commands (7:13).

positive admonitions for the day: It was to be a day of rest and it was to be considered holy. Yet, those calls were too vague to assure the Jews of being compliant. Even in the places where the Old Testament details Sabbath day prohibitions (Exod. 16:22–30; 34:21; 35:2–3; Num. 15:32–36; Neh. 13:15–22), one cannot find a concise definition of what is actually being forbidden. For example, what does "you shall not do any work"

BACKGROUND
MISHNA

Compiled around 200 C.E., the Mishnah was the first authoritative collection of the oral law (traditions of men, see Mark 7:5, 8, 13), which was traditionally given to Moses on Mount Sinai. It was built off the teachings of the Old Testament, and, citing well over one hundred renowned Jewish teachers, it sought to shed light on ambiguous elements of the Torah. The Mishnah's endurance was solidified as it served as the foundation for later rabbinic thought, that is, the Talmud.

(Exod. 20:10; Deut. 5:14) mean? The teaching that addresses these issues was ultimately codified in the Mishnah by the end of the second century A.D.

Yet there is no reason to think that the oral tradition of the Jews, which was the basis for these principles, was not well established for use by the Pharisees in Jesus' day. The task of the Jewish religious leaders was to leave nothing to chance when it came to identifying to the Jewish people what prescribed Sabbath obedience. Most conceivable possibilities from everyday life were explored and then documented. These came to be documented in the Mishnaic tractate known as the *Šabbāt* and contained thirty-nine forbidden acts for Sabbath keeping, one of which included "reaping," the focus of this passage. A modern reader should not assume that there was no room for debate within the disparate groups in Judaism regarding the application of Sabbath practices. But the Jewish problem with Jesus seemed to be that He simply did not want to debate the Sabbath issue. Rather He swept aside the whole matter, placing it under the rubric of His own authority, climaxing in the second Son of Man declaration: **"the Son of Man is Lord even of the Sabbath"** (2:28).

Jesus' response was a somewhat cryptic appeal to Scripture (1 Sam. 21): **"Have you never read what David did when he and his companions were hungry and in need? . . . [H]e entered the house of God and ate the consecrated bread . . . he also gave some to his companions"** (2:25–26). Jesus appealed to the precedent set by David and supported by Scripture that human necessity trumps legal restrictions. Garland says it this way: "The Scripture tacitly sanctions his actions by not condemning him."[7] But the implied nuance of Jesus' interpretation was not that David was simply hungry and this justified the breaking of the Law. That would mean merely that David (and by implication Jesus) was justifying law-breaking based solely upon need, thereby relegating the Law to a quasi-situational ethic. David's action in eating the consecrated bread and the disciples' reaping grain was "forbidden" on the Sabbath. Rabbinic exegetes explained this as necessity over regulation, saving of life over law. Yet in neither story was the threat of the loss of life imminent.

So, what is the real issue in the debate? It can be placed into two categories. First, Mark was demonstrating to his readers that Jesus and His disciples had not adopted the strict regulations of the oral tradition. As will be discussed in chapter 7, the oral tradition (also called "traditions of men," 7:8) was created by the Pharisees to create a protective hedge around the

Law to prevent Jewish people from unknowingly transgressing it. Yet, from Jesus' perspective, these teachings of men detracted from the real purpose of the commandments of God regarding the Sabbath. It was not "to do" rules but to abide in His rest. The Pharisees had failed to understand that **"The Sabbath was made for man, not man for the Sabbath"** (2:27).

The second issue that Jesus revealed in this passage is found in the climactic declaration, **"the Son of Man is Lord even of the Sabbath"** (2:28). This causal link is significant. If the Sabbath was made for man (an expression meaning that the Sabbath was made for Israel), then the Son of Man, who represented the ideal representative of Israel, was Lord of the Sabbath. Thus, Jesus declared He alone had the authority to interpret proper religious practice in perfect harmony with the Law of God.

5. SECOND SABBATH CONTROVERSY 3:1–6

The series of controversy stories reaches its climax in this passage (2:1–3:6). This is accomplished with the careful integration of subject matter. The first six verses of chapter 3 are about a healing in a synagogue much like 2:1–12. The controversy was not merely about Jesus' authority but about when the healing took place, on the Sabbath (as did the incident in 2:23–28). Also, the onlookers were certainly the Pharisees from the previous episode in the fields, who **were looking for a reason to accuse Jesus, so they watched him closely to see if he would heal him on the Sabbath** (3:2). The level of accusation directed toward Jesus had risen from the scribal self-talk of 2:6 to the sidebar conversation with Jesus' disciples (2:16) to their questioning of Jesus about His disciples (2:18, 24). Here, the Pharisees believed they were watching a lawbreaker in action.

With the simple interjection of the phrase **another time** (3:1), Mark linked this event with the disciples' return from their confrontational journey in the grainfields in the previous passage. It may be assumed that this synagogue is the same one in which the people of Capernaum witnessed the display of Jesus' authority not long before (2:1–12).

Irony underscores the passage, for the Pharisees apparently took Jesus' power to heal for granted; they simply wanted to know if He would do so on the Sabbath. Jesus did not disappoint the onlookers; He did not wait for a more private moment to deal with **a man with a shriveled hand** (3:1) but called for a public referendum by commanding the man, **"Stand up in front of everyone"** (3:3). In the parallel passages in Matthew (12:11–12) and Luke (13:15; 14:5), when questioned about healing on the Sabbath, Jesus presented the well-accepted argument that on the Sabbath, the relief of animal suffering is permitted. Here Jesus laid the matter out in a more generic, rhetorical question: **"Which is lawful on the Sabbath: to do good or to do evil, to save life or to kill?"** (3:4). The Pharisees' silence is revealing, for they neither wanted to be accused of Sabbath breaking themselves nor of sponsoring the taking a life.

Mark provided insider information regarding the emotions of Jesus at this point. **He looked around at them in anger and, deeply distressed at their stubborn hearts** (3:5). The cause for anger is linked directly to their stubborn hearts, a phrase employed throughout the New Testament to depict the Jewish nation's blindness to recognize Jesus as the Messiah (Rom. 11:7, 25; 2 Cor. 3:14; John 12:40). Moreover, Mark used the same concept to describe the disciples' inability to grasp the meaning of Jesus' feeding miracles (6:52; 8:17). Thus, stubborn hearts may describe an overall human dilemma that can only be overcome by divine transformation.

As the Pharisees froze in their response to Jesus, the man with the withered hand immediately **stretched it out, and his hand was completely restored** (3:5). The narration of the cure seems to be relegated to the background of the passage. The man extended an injured hand (arm?), and Jesus restored it without a touch, only a word. The real stretch was for the Pharisees to construe this as Sabbath work. Yet the agenda of the onlookers had been set from the beginning: to find a reason to accuse Jesus. **Then the Pharisees went out and began to plot with the Herodians how they might kill Jesus** (3:6). The surprising turn of events in the story is not the hard-heartedness of the Pharisees, but their association with the Herodians.

BACKGROUND

WHO WERE THE HERODIANS?

The Herodians were a group of people committed to the endurance of Herod's reign in Galilee. In essence they were political activists; likely they were religiously and economically affiliated with the Sadducees.

The earlier public silence of the Pharisees leads to private horror for the readers, who find the Pharisees departing the synagogue to collaborate with their political enemies, the Herodians. The NIV chooses not to translate the simple Greek adverb "immediately." One should not overlook the irony of the fact that as Jesus chose to heal on the Sabbath, they likewise conspired to take Jesus' life on the same day.

ENDNOTES

1. Note that the accusation of blasphemy is unstated here, but will return in Jesus' trial with the high priest's charge in 14:64.

2. The Old Testament repeatedly records that God knows the heart (1 Sam. 16:7; 1 Chron. 28:9; Ps. 139:1–2; Jer. 17:9–10). The New Testament reports the same (Luke 16:15; Acts 1:24).

3. The Greek is not nearly as clear as to who the subject of the verb is in 2:15 and who precisely the owner of the house was. It simply reads "he" was eating at "his" house. Nowhere else does Mark refer to the house in Capernaum as Jesus' house (only as Simon's), so it might be strange to assume that this was anyone's other than Levi's house. This enhances the offense. Mark may have been vague in the matter intentionally, thereby raising the issue of who is the host of this dinner. Possibly Jesus was being implied, for when a meal was given, Jesus seemed to become the official or unofficial host no matter where it transpired.

4. Mark uses "tax collectors and sinners" on the first and third occurrence and "sinners and tax collectors" in the middle.

5. In the previous passage (2:1–12) the scribes talked to themselves about the matter of Jesus forgiving sins (2:6). Here, they ask the disciples (2:16). It is not until the next passage that anyone directly asks Jesus a question.

6. The only prescribed fast for Jews is on the Day of Atonement, and Zechariah 8:19 indicates that in the post-exilic period there were four additional fasts. It is in the New Testament (Luke 18:12) that one discovers that the Pharisees moved to practicing twice weekly fasts.

7. David Garland, *Mark: The NIV Application Commentary* (Grand Rapids, Mich.: Zondervan, 1996), p. 106.

4

THE CROWDS GATHER

Mark 3:7-35

1. SUMMARY OF SUCCESS 3:7-12

Mark 3:7-12 subtly shifts from the synagogue to the outdoor ministry by the lake, where Jesus was not limited by space or the disapproval of officials. Through this section, readers observe the increasing contrast of opinions regarding Jesus between the Jewish leaders and the masses. The lengthy summary of Jesus' activities (see also 6:53-56; 1:14-15; 1:32-34) causes the reader to focus in on Jesus' miracles (**all he was doing**, 3:8). Though Mark would return to Jesus' teaching, Jesus' initial popularity did not arise from His words, but from His deeds. The crowds gathered for healing and deliverance, which gave rise to the opportunity to teach. Thus, the **large crowd from Galilee** [that] **followed** (3:7) Jesus was augmented by all who flowed in to see Him **from Judea, Jerusalem, Idumea, and the regions across the Jordan and around Tyre and Sidon** (3:8). The geographic region stretched to the farthest recesses of Jewish territory and into Gentile territory. John the Baptist was said to draw out Judea and Jerusalem to the desert for baptism (1:5). Here, the one who is greater than he—Jesus—drew crowds from every corner of the Jewish map, indicating just how far His popularity had spread.

Because of the crowd he told his disciples to have a small boat ready for him, to keep the people from crowding him (3:9). The demands of the crowd have come up before (1:45; 2:2-4), and Jesus took precautionary measures by calling for a boat to serve as a mobile lectern.

It seems as if the people had taken their healing needs to another level as **those with diseases were pushing forward to touch him** (3:10). Mark's language is dramatic and describes a chaotic scene as people are literally "falling over" Jesus to touch Him. The almost "magical" quality the people projected onto Jesus repeated in the life of Peter in Acts 5:15–16 and later with Paul in Acts 19:11–12. **Whenever the evil spirits saw him, they fell down before him and cried out, "You are the Son of God"** (3:11). Mark discussed the unclean spirits separately from disease. But their exorcism is submerged beneath their recognition of the true identity of Jesus. Rather than speaking words of expulsion, Jesus commanded silence. Mark set up a contrast between the demons who knew Jesus and the people who missed what the cosmic world already knew: He is the Son of God. This title has been introduced earlier in the Gospel title (1:1) and by the declaration from heaven, "You are my Son" (1:11). An earlier unclean spirit confessed Jesus as the "Holy One of God" (1:24), but this title seems to supplant it in Christological importance since it will be the ultimate revelation of Jesus again at the Transfiguration (9:7), at His trial (14:61–62), and the confession of the centurion at the crucifixion (15:39). The ironic undertone of this passage is that the demons were ready to fall before Jesus and confess He is the Son of God, while humanity stumbled over Jesus' identity.

2. APPOINTMENT OF THE TWELVE 3:13–19

Thus far in the Gospel the reader has been introduced to five followers who officially were called by Jesus (1:16–20; 2:14). Though many would respond to Jesus, Mark faithfully kept a distinction between the Twelve and all others.[1] As the story becomes more and more focused on the identity of Jesus (especially in 8:22–10:52), Jesus appears to separate himself with the Twelve, and Mark makes it clear when there are others invited (see 8:34). Two issues are important to note. First, the entire group is male. This is due to the social norms of the day rather than Jesus imposing theological conclusions on gender distinctions. For men to travel closely with women other than their wives was taboo. However, several comments are made throughout Jesus' itinerant ministry in which women are highlighted for

their faithfulness (Luke 8:2–3; 10:38–42), they were present at the crucifixion (15:40–41), and they were first to hear the good news of His
resurrection (16:1–8). Second, the number twelve is more certainly symbolic. Though Mark did not make the explicit claim to the disciples'
representing the restoration of Israel that Matthew (19:28) and Luke
(22:30) did, it nevertheless is not an arbitrary number. Moreover, though
the names of the disciples in the New Testament lists vary in each presentation (Mark 3; Matt. 10; Luke 6; Acts 1), their number and corporate
nature stands unwavering.

**Jesus went up on a mountainside and called to him those he
wanted, and they came to him** (3:13). The exact location is not identified. Once again, Jesus seems to have been setting himself (1:35) and His
followers apart from the crowds (6:32; 7:24; 8:27). Additionally, since
the number twelve plays more than a cursory role, this passage may echo
many of the formative mountaintop experiences in the history of Israel
(Exod. 3: 9–20; 1 Kings 19). **He appointed twelve—designating them
apostles—that they might be with him and that he might send them
out to preach and to have authority to drive out demons** (3:14–15).
The term "appoint" is used in conjunction with the word "designating"
(literally, naming), but both are being further enhanced by two clear purpose clauses.

The first purpose is to be with Jesus, which can be simply understood
as being traveling companions of Jesus. But note how Mark utilized the
terminology being "with Jesus" throughout the rest of the gospel. For
being "with Him" would take on a fuller and deeper meaning as Jesus'
identity and the call He placed upon His followers was fleshed out. Being
designated as a disciple would not merely be a matter of physical location, but it would constitute abandoning one's own agenda and fully
adopting Jesus'. The discipleship training material in chapters 8–10 elaborates on the identity-call issue, but the true challenge for being "with
Jesus" would come to a climax in the Passion narrative (chapters 14–16).
During Jesus' arrest immediately following Gethsemane (14:43–52),
Mark's readers find all the disciples fled from Jesus. Then, the three-fold
denial of Peter began: "You also were *with* that Nazarene, Jesus" (14:67,
italics added). Thus, the call to discipleship is a call to be "with Jesus"

both in terms of physical location, but even more intimately it is a way of describing one's life mission and ultimate loyalty.

The second purpose for Jesus' call to discipleship could be termed occupational, but that designation is far too cold, since this call was for His disciples to join in His own missional thrust in the ushering in of the kingdom of God. The call of the Twelve was principally to participate with what Jesus had already performed in the gospel, preaching (1:14–15, 38) and casting out demons (1:24). Additionally, for the disciples to fulfill this ministry, they needed to be given the same "authority" that had been uniquely Jesus' thus far (1:22, 27; 2:10). The tension in the gospel would soon be posed in a question: "Are they ready to assume such a responsibility?" The disciples themselves put into action this second function of their call once they were sent out two by two (6:7). Upon returning from their first successful mission, apparently the transfer of authority had occurred. Yet, when they were later called upon to exorcise a demon (9:14–29), they were powerless. Thus, the efficacy of the disciples' mission

CHART

COMPARATIVE LIST OF DISCIPLES

Matthew 10	Mark 3	Luke 6	Acts 1
Simon (Peter)	Simon (Peter)	Simon (Peter)	Peter
Andrew	James	Andrew	John
James (son of Zebedee)	John	James	James
John	Andrew	John	Andrew
Philip	Philip	Philip	Philip
Bartholomew	Bartholomew	Bartholomew	Thomas
Thomas	Matthew	Matthew	Bartholomew
Matthew	Thomas	Thomas	Matthew
James (son of Alphaeus)	James (son of Alphaeus)	James (son of Alphaeus)	James (son of Alphaeus)
Thaddeus	Thaddeus	Simon the Zealot	Simon the Zelot
Simon the Zealot	Simon the Zealot	Judas (son of James)	Judas (son of James)
Judas Iscariot	Judas Iscariot	Judas Iscariot	———

had to be further refined with a clearer understanding of the mission of Jesus; authority and the dissemination of power had to be tempered with servanthood and the relinquishment of personal honor.

Reconciling this specific list of the disciples in Mark 3 with the others in the New Testament remains a hermeneutical puzzle, yet the names and nicknames point toward the disciples' roles in the remainder of the book. **Simon (to whom he gave the name Peter) James son of Zebedee and his brother John (to them he gave the name Boanerges, which means Sons of Thunder)** (3:16–17). The first in the list, Simon, was named Peter (*petros*, meaning rock). The next two, James and John were given both family lineage as well as a title that would be descriptive of future behavior (for example, 10:35–45). The first three men also formed what might be termed Jesus' inner circle of three who would be with Him at His most significant and revealing points in the gospel: the raising of Jairus's daughter (5:37), the Transfiguration (9:2), and in Gethsemane (14:33). Though this may have afforded them more of an opportunity to witness Jesus at His high points, it did not afford them any meaningful understanding (9:6, 9–10; 14:37) beyond the rest of the group. Next comes in rapid-fire succession **Andrew, Philip, Bartholomew, Matthew, Thomas, James son of Alphaeus, Thaddaeus, Simon the Zealot and Judas Iscariot, who betrayed him** (3:18–19). Andrew, mentioned in the opening call narratives (1:16, 29) was seemingly disconnected from the first tier.[2] None of the others would be mentioned by name again, except of course, Judas Iscariot. The meaning of his "last" name has most often been understood regionally, a "man of Kerioth." This might make Judas the only non-Galilean among the Twelve. Another suggestion links Judas with the zealot-bandit movement (akin to Simon the Zealot), whose primary political agenda was to overthrow the Roman oppressors from power in Jewish land.[3] Yet Mark refocused his readers' questions from a name or a place designation to an act: **who betrayed him**. Whenever Judas was named in the remainder of the Gospel, he was known by this act (14:10, 43, 45) or by being linked to the Twelve.

While Judas is known specifically as the "betrayer," the Greek word *paradidōmi* is associated with many other people and settings than simply Judas. It describes the arrest of John the Baptist (1:14). It depicts the act of the Jewish leaders who "handed over" Jesus to the Romans for crucifixion (9:31; 15:1, 10), the works of the Jewish officials in the lives of the disciples after the death of Jesus (13:9, 11), and even of Pilate who "handed over" Jesus to the soldiers for scourging and crucifixion (15:15). It may be fair to say that Mark was indicating that *paradidōmi* may be not only a "Judas" problem but also a human moral dilemma.

3. TRANSFERENCE OF DEMONIC ROLE TO OPPONENTS 3:20–35

This section naturally breaks into three component parts. The passage of 3:20–21 introduces the theme of Jesus' family, heretofore unmentioned in the Gospel. Jesus was previously associated with His city of origin, Nazareth (1:9, 24). Apart from the completion of this story in 3:31–35, any reference of His family only briefly resurfaces during Jesus' rejection in Nazareth (6:3). Mark described Jesus' mother and brothers as outsiders[4] to the Kingdom (3:31). They appear to have so misunderstood the call of God on Jesus' life that they traveled to Capernaum to rescue Him from His own "insane" agenda.

This family argument seems to have been interrupted by the chaotic exchange of words and accusations between Jesus and the scribes of 3:22–30, only to return to family matters in 3:31–35. This technique of "sandwiching"[5] material is a common practice in Mark's writing. He took apparently unrelated material, such as family matters and exorcism debates, and linked it into a unit that forces his readers to deal with both matters simultaneously. Thus, for Mark, one could not understand family loyalty apart from the issues of a kingdom divided against itself. Furthermore, Mark's readers should also remember to integrate the previous "call" narrative as Jesus formed a new set of companions who are called first and foremost to be with Him (3:14).

Then Jesus entered a house, and again a crowd gathered, so that he and his disciples were not even able to eat (3:20). Realistically, this could be any random dwelling place in Galilee, but thus far the term "house" has only been connected with the home of Simon and Andrew in Capernaum (1:29), probably the one they returned to in 2:1. The interjection of the word **again** hints at a repeat performance of a capacity crowd drawn by His popularity that was so intrusive that it prevented the disciples and Jesus from eating.

JESUS ACCUSED OF INSANITY

Now come some of the most difficult words in the gospel: **When his family heard about this, they went to take charge of him, for they said, "He is out of his mind"** (3:21). The words are so inflammatory that scholars have struggled for sound exegetical ways to tone down their rhetoric. The problematic core is translating the phrase the NIV renders "family," which has been the traditional way of interpreting the passage. The words literally read "the ones with him." The generic meaning might be His "associates" or even His disciples, yet we know they were already inside with Him attempting to eat. The context must be the deciding factor on the precise rendering of the phrase. Since the following passage in our Markan "sandwich" tells the reader that **Jesus' mother and brothers arrived** (3:31), the reader must deduce that the ones who once were so close to Him—His family—stood outside with the crowd, asking for Him to come out. The crowd itself wanted Him for the sake of miracles or teaching, but this passage informs the readers that His blood family wanted to **take charge of him, for they said, "He is out of his mind."** The phrase **take charge** connotes force (6:17; 12:12; 14:51), associated by Mark with Jesus' arrest (14:1, 44, 46). His family wanted to seize Jesus because they thought He was "out of his mind."[6] Though many scholars have attempted to soften the meaning of this phrase,[7] its traditional meaning is with reference to insanity. Moreover, since Mark syntactically linked Jesus' family's reaction to parallel with the

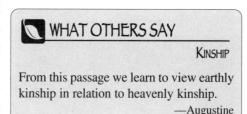

WHAT OTHERS SAY

KINSHIP

From this passage we learn to view earthly kinship in relation to heavenly kinship.
—Augustine

disbelieving scribes, it is fair to assume that His mother and brothers likened Jesus' behavior to demon possession (3:22). Jesus' family stood outside, looking in with skepticism at best and more probably outright rejection of His agenda.

JESUS ACCUSED OF DEMON POSSESSION

In 3:21–30 the reader encounters **the teachers of the law who came down from Jerusalem** (3:22). Jesus' confrontation with His family may have been disappointing, but this new set of accusers came directly from Jerusalem. They claimed, **"He is possessed by Beelzebub! By the prince of demons he is driving out demons"** (3:22).The teachers of the law from Jerusalem were ignorant as to the origin of Jesus' power and authority. Their accusation was clear: The scribes placed Jesus in league with Satan.[8] Though the scribes did not know the source of His power, we know that it is first of all from His person, the Son of God. But secondly, it springs from the Holy Spirit who dwells within Him (1:9–10). The demons recognized this fact as He commanded them to leave their human victims as well as to remain silent.

So Jesus called them and spoke to them in parables (3:23). Jesus immediately responded by calling for their attention. It appears that these men were either talking with one another or the crowds, but Jesus demanded personal interaction. Moreover Jesus chose to relate to them **in parables**. The word points to the next chapter, where Jesus used colorful, figurative language, often puzzle-like and difficult to discern. In chapter 4, the key to comprehending the parable was being "with Jesus." Just prior to interpreting the parables for the disciples, Jesus said, "The secret of the kingdom of God has been given to you. But to those on *the outside* everything is said in parables" (4:11, italics added). Mark carefully informed his readers that the view or perspective of the teachers from Jerusalem was that of an outsider. Their frame of reference was so distorted that a lie—the origin of Jesus' power is from the demonic world—had become to them the truth. The statement of the scribes is only a logical assumption for those who reject Jesus' connection to the kingdom to God. Jesus corrected this grievous error: **"How can Satan drive out Satan?"** (3:23). In 3:23–26 Jesus attacked the illogical nature of their argument: Any force that turns upon itself is doomed to failure and **"that kingdom cannot stand"** (3:24).

Jesus made yet another parabolic statement: **"In fact, no one can enter a strong man's house and carry off his possessions unless he first ties up the strong man. Then he can rob his house"** (3:27). This image contrasts to the argument of 3:23–26. Jesus' ministry thus far had been an overt thrust into the realm of the demons, and His miracles, especially the exorcisms, were His way of reclaiming enemy territory (1:16–45; 2:1–12; 3:1–6). The house of the **strong man** (most assuredly Satan) had been entered and his possessions carried off. This parable illustrates that Jesus was in conflict with the strong man, not possessed by him. And as the "stronger man" He would most certainly prevail.

Jesus climaxed His teaching with the forceful statement **"I tell you the truth"** (3:28). In typical gospel pronouncement language, Jesus began with the Hebrew word "Amen," gathering attention for this authoritative announcement.[9] Words of grace preceded as He stated, **"all the sins and blasphemies of men will be forgiven them."** He turned their attention to the term blasphemy: **"But whoever blasphemes against the Holy Spirit will never be forgiven"** (3:29). It is in this passage that once again Mark's readers are reacquainted with the three key players of the baptismal-temptation scene: Jesus, Satan, and the Spirit. However, here the scribes misconstrued the relationships. They see Jesus in collusion with Satan rather than in partnership with the Holy Spirit. As they equated Jesus' work through the power of the Holy Spirit with Satan, they not only ostracized themselves from God's forgiveness, they simultaneously aligned themselves with the demonic agenda. Thus, to maintain that Jesus' authority over the demons arose from any source other than the Holy Spirit himself was to deny the very presence of the Holy Spirit in Christ. This person is guilty of an eternal sin, never to be forgiven. If the Holy Spirit is rejected, how can there be forgiveness? In the end, Mark summarized the attitudes of the scribes: **they were saying, "He has an evil spirit"** (3:30). R. T. France says, "The allegation that Jesus is empowered in his exorcistic ministry not by the Spirit of God but by the chief spirit of evil suggests that this allegation involves a total perversion of the truth and the repudiation of the rule of God."[10]

As a closing application, one should be cautious concerning unpardonable sin. The meaning of 3:28–29 is set within the framework of total rejection of Jesus and His ministry. Thus, from a counseling perspective, wise counselors will refrain from employing it to terrify those who are weak in faith and fearful that they may have committed the unpardonable sin. This sin seems to be reserved for those who intentionally attribute demonic origin to the works of Jesus.

The readers are well informed about who Jesus is, and they have read previously that Jesus' mission is distinctly aligned with God against Satan. Further, they will be able to discern that each future scribal debate with Jesus will have a demonic overtone to it. This can be seen specifically as the debates between Jesus and the Jewish authorities are called temptations,[11] thus making their evil intentions clear. The opposition of the Jewish leaders to Jesus is seen in Mark's gospel as a continuation of the demonic plan, first introduced at the baptism-temptation, continued in the exorcisms, and subversively concealed in the verbal confrontations with the authorities. Mark's intention was to depict Satan as the overseer of this diabolical plot and as Jesus' chief adversary (see Eph. 6:12).

JESUS' TRUE FAMILY

Then Jesus' mother and brothers arrived. Standing outside, they sent someone in to call him (3:31). Mark returned to the material originally encountered in 3:20–21, where Jesus' family was trying to take hold of Him (literally, seize) because they believed Him to be insane. The vague family reference of 3:21[12] is made explicit here with the identification of Jesus' mother and brothers. As mentioned above, this house was full to capacity (3:20, and similar events in 2:2–4), thus necessitating the sending in of a messenger. Note the subtle yet significant location clue: They were outsiders at this gathering. Ironically, in the earlier passage (3:20–21) they were not described by the literal term "family" but by a traditional one that reads "the ones around Him." They were on the outside looking in. Perhaps implied is that Jesus' family had more in common with the scribes from Jerusalem than with Jesus of Nazareth.

A crowd was sitting around him, and they told him, "Your mother and brothers are outside looking for you" (3:32). The family was outside and the crowd surrounded Him. Location and proximity to Him is the key; the family had no access to Jesus except through the crowd.

Jesus posed a rhetorical question to the people around Him: **"Who are my mother and my brothers?"** (3:33). He then answered with a gaze and a word: **"Here are my mother and my brothers!"** (3:34). Jesus' actions may have seemed downright insulting, for in a culture that commemorates the virtue of hospitality, Jesus did not even welcome His family to join the inner circle. Moreover, they never again enter into the narrative of Mark.

"Whoever does God's will is my brother and sister and mother" (3:35). Jesus pushed the issue of new family loyalty to new heights. It was no longer to be based on location (read that as bloodlines or heritage), but became solely an expression of one's obedience to the will of God. This may not have been surprising to a first-century Jew, since doing the will of God was axiomatic. But Jesus personified obedience in a new way, for He and He alone became the purveyor of God's will on earth. Membership in Jesus' newly formed family was not to be based upon blood (3:20–21) or tradition (3:22–30) but by doing the will of God as revealed in the preaching and teaching of the only Son; the Kingdom can only be found in Jesus.

I offer two statements in closing. First, Jesus did not depict himself as just another member of God's family. It would be exegetically incorrect to read this passage as one big happy family with Jesus as simply one of the brothers. Jesus' position is the head of the household. Note how in the closing verse of the chapter, Jesus did not describe who His Father is, but rather who are His mother and brothers and sisters (3:35). This leads to the second observation: Jesus surprisingly invited many beyond the scope of the Twelve into the fellowship of His inner circle. Moreover, He unashamedly included "sisters." It is not until this closing verse that Jesus mentioned anyone other than His mother and brothers, which may at this point have been describing His own blood family. But in this reconstitution of Jesus' family, women, called here sisters, are just as welcome.[13]

ENDNOTES

1. The distinction is never clearer than in 4:10: "When he was alone, the Twelve and the others around him asked him about the parables."

2. He would once again be partnered with the inner circle in 13:3, but never again in a primary role.

3. For a full list of options on the meaning if "Iscariot," see Raymond E. Brown, *Death of the Messiah*, The Anchor Bible (New York: Doubleday, 1994) pp. 1410–1416.

4. The term "outsiders" becomes almost a technical term for those who are not part of Jesus' kingdom-building group. See the description of 3:30–31 and 4:10–11.

5. Other examples can be found in 5:21–43 and 14:1–11.

6. NASB: "He has lost His senses"; NRSV: "He has gone out of his mind."

7. It is true that three other times in Mark (2:12; 5:42; 6:51) the word is equated with the people's amazement with Jesus' miracles.

8. The origin of the name Beelzebub (alternative reading, Beelzebul) is difficult to pinpoint. It may derive from the name of a Philistine god—"Baal of the flies"—or it may come from another similar name, which can be translated "Baal of the height" or "Baal of the house."

9. This construction occurs frequently in Matthew and Mark, less so in Luke. The "Amen" is doubled in John. This is an authoritative statement, as though Jesus is speaking for himself, self-authenticating.

10. R. T. France, *The Gospel of Mark: New International Commentary on the Greek Testament* (Grand Rapids, Mich.: William B. Eerdmans), p. 177.

11. Mark 8:11; 10:2; 12:15 all contain the word for tempt or test (Greek: *teirazō*). Mark was trying to indicate that the Jewish leaders were enticing Jesus just as Satan tempted Jesus in wilderness in 1:13

12. The literal reading is "the ones around him," not family as the NIV reads.

13. Women played an important role in the dissemination of the gospel. First they were commended in Luke 8:1–3 for not only being followers, but also primary financial supporters of Jesus' ministry. Moreover, in Mark's gospel, women seemed to understand what the disciples and other of the inner circle missed (for example, the woman with the issue of blood [5:25–34]; the Syrophoenician woman [7:24–30]; the woman who anointed Jesus [14:3–9]; and the women who witnessed Jesus' death [15:40–41] and heard the proclamation of the resurrection [16:1–8]). Finally, throughout Paul's ministry, as documented in the book of Acts and in his own correspondence, women played a central role.

5

THE KINGDOM IN PARABLES

Mark 4:1–34

1. PARABLE INTRODUCTION 4:1–2

Mark spent considerable time describing Jesus as a teacher,[1] yet few of Jesus' words have been preserved in the second gospel. Thus far there has been a wide spectrum of response to Jesus' proclamation of the Kingdom. Initially, the disciples followed without hesitation. There had also been a constant crowd nearby because of His miraculous actions. Yet the people who one might expect to be best prepared to acknowledge Him, His family and the religion leaders, rejected Him as insane (3:21) and as demon possessed (3:22, 30). If the demons themselves could see Him to be the Son of God (1:24; 3:11), why was humanity so deaf and so blind? This parable will give a foundation for the multifaceted response to Jesus.

He taught them many things by parables (4:2). The classic definition of a parable, "an earthly story with a heavenly meaning," falls short of what the reader will soon encounter from Jesus, for there was nothing self-interpreting about Jesus' parables. From the disciples' response in 4:10, we see that the parable of the sower confused or puzzled them rather than making clear Jesus' instruction. Moreover, Jesus' explanation regarding the purpose of teaching in parables (4:11–12) may be the most baffling passage in the entire book. Jesus' parables tended to challenge the status quo rather than offer straightforward, story-like explanations.

Parabolic teaching was not original with Jesus. In the Old Testament, the word "parable" may be used in conjunction with other terms such as

101

proverbs, illustrative stories, or even used in conjunction with the concept of "riddle, as if one word is helping to define the other."[2] Understanding the meaning and the application of a parable may be best explained by how it compares with other parts of the New Testament. For example, many Christians may find themselves more comfortable when they read the letters of Paul or James, which appear to be based more on principles, precepts, or instructions to follow than on stories that need to be carefully interpreted. Therefore, it might be fair to say that some folks are more "Pauline" in their orientation, while others may find themselves more "gospel" people.[3] Though there are most certainly narratives that stand directly behind Paul's letters, his epistle writing technique is much more prescriptive as he outlines propositional truths that should be integrated into a Christian life. Mark, however, is fashioned into the form of a story. On a whole, it is a parabolic story of the Kingdom, with meaning that does not lie on the surface but demands inquiry to gain insight and requires faith to follow.

But though it may be considered a story, this section should not be understood to be haphazard in its construction. Its beginning (4:1–2) and ending (4:33–34) form bookends to the parables. The passage opens by explaining the overall makeup of the crowd: **all the people were along**

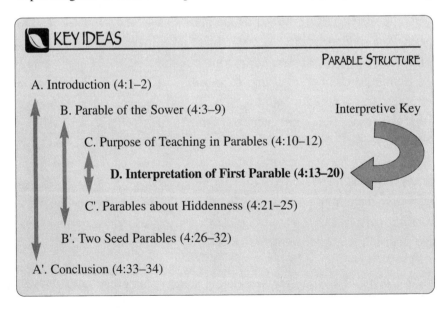

KEY IDEAS

PARABLE STRUCTURE

A. Introduction (4:1–2)

   B. Parable of the Sower (4:3–9)   Interpretive Key

      C. Purpose of Teaching in Parables (4:10–12)

         D. Interpretation of First Parable (4:13–20)

      C'. Parables about Hiddenness (4:21–25)

   B'. Two Seed Parables (4:26–32)

A'. Conclusion (4:33–34)

the shore at the water's edge (4:1) and desired to hear. The passage closes with the description of the division that was created within the group: those designated as "outsiders" and those who will be called "insiders."[4] The layout of Jesus' parabolic instruction is a common form in the ancient world known as a chiasm. The beginning and ending correspond to one another.

The crowd that gathered around him was so large that he got into a boat and sat in it out on the lake (4:1). Jesus' early ministry in the Galilean region was defined by a pressing crowd, and this teaching moment was no different. **All the people were along the shore at the water's edge** (4:1). There is a subtle sense of irony with Mark's choice of the word "shore." Literally, the word is "soil," the same one Jesus employed nine times throughout the chapter. The crowds that sat on the "soil" are representative of the four soils Jesus illustrated. This is also true of every subsequent reader of this parable.

He taught them many things by parables (4:2). Mark centered on Jesus as "teacher." In these first two verses, the verb "to teach" occurs twice and the noun "teaching" once.[5] However, the focal point is the methodology by which Jesus taught: **by** [means of] **parables**. If we assume Jesus simply taught by telling stories, we will miss the nature of the ambiguity of the term "parable." For in 4:11 Jesus states the reason for using parables was apparently to prevent some of the people from fully comprehending the kingdom of God, thus to have them remain "outside." Thus, it may be fair to translate the phrase "by parables" within a range of meaning stretching from "by means of riddles" to "mysteriously" or "ambiguously." Simply put, the following well-known parable did not clarify the nature of the Kingdom to its hearers, but mystified both the crowd and the disciples.

2. PARABLE OF THE SOWER 4:3–9

"Listen! A farmer went out to sow his seed" (4:3). A brief preface may be in order before discussing the parable itself. First, the primary focus should be placed on the fate of the seed and the different kinds of soils upon which it falls rather than the sower. Second, one must remove any preconceived notions about the application of the passage. One of the chief commands in the book of Mark, "to listen" or "to hear," sets the tone for Jesus as teacher and disciple. This is not a new instruction for first-century Jews since the command "to listen" is also the first word of the prayer every faithful Jew was to recite daily, the *Shema* (Deut. 6:4). Thus, Jesus' words form an uninterrupted link with the ancient words of Moses.

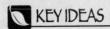

KEY IDEAS

SHEMA

Shema is the first word in Deuteronomy 6:4 and used as a title for the Jewish daily prayers. Deuteronomy 6:4–9, 11:13–21, and Numbers 15:37–41 are to be quoted in the morning and the evening. With every recurrence, the pietistic Jews are reminded of their allegiance to God and the covenant with its obligations.

The word "listen" also occurs twice in the enigmatic quotation of Isaiah 6:9 in Mark 4:12, which forms Jesus' explanation why "by parables" was the form He chose for revealing the secret of the Kingdom. It is interesting to note that Jesus did not emphasize becoming good soil. Obviously, each of the soil types heard and responded to the Word differently (4:15, 16, 18, 20). Yet in this parable, there was not a command to be "good" soil. The only imperative in the parable was to "listen." It seems to be the hinge upon which all else rotates. Here, the teaching of Jesus begins slowly to take preeminence over His miracles.

This sower did his work with reckless abandon as he scattered and wasted good seed on bad soil. The broadcast method was the farming option of the day. The ground was plowed and then seed was cast liberally. Every farmer knew the risks; some seed would germinate and grow into a healthy harvest, while other seed would be lost for any number of reasons. Nevertheless, the sower was not afraid to sow seed profusely. Thus, Jesus anticipated repeated failure to some degree, even in His own ministry.

Patient endurance in the face of defeat is the call of this parable. Evil certainly falls under the lordship of Jesus, but it does not immediately disappear any more than people will universally respond to the Word of God. Seed is vulnerable to be devoured by birds (4:4), to be scorched by the sun (4:6), or to be choked by other plants (4:7). The closing words, **"He who has ears to hear, let him hear"** (4:9), imply that not everyone had ears attuned to Jesus, so not all who encountered His teaching would benefit from Him.

3. PARABOLIC (MIS)INFORMATION 4:10–12

When he was alone, the Twelve and the others around him asked him about the parables (4:10). The context for Jesus' explanation of the purpose of His parabolic teaching includes a limited crowd who asked Him about the meaning of the parables and His exclusionary principle.

"The secret of the kingdom of God has been given to you. But to those on the outside everything is said in parables" (4:11). To whom was Jesus referring when He said "to you" (4:11)? Mark placed the "to you" group in direct contrast with another group designated as the "outsiders," whose cardinal trait was characterized by a perception dilemma: **"they may be ever seeing but never perceiving, and ever hearing but never understanding"** (4:12). At no time did Mark make the direct contrast between outsiders and insiders. Rather the contrast was between the "outsiders" and the referentially powerful term "to you."

Three simple observations may assist in the interpretation of this difficult passage. First, the parable as a whole of chapter 4 was given to everyone within earshot of Jesus (the crowd, 4:1), while Jesus' explanation was given in private to the disciples and a select few. Second, the parable of the sower is placed within the context of teaching (4:1–2). Mark explained that all of Jesus' speech fell within the context of parabolic instruction (4:33–34). Thus, if one aspect of the meaning of the word "parable" is to be equated with the term "riddle," then much of Jesus' teaching will be quite difficult to comprehend. At the very least, it will demand interpretation. Third, this chapter is shaped for a listening audience (4:3, 9, 23). Thus, the modern reader hears or overhears the disciples being given privileged information regarding the parable that was withheld from the rest of the crowd. Moreover, Jesus' parabolic interpretation (4:13–20) transformed the parable from an agricultural metaphor to one centered on proclamation, hearing, and response.

Jesus described the parables as a mystery that **"has been given to you."** Jesus housed this in the passive voice. Thus, the mystery of the

Kingdom does not come to humankind via self-discovery at the end of an arduous intellectual pilgrimage. Rather, the passive voice denotes that, in the end, it can only come about through God's own revelation.[6] Thus, this mystery came in a veiled form in the parable and could not be comprehended apart from Jesus' interpretation. Everything, especially His miracles, requires some degree of interpretation (see 3:22–30; 6:2–3; 6:49, 6:51–52; 8:14–21). "Virtually all the events of 4:35–8:26 are parabolic events, pointing beyond themselves to the Kingdom in process of coming."[7] In actuality, the parables did not cloud the issue; they merely revealed the state of human blindness. Among the blind were the Pharisees and scribes (2:1–3:6; 3:22–30) and Jesus' immediate family (3:21, 31–35), and soon even His disciples would be defined by their sightlessness (8:14–21). Their blindness was not due to ignorance but to a hardened heart (6:51–52) and to a proclivity to evaluate issues from a mere human perception (8:33).

One of the most troubling passages in the entire Gospel is Jesus' quotation of Isaiah 6:9–10, which He cited as scriptural support for His parabolic teaching model: **"so that, they may be ever seeing but never perceiving, and ever hearing but never understanding; otherwise they might turn and be forgiven!"** (4:12). It is possible to suggest that Jesus was being intentionally hard to understand, thereby excluding individuals from repentance and forgiveness. The original setting of the Isaianic prophecy will illuminate Jesus' adoption of the quotation. The opening of the book of Isaiah describes the nation of Israel in rebellion against their God (1:2, 5, 23) and living in ignorance (1:3). After five long chapters, the reader senses hopefulness as God revealed himself to the prophet Isaiah in the Temple (6:1–13). In the midst of his call narrative, God informed Isaiah that his preaching would only harden the hearts of the people until God carried out His punishment. Isaiah's people were just as spiritually blind as the people in Jesus' day.[8] The kingdom of God is concealed not by God's divine choice but by human will. In the case of the Israelites in Isaiah's day, revelation did not come until destruction and expulsion from the land opened their eyes to reality (Isa. 6:11–13). In Jesus' day, the mystery of the Kingdom remained concealed to onlookers until they comprehended that it was ushered in by suffering (Mark 8:31;

9:31; 10:33–34) and servanthood (8:34–38; 10:31, 45). Moreover, this could not be fully realized until after Jesus' death and resurrection (9:9–10).

4. THE PARABLE EXPLAINED 4:13–20

The favorable impression of being earmarked as part of the "to you" group is short lived. Jesus transitioned His listeners from the purpose of His parabolic instruction to His explanation with the questions **"Don't you understand this parable? How then will you understand any parable?"** (4:13). If they had been given the mystery of the Kingdom, how could they fail to grasp this straightforward parable, since they have the "interpretative key"? This rebuke may seem harsh in light of Jesus' private revelation in the previous verse, yet it discloses an aspect of the mystery that had thus gone undetected. The giving of this mystery does not equate with an instantaneous reception. It would take the rest of Jesus' earthly ministry to flesh out even in part.

"Some people are like seed along the path, where the word is sown. As soon as they hear it, Satan comes and takes away the word that was sown in them" (4:15). Jesus' interpretation reframed the metaphor with clear, evangelistic thrusts. Each seed was equated with different types of people and their respective responses to the gospel. Jesus did not allow the parable to be understood as describing a mere intellectual challenge. Rather, what was unfolding was a cosmic battle being waged between God and Satan.

The seed **along the path** alerts the readers of Mark that Satan comes quickly to snatch away the Word and distort the message. The rest of Mark

 **BACKGROUND**

SATAN

The term "Satan" has its origin in Hebrew literature. It is derived from a Hebrew word roughly meaning "accuser." Likewise, its verb form generally means "to accuse." In early biblical literature, this concept was applied to humanity (Num. 22:22, 32; 1 Sam. 29:4; 2 Sam. 19:23; 1 Kings 5:18; 11:14, 23, 25; Ps. 38:20; 71:13; 109:4, 20, 29). It was in later biblical, apocryphal, and post-biblical literature that this concept began to represent a cosmic force responsible for evil (Job 1–2; Zech. 3:1–2; Enoch 15–16; Wis. 2:4).

depicts many such people, predominantly displayed in the behavior of the Pharisees, the teachers of the law, the Herodians, and later in narrative with the chief priests. Upon hearing Jesus, they sought to destroy Him (3:6, 11:18; 12:13; 14:1, 55). Jesus was stating emphatically that disregarding the clear teaching (words) of Jesus is equivalent to having Satan snatch away the word and leave only a human perspective of the world in its place.

"Others, like seed sown on rocky places, hear the word and at once receive it with joy" (4:16). But they are incapable of establishing deep roots. **"When trouble or persecution comes because of the word, they quickly fall away"** (4:17). The term "fall away" is a key to determining the identity of these people. Many people are initially amazed with Jesus but quickly turn away once trouble appears on the horizon. The people in Jesus' hometown of Nazareth were offended (same word, literally "scandalized") by Him. Later, at the Last Supper, Jesus predicted that all His disciples will be offended by Him once they discovered His true nature and mission (14:27, 29).

"Still others, like seed sown among thorns, hear the word; but the worries of this life, the deceitfulness of wealth and the desires for other things come in and choke the word, making it unfruitful (4:18–19). Several persons in Mark's story epitomize this third soil. For example, the rich ruler who came to Jesus seeking answers to eternal questions sensed that the cost of discipleship was far too expensive (10:17–22). The same qualities can be found in the person of Herod, who demonstrated high regard for John the Baptist's teaching and ministry (6:20), but when life called for him to act on his beliefs, his lust for personal honor choked out any spiritual awakening (6:21–29).

The spiritually aware readers will be simultaneously determining their own soil fate, asking the question, "Where do I stand with reference to Jesus?" The answer is best found in the description of the third soil, the seed sown among thorns. Thomas Boomershine writes insightfully:

The description of the responses of the listeners begins with those who are troubled by the possibility of persecution and progresses to those who allow other concerns such as money or pleasure to affect their hearing of the parables or the Gospel. I would argue, for example, that no listener in the entire history of the reading of Mark's Gospel from then until now can honestly say that their hearing of parables of the Gospel has not been affected by the possibility of persecution or tribulation, the anxieties of this world, the delight in riches, and the desire for other things.[9]

According to Boomershine, no listener can conclude candidly, "I am the good soil." The logical progression of the parable prevents it. Thus, Mark subtly led his readers to assume the role of "outsiders." Furthermore, the dullness of the disciples in later parts of the narrative[10] shows that possessing the mystery itself in no way guarantees proper alignment with the expectations of God.

Finally, some people, **"like seed sown on good soil, hear the word, accept it, and produce a crop"** (4:20). One might expect a detailed explanation to the success of these people. Yet, all Jesus revealed is that they "accept it" (present tense meaning "continually receive it") and "produce a crop" (present tense meaning "continually bearing fruit").

Jesus taught that it is one's obedience to the will of God that is the essence of one's position in the Kingdom (3:31–35). Mark's readers will hear the disciples' behavior analogous with that of "outsiders." To these twelve men, Jesus had given and interpreted the secret of the kingdom of God. Yet the narrative displays their hubris and hard hearts to be the cause

CHART

CONTRASTING THE GOOD SOIL TO THE OTHERS

	Failed Soils	Good Soil
How it was received	Birds (Satan) snatch the seed away as soon as it falls	At once accepts it
How the roots develop	Shallow, poor roots that could not withstand trouble or persecution (scorching heat)	Developed deep roots that allowed crop to grow and fruit to mature
What grows	Thorns grow with the seed and (worries of life) choke it	Good crop grows and produces a harvest

of their ultimate downfall, finally depicted in their total abandonment of Jesus in 14:50. They trusted Jesus on their own terms and primarily on their own comprehension of the events. May we be on guard of falling into a similar fate.

5. PARABLES ABOUT HIDDENNESS 4:21–25

Following the parable of the soils, Jesus turned to a series of several short aphorisms, neatly tied together with the theme of hearing: **"If anyone has ears to hear, let him hear. Consider carefully what you hear"** (4:23–24). The first saying begins with a double question. In Greek, a question can be framed with words to indicate how it is to be answered. Thus, the first question, **"Do you bring in a lamp to put it under a bowl or a bed?"** (4:21) is rhetorically answered with an emphatic no! The second question, **"don't you put it on its stand?"** asks for a yes response. It seems clear that the light to which Jesus referred is the mystery of the Kingdom, the light that distinguishes insiders from outsiders. If this is true, then it suggests that the "messianic secret" was not to take a permanent role but only a temporal role until one deciphered the meaning of the mystery.

This argument is supported by the next verse, which begins with the simple conjunction "for." **"For whatever is hidden is meant to be disclosed, and whatever is concealed is meant to be brought out into the open"** (4:22). This verse can be divided into halves, one bringing clarity to the inherent ambiguity of the other.[11] Thus, *hidden* is to be understood as a synonym to *conceal*, and *disclose* is placed in parallel with *open*. The goal of God is not to remain hidden to outsiders but to reveal himself and His way to all people, so ultimately they can "turn and be forgiven" (4:12).

The phrase **"consider carefully what you hear"** (4:24) is an interesting construction, for it literally reads, "see what you hear," combining the dual warnings of 4:12 into one thought: "they may be ever *seeing* but never perceiving, and ever *hearing* but never understanding" (italics added). The rendering of the phrase by the NIV is quite accurate, for the entire parabolic passage is about the difference between how insiders and outsiders hear the same message.

One must carefully connect the next passage to the previous context. **"With the measure you use, it will be measured to you—and even more"** (4:24). In the ancient world, food and supplies were measured out into customary-size containers that were brought to the marketplace by the purchaser. Thus, they received the measure based on the vessel they brought. **"Whoever has will be given more; whoever does not have, even what he has will be taken from him"** (4:25). Just as 4:22 was linked to 4:21 with the conjunction "for," 4:25 is linked to 4:24 with the same Greek word, though not translated by the NIV. Thus, the rich in hearing (insiders) would be given more insight, while those outside who have closed their ears to Jesus' words would lose all privileges to the Kingdom. There is a tension between the positive understanding of 4:21–22, that whatever was hidden would come to light, and the somewhat negative tone to 4:24–25, that some would simply fail to hear and all would be lost. It is that uneasiness that cloaks Jesus' parabolic interpretation. All have access to the mystery if only they do not turn a deaf ear to it.

6. TWO SEED PARABLES 4:26–32

Consider two initial thoughts. First, there is a close connection between these two parables. They both begin with almost exactly the same words: (1) **He also said, "This is what the kingdom of God is like . . ."** (4:26); (2) **Again he said, "What shall we say the kingdom of God is like . . ."** (4:30).

Second, if one considers the chiastic structure of the entire parabolic passage discussed at the beginning of this passage, this section parallels the parable of the sower (4:3–9). Thus, Mark returned to the theme of "growing" and seeds. The first parable in this closing passage illustrates that human effort has nothing to do with the seed's growth. The harvest is based on Jesus' presence (4:3–9; 14–20) and the grace of God. Ironically, the beneficiary of the growth has nothing to offer to the process beyond sowing. Moreover, one should not be concerned with the uncertainty of fully comprehending the workings of God (4:10–13; 21–25). Proper understanding does not impede the coming Kingdom, nor does logic expedite the process.

Though quite similar, the introduction of the second seed parable is a bit more elaborate than the first, for there are two introductory questions: **"What shall we say the kingdom of God is like, or what parable shall we use to describe it?"** (4:30). This parable continues on a similar growth theme with an interesting sense of hopefulness. The kingdom starts out small (1:14–15); **"it is like a mustard seed, which is the smallest seed"** (4:31). Yet in spite of numerous human obstacles (2:1–3:6), demonic attacks (1:21–28; 3:11–12), and even family misunderstandings (3:20–21), **"it grows and becomes the largest of all garden plants"** (4:32). No one should underestimate the effect of the proclamation of the Kingdom, no matter how unimpressive its beginning might have been. These two parables placed back to back should establish a true sense of confidence to any and all disciples who may have become disheartened over a lack of growth in the seeds they have planted. There is much going on beneath the surface.

All the parables in this closing section describe the deceptive and ignominious beginning to the Kingdom. Would anyone have guessed that God would work through failure, defeat, rejection, even through crucifixion?

7. CONCLUSION 4:33–34

Mark closed off the parabolic material with his own editorial comments: **With many similar parables Jesus spoke the word to them** (4:33). Jesus' parabolic teaching material in any extended fashion is limited to chapters 4 and 12. Yet the wording of this closing remark indicates that it was a normal practice, not just a temporary methodology.[12] **He did not say anything to them without using a parable** (4:34). If this passage was being interpreted alone, it might be possible to understand Jesus' choice of parables to be one to bring clarity to the average listener. However, these comments come at the end of a lengthy discourse depicting people who seemed to be hard of hearing. Moreover, in this closing verse, Mark contrasted the pronoun "them" (outsiders) with the "disciples" (insiders), who only comprehended because **when he was alone with his own disciples, he explained everything** (4:34).

Thus, it seems fair to draw the following conclusions. First, there were some who were not able to hear what Jesus was saying. The parable of the sower would be better named the "parable of the soils" to describe the listening disorders associated with the people within the narrative world of Mark, and who are thus portrayed in the contemporary world today. Second, Jesus' words and actions demanded an interpretation. One can draw contrasting conclusions depending upon one's perspective. To be certain, one must listen and adhere to the worldview of the Kingdom reported by Jesus the Son.

ENDNOTES

1. "Teacher" is the favorite title of Jesus in the gospel of Mark (twelve times). Yet ironically, Mark recorded less of the content of His teaching than in any other gospel. In Matthew, there are five great didactic sections of material: Sermon on Mount (Matt. 5–7), Mission of the Twelve (Matt. 10), Parabolic Instruction (Matt. 13), Community Discourse (Matt. 18), and the Eschatological Discourse (Matt. 14–25). In Luke, the middle section of the gospel (Luke 9–19) contains more parabolic instruction than the other three gospels. In John, nearly one third of the gospel consists of the actual words of Jesus.

2. The Hebrew word for "parable" (*māšsāl*) is used several times in parallel with the word "riddle" (*hîdâ*). See Psalm 49:5; 78:2; Proverbs 1:6; and Ezekiel 17:2.

3. No devoted follower of Jesus ever exclusively read only the Epistles or only the Gospels. But each of us is wired differently, and each of us has personal tastes when it comes to books of the Bible. So, are you a person who prefers to read and follow the precepts and principles of Paul or to linger over the stories of Jesus? The answer can be quite revealing.

4. The designation of insiders and outsiders is more carefully delineated in Jesus' explanation for teaching in parables (4:10–12). "The secret of the kingdom of God has been given *to you*. But to those on the *outside* everything is said in parables" (italics added).

5. In Matthew's parallel material (13:1–2), he does not employ the word "teach" at all.

6. It is of interest that 4:11 does not literally read "but to those on the outside everything is *said* in parables" but that "everything comes/becomes/is in parables." Thus, the answer cannot be expressed in words alone, but must include more than mere reason.

7. Timothy Geddert, *Watchwords: Mark 13 in Markan Eschatology,* Journal for the Study of the New Testament (Sheffield, England: Sheffield Academic Press, 1989), p. 154.

8. This was just as true in Ezekiel's day. He was called to preach to rebellious people (Ezek. 2:5–8), and they were seemingly deaf to God's word (Ezek. 12:2–3). Ezekiel himself expressed regret that his preaching was beyond their grasp, as if spoken in allegories and parables (Ezek. 17:2; 20:49).

9. Thomas Boomershine, "Epistemology at the Turn of the Ages," *Apocalyptic and the New Testament,* ed. J. Marcus and M. Soards, Journal for the Study of the New Testament Suppliments 24 (Sheffield, England: Sheffield Academic Press, 1989), p. 163.

10. See below for a discussion of the boat and feeding stories.

11. This is common practice in Greek and Hebrew literature and is referred to as synonymous parallelism.

12. This was made clear with Mark's use of the imperfect tense in all four verbs in these two verses (spoke, understand, say, explained), which indicates continuing or habitual action.

6

LORD OVER ALL

Mark 4:35—5:43

C hapter and verse divisions were added to the Bible and were not completed until the mid 1500s. Though necessary tools to discuss the biblical text, there is nothing inherently sacred about them. As a matter of fact, sometimes chapter divisions create interpretive problems, since one might easily equate the end of a chapter as a clear dividing line in an author's thought. Such is the case with the division of chapters 4 and 5 in the gospel of Mark. This last portion of chapter 4 (verses 35–41) is intimately linked with chapter 5. Jesus' authority has been well established in the first four chapters, but the issue is revisited as it is framed in the first of Jesus' nature miracles.

1. WHO IS THIS MAN? 4:35–41

Other individuals in the narrative thus far have raised a similar question (1:27; 2:7–12; 3:11–12), but in this passage, the disciples asked their first true Christological question regarding Jesus' identity: **"Who is this? Even the wind and the waves obey him!"** (4:41). Mark did not intend for his readers to speculate for themselves regarding the answer; he wants Jesus' action recorded in chapter 5 to fashion the answer.

The overall structure is straightforward: 4:35–41 (question), 5:1–43 (answer). Moreover, this is portrayed in the form of a travel narrative, as Jesus traversed the Sea of Galilee. **That day when evening came, he said to his disciples, "Let us go over to the other side"** (4:35). The story begins with His leaving immediately upon concluding His parabolic teaching (4:1–34) from the western shore of the Sea of Galilee, Jewish territory. The storm scene (4:35–41) took place during this crossing. This lake miracle (and the other recorded in 6:45–52) may lift Jesus to a more divine-like role than any other miracle in the Gospel. In the first century, control of nature was attributed exclusively to God.

Leaving the crowd behind, they took him along (4:36). Jesus appears to have moved to the other side of the lake only with His disciples (contrast with 4:1). **A furious squall came up, and the waves broke over the boat, so that it was nearly swamped** (4:37). Mark indicates a hopeless situation; the men were powerless to do anything. This same hopeless scenario will be repeated in each of the subsequent stories of chapter 5. In each scene, hopelessness abounds, and in each situation Jesus dramatically intervenes.

Jesus was asleep in the midst of the storm (4:38), an incident in need of explanation. First, it directly contrasts with the obvious panic of the disciples: He was at rest; they were in distress. Second, recall Jonah (Jonah 1:5–6), who slept while the crew of pagan sailors helplessly fought for survival. Third, at the end of chapter 5, when Jesus took Peter, James, and John to witness the healing of Jairus's young daughter, they overheard Jesus say, "The child is not dead but asleep" (5:39). Thus, in the presence of Jesus, things may not be as they naturally appear. Death has been transformed into mere sleep. It has lost its sting (1 Cor. 15:55). Finally, that fact that Jesus was asleep in the stern of the boat cannot be equated with His unconcern for the disciples' well-being. Nevertheless, the disciples as a group formed an uncompassionate opinion of Jesus as they rudely awakened Him with this question: **"Teacher, don't you care if we drown?"** (4:38). The precise wording is revealing. Twice earlier in Mark, the word translated as "drown" has been used. Initially, it appears in the first exorcism scene when the demon recognized Jesus as the Holy One of God and rhetorically asked, "Have you come to *destroy* us?" (italics added). The answer was a resounding yes, due largely to the compassion Jesus had for the person suffering demonic possession. The coming Kingdom destroyed the works of the evil one (1 John 3:8). The next use of the word "drown-destroy" is found on the lips of the Pharisees (3:6), who were conspiring with the Herodians how they "might kill Jesus" (2:1–3:6). So, now one can understand the true nature of the disciples' question as they awakened

Him during the storm: "Are You just going sleep? Are You just going to take care of Your own needs? Do You not care if we perish?" All the while, they had forgotten (been blind to?) the times Jesus had destroyed the evil that haunted them and others around them.

Jesus said nothing to them. Instead, He instantly responded to the enemy standing before them: the sea. **He got up, rebuked the wind and said to the waves, "Quiet! Be still!"** (4:39). Jesus spoke two words in Greek, both commands. The word "rebuke" and the command "be still" duplicate Jesus' command to the unclean spirit at the first exorcism (1:25). This is another episode where Jesus displayed His ultimate authority over a force that the disciples were helpless to control. Moreover, they witnessed His acting for the first time on their behalf rather than witnessing His performing a healing miracle for others.

Then the wind died down and it was completely calm (4:39). As will be shown later, this seems to reflect the similar result of the demoniac healing in the next story. Then Jesus posed a key question to His disciples: **"Why are you so afraid? Do you still have no faith?"** (4:40). The Greek of the verse is quite clear: "Why

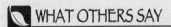

WHAT OTHERS SAY

THE WINDS OF LIFE

When you have to listen to abuse, that means you are being buffeted by the wind. When your anger is roused, you are being tossed by the waves. . . . Rouse him, then; remember him, let him keep watch within you, pay heed to him. . . . A temptation arises, it is the wind. It disturbs you; it is the surging of the sea. This is the moment to awaken Christ and let him remind you of those words, "Who can this be? Even the winds and the seas obey him."

—Augustine

are you [present tense] timid-cowardly? Why do you [present tense] have no faith?" The question may even be more accurately translated "Why are you *now* afraid?" Ironically, both the disciples in this boat scene and the people in 5:15 who witnessed Jesus casting out the legion of demons were not nearly as fearful of the storm or of the demons as they were of being in the presence of the One who had control over these elements. The second question by Jesus parallels the first: **"Do you still have no faith?"** He equated fear with faithlessness. What they lacked was confidence or faith in the power of God working in and through Jesus.

The disciples' reaction is framed in a synonym to Jesus' choice of words for fear: **they were terrified** (4:41).[1] Eduard Schweizer expands the meaning with this translation of the disciples' fright to "a fear that was greater than any fear of the storm."[2] Fear would be an ongoing reaction to the presence of Jesus. It enters as a key part of each encounter of Jesus in chapter 5, and it seems to appear at key moments throughout the remainder of the book (6:20, 50; 9:32; 10:32; 11:18, 32; 12:12; 16:8).

The end of this chapter displays the highest view of Jesus thus far in the book. Only God, and God alone, has the power and might to calm the seas. Yet the disciples' question, **"Who is this? Even the wind and the waves obey him!"** went unanswered. They wrongly **asked each other** the question rather than posing it to one who answered all their parabolic questions. Jesus' miracles, just like His parables, require an interpretation. In the end, the disciples who were considered privileged "insiders" of the parables (4:10–11) appeared far outside the bounds of recognizing the mystery that stands boldly before them in human form.

2. LORD OVER DEMONS 5:1–20

Mark told an amazing story about Jesus' victory over the winds and the waves. Next an equally impressive account unfolds with Jesus' exorcism of not one demon but an entire legion of unclean spirits. The casting out of demons had been a central part of Jesus' ministry. His first miracle in Mark was the casting out of a demon (1:21–28); twice summaries detail this ministry (1:32–34; 3:11–12), and one major controversy describes the Jerusalem's leaders' misunderstanding of the source of His power to accomplish these feats (3:22–30).[3]

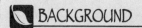

BACKGROUND

DECAPOLIS

It is hard to determine an exact list of the cities that existed within this region. What can be determined is that the initial settlements in this region date back to Alexander the Great. These locations were chosen for their military and economic advantages. After their development under Seleucid control, these settlements fell into anarchy until Pompey's conquest allowed for resolution. By the first century, Hellenistic influence marked the region's cultic and social structures as well as its architecture.

Mark 5:1–2 sets the tone for the story. Jesus crossed the Sea of Galilee to the eastern shore, Gentile territory. A man with an evil spirit (literally, "unclean spirit," see 1:23) came out of the tombs, a ceremonially unclean place, to meet Him. The next three verses serve as a parenthetical statement, detailing the hopelessness of the situation. Men had tried to bind him to no avail; no one was strong enough (see 1:7; 3:27). **Night and day among the tombs and in the hills he would cry out and cut himself with stones** (5:5). It appears as if his behavior was primarily self-destructive, maybe of no inherent danger to the town.

When he saw Jesus from a distance, he ran and fell on his knees in front of him (5:6). This is unusual language for Mark's gospel, for the term rendered "fell on his knees" is used elsewhere in the New Testament as a term of worship (Matt. 2:11; 14:33; John 4:20, 23; 1 Cor. 14:25; Rev. 4:10). The only other place in Mark where it appears is in the soldiers' mocking of Jesus during His flogging (15:19). Is this to be seen as an act of obeisance by the demons, or were they simply acknowledging His superiority? **He shouted at the top of his voice, "What do you want with me, Jesus, Son of the Most High God? Swear to God that you won't torture me!"** (5:7). The wording of the demon's question-request is similar to that of the earlier encounter in 1:23–24. However, this time the demon seems to have been trying to reverse the roles, attempting to bind Jesus with an oath. In the ancient world, to know and declare one's name was to give one power over another. This may have much to do with the demon's approach to Jesus. Yet Jesus quickly turned the tables on it as He demanded to know, **"What is your name?" "My name is Legion," he replied, "for we are many"** (5:9). This was not one demon, but an entire army encamped within this man, destroying his very person. This was the first time in the conversation between Jesus and the possessed man that the subject and verb are in the plural: **"we are many."** Had Jesus' earlier conversation been primarily with the man, and next Jesus engaged with the demonic powers directly? Or was the voice of the man merely an agency employed by the demons, thereby getting at the heart of demon possession; this was a matter of alien occupation[4] that had rendered the man incapable of functioning on his own.

And he begged Jesus . . . not to send them out of the area (5:10). At this point in the exchange, the demons know they have lost, but they seem to be negotiating for the best feasible solution short of destruction. **"Send us among the pigs; allow us to go into them"** (5:12). Here the theme of "uncleanness" is taken to a new level; Jesus was in an unclean territory; He was confronted by an unclean spirit who dwelt in a man who lived in the unclean graveyard, and the demon demanded to be placed in unclean animals. Jesus accepted, **and the evil spirits came out and went into the pigs** (5:13). There is no mention by Mark (or Matthew or Luke) regarding the moral issue of destroying two thousand pigs. One interpreter argues that the destruction of the "unclean" animals was in fact an act of "deliverance of the land" as Jesus' initial removal of uncleanness from Gentile territory.[5] It appears that the united demonic force in the man was divided into individual pigs; they stampeded down into the water, destroying both swine and demon in the very sea that was previously seen by the disciples as their own stormy enemy.

Those tending the pigs . . . reported . . . , and the people went out to see (5:14). In many similar Markan episodes, the reaction of the crowd is described as "amazed" (1:22; 27). This is the longest explanation about the response of onlookers toward Jesus. The people were naturally curious. **When they came to Jesus, they saw the man . . . ; and they were afraid** (5:15). The sight of the transformed demoniac brought about corporate fear. Mark described the man—**sitting . . . , dressed and in his right mind**—as a polar opposite from the opening description (5:3–5). The reaction of the people was the same as the disciples who failed to recognize the manifestation of the kingdom of God in the person of Jesus: fear (4:41). **Those who had seen it told the people** (5:16). Interestingly, the conversation was centered on the man and the pigs; they discussed the social and economic effects of Jesus' presence. **Then the people began to plead with Jesus to leave their region** (5:17). Mark's choice of words is enlightening; the people pled with Jesus just as the demons did earlier (same Greek word, 5:10, 12). Furthermore, they requested that He leave the region where the demons pled to remain. The people seem to have been more comfortable with the demons they knew rather than the God whom they did not; and fear was at the heart of their rejection.

This passage ends with another poignant request-plea, but this time with a positive bent as **the man who had been demon-possessed begged**

to go with him (5:18). The meaning may be somewhat hidden, as the man asked to be "with him," a characteristic phrasing of discipleship. This concept epitomizes the act of "follower-ship." The man wanted to be with Jesus on His journey. Strangely, **Jesus did not let him, but said, "Go home to your family and tell them how much the Lord has done for you, and how he has had mercy on you"** (5:19). At this juncture, a Gentile on the journey to Jerusalem with Jesus and His present followers was not part of the plan, so Jesus gave the man another outlet for his passion: Go home and announce[6]

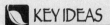

KEY IDEAS

HOPELESSNESS DROVE PEOPLE TO JESUS

- The disciples during the storm wondered if Jesus even cared if they drowned (4:38).

- The scene in the graveyard contains the extended description of the demoniac, where everything humanly possible had been tried to manage his situation (5:3–5).

- Jairus pled with Jesus, "My little daughter is dying. Please come and put your hands on her so that she will be healed and live" (5:23).

- The woman with the blood flow exhausted all her financial resources searching for a medical cure, yet still remained "unclean" (5:25–28).

All is lost by human standards, but with Jesus hope is restored.

the mercy of the Lord. The man was asked to accomplish what Jesus himself had not been welcome to do. As an aside, Jesus' instruction is for the man to announce what the "Lord" had done, referring to God, not himself.[7] Thus, Jesus is not covertly breaking His command to silence about His own accomplishments (1:44, and after in 5:53; 7:36; 8:26). Rather, He desires the goodness of God to spread throughout the world. **So the man went away and began to tell in the Decapolis how much Jesus had done for him** (5:20). The man was not merely "telling," but this is the word for "preaching." He did the same thing John the Baptist (1:7), Jesus (1:14–15; 1:38–39), the healed leper (1:45), and the disciples (3:14; 6:12) did. There is one subtle difference between the command of Jesus and the act of the man: He attributed the mercy of "the Lord" to Jesus. The result was that **all the people were amazed,** usually an effect attributed to the ministry of Jesus.

3. LORD OVER DISEASE; LORD OVER DEATH 5:21-43

The next two episodes—Jairus's daughter and the woman with the issue of blood—are linked together, creating one breathtaking final statement about Jesus' authority and identity as they climactically answer the disciples' question, "Who is this man?" (4:41). Uncleanness is a thematic connection that unites these two passages with the previous healing of the demon-possessed man. Jesus came into physical contact with a woman with a bleeding disorder and with a dead girl. He touched and made the unclean clean. It is not that Jesus had a casual regard for the purity laws of Israel, but the reader is introduced to and will return to in chapter 7 the issues of what truly makes one clean or unclean.

In the beginning of this passage, Jesus has **crossed over by boat to the other side of the lake** (5:21), returning to the western shore, most likely around Capernaum. As was customary, **a large crowd gathered around him**, presumably for teaching or expecting miracles. But surprisingly, **one of the synagogue rulers** (5:22) came to see Jesus. Another surprise is that Mark recorded his name. Few characters besides the disciples and historically important people (such as Herod and Pilate) are named in this book. Interjecting the name Jairus may demonstrate how important or recognized he was in Capernaum. With that said, it is difficult to discuss his position—synagogue leader—with precision. The title only occurs in Mark and in Luke-Acts,[8] and it can be interpreted to mean the president of the synagogue or one among many leaders. Nevertheless, the importance for this passage is that this named man recognized publicly who Jesus is and **fell at his feet**. This phrase unites each of the characters in this composite story physically: the demon-possessed man "fell on his knees in front of him" (5:6); Jairus **fell at [Jesus'] feet** (5:22); and the woman with the blood disorder **fell at his feet** (5:33). Though set apart by differing social norms, they are strangely united in their personal need.

Jairus pled for Jesus to come to heal his daughter, and **Jesus went with him** (5:24). The ever-present **crowd followed and pressed around him,** allowing the unclean woman to approach Jesus and be healed without other people noticing that she contacted Him.[9] Since she **had**

been subject to bleeding for twelve years (5:25), she had been isolated from society. This kind of impurity was addressed in the Old Testament (Lev. 15:19–33), detailing that people were to avoid any kind of association with a woman who had this kind of disorder. This biblically commanded isolation added the stigma of being a social and religious outcast to the trauma of her lengthy physical ordeal. Thus, Mark portrayed her as a complete outcast in every aspect, unable to approach people and ceremonially unfit to approach God.

When she heard about Jesus, she came up behind him in the crowd and touched his cloak, because she thought, "If I just touch his clothes, I will be healed" (5:27–28). This woman heard about Jesus from some source, and hope returned. She seems to have had a magical view of touching His clothes. Nevertheless, Jesus seems to have been more concerned with her need and her persistence, which He later defined as faith. **Immediately her bleeding stopped and . . . she was freed from her suffering** (5:29). The instant she was aware of her healing, Jesus responded similarly: **At once Jesus realized that power had gone out from him** (5:30).[10] Jesus then inquired, **"Who touched my clothes?"** The disciples missed the point of the question when they responded on a merely human level (5:31). They saw a crowded marketplace with many people touching one another and said, **"You see the people crowding against you . . . and yet you can ask, 'Who touched me?'"** Jesus recognized that a person of faith had approached Him and sensed a spiritual encounter. Jesus did not instantly recognize the identity of the woman and **kept looking around to see who had done it** (5:32). Somehow, this compelled her to fall **at his feet and, trembling with fear, told him the whole truth** (5:33). The source of her fear may be the same as that of the disciples in the boat (4:41); they both stood in the presence of a divine-like miracle worker. Yet, she also recognized that by touching Jesus, she had defiled Him. She expected to be punished for this act. Instead, Jesus informed her of the power of faith: **"Daughter, your faith has healed you. Go in peace and be freed from your suffering"** (5:34). The reader should not minimize this event as a simple transference of power from Jesus to the woman, for her faith is a key ingredient in this healing miracle.[11] The issue of faith would be revisited when Jesus returned to

Nazareth, since there His miracles were severely limited because of the people's lack of faith (6:5–6).

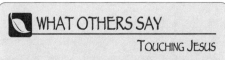

WHAT OTHERS SAY

TOUCHING JESUS

Few are they who by faith touch him; multitudes are they who throng about him.

—Augustine

Jesus' unanticipated interruption with the woman created a fatal result: **While Jesus was still speaking, some men came from the house of Jairus, the synagogue ruler. "Your daughter is dead"** (5:35). Mark recorded Jesus' **ignoring what they said** (5:36). Literally, this reads, "Jesus refused to listen to the words they were saying." Throughout the entire book, "listening" is a key to understanding Jesus. Now we learn that in part, the secret to comprehending the movement of God in our midst is being able to discern which voices are contradictory to the truth of the Kingdom. Jesus immediately took action to challenge the human perspective of this hopeless situation. Without giving the father time to grieve, He stated, **"Don't be afraid; just believe"** (5:36). Jesus' audience had just heard Jesus employ the word "faith" with the woman's illness (5:34).[12] But this call of Jesus is to do something contrary to human reason: Do not be afraid of death.

Jesus limited His followers to **Peter, James and John the brother of James** (5:37). These three witnessed some of Jesus' greatest revelatory acts: They saw His Transfiguration (9:2), heard His eschatological discourse (13:3), accompanied Him to Gethsemane (14:33), and witnessed the raising of Jairus's daughter from the dead. **When they came to the home of the synagogue ruler, Jesus saw a commotion, with people crying and wailing loudly** (5:38). The faith of the father must have been seriously tested by the uproar in his home. Emotion had set the agenda, but Jesus rearranged the stage with His declaration, **"The child is not dead but asleep"** (5:39). Jesus used a well-known biblical metaphor for death as a catalyst to encourage the father's faith. **But they laughed at him** (5:40). The antecedent of the pronoun "they" is not explicit, but it is to be understood as the mourners, whose tradition demanded that death be received with great signs of sorrow. Yet they were unaware that the Jesus whom they are mocking had vanquished a powerful storm, restored to life a demon-possessed man, and cured an illness that was untreatable by human doctors. These mourners acted within a "normal" human frame of reference (8:33). It is their disbelief and skepticism that caused Jesus to **put them all out** of the house, for they were faith distractions for the parents and for the three disciples.

The miracle itself took place in private, with minimal fanfare.[13] There is a subdued description of a touch (**He took her by the hand**, 5:41) and a word (**said to her, "Talitha koum!"**). Yet both played a role in answering the question once again, "Who is this? Even the wind and the waves obey him!" (4:41). First, Jesus touched the young girl. He acted similarly when he was touched by the woman who was defiled by her bleeding (5:30). Jewish law demanded that people avoid those who were unclean or to purify themselves following contact, since uncleanness infringes upon the realm of God's holiness.[14] However, Jesus demonstrated He was unaffected by coming into contact with human impurity. Moreover, He cleansed the unclean and sinful ones and restored them to wholeness and to life in the community. Second, Jesus spoke to the dead girl. His words have power over death itself. The word for "get up" is used to denote the raising from the dead of John the Baptist (6:14, 16), of an apparently dead demon-possessed boy (9:27), and of Jesus' own resurrection (14:28; 16:6). This was Mark's way of establishing that Jesus' words contain the elements of eternal life, and turning a deaf ear to His teaching is analogous to rejecting God's means of salvation.

In closing, it is vital to see how Mark carefully interwove these two stories with vastly different backgrounds and similar destinies. One person had been afflicted for twelve years (5:25); the other's daughter was simply twelve years old (5:42). One was a well-bred father named Jairus, who came to make a public intercession on his daughter's behalf; the other was a nameless woman with no advocate, whose affliction isolated her from society. Jairus was a man of wealth and social privilege, demonstrated by his numerous servants; the woman was destitute because she had spent all her funds on her failed medical treatment. Yet as one of life's great ironies, both were equally helpless in their respective situations. The man must certainly have taken the matter of his daughter to his synagogue with no avail. The woman was cut off from

Temple sacrifices and God due to her impurity. Both then fell at the feet of Jesus (5:23, 33) begging for His assistance. As Mark blends these stories, being male, pure, and wealthy is no advantage over being female, unclean, and destitute. In the kingdom of God, faith enables all to meet Jesus with equity.

ENDNOTES

1. Literally, "they feared a great fear."

2. Eduard Schweizer, *The Good News According to Mark* (London: SPCK Publishing, 1971), p. 110.

3. R. T. France, *The Gospel of Mark: New International Commentary on the Greek Testament* (Grand Rapids, Mich.: William B. Eerdmans, 2002), p. 226.

4. France, *Mark*, p. 230.

5. Robert Guelich, *Mark 1–8:26: Word Biblical Commentary* (Nashville: Nelson, 1989), p. 238.

6. This is the same Greek word used to describe what those tending the pigs did after Jesus cast out the legion of demons from the man. Possibly, Jesus was asking the man to reverse public opinion in the region He had been asked to leave.

7. Luke in his parallel passage explicitly wrote "God" (Luke 8:39).

8. Mark 5:22, 35, 38; Luke 8:49; 13:14; Acts 13:15; 18:8, 17.

9. It is interesting that as the woman was introduced by Mark, he places seven participles back to back before using the main verb: "If I just *touch* his clothes, I will be healed." Mark is compounding the woman's dilemma, piling up all her failed attempts to solve her problems with human answers before she comes to Jesus. See C. D. Marshall, *Faith as a Theme in Mark's Narrative* (Cambridge: Cambridge University Press, 1989), p. 104.

10. The words "she felt" and "Jesus realized" come from the same Greek root, to know.

11. For the linking of faith and healings, see especially 10:52 and 2:5; 5:36; 9:23–24.

12. The word "believe" is the verb form of the noun "faith."

13. This is certainly in line with many Old Testament miracles of Elijah (1 Kings 17:17–24) and Elisha (2 Kings 4:29–37).

14. David Garland, *Mark: The NIV Application Commentary* (Grand Rapids, Mich.: Zondervan, 1996), p. 225.

7

VALLEYS AND PEAKS IN MINISTRY

Mark 6:1–56

1. A PROPHET WITHOUT HONOR 6:1–6

Jesus left there and went to his hometown, accompanied by his disciples (6:1). Since He began preaching in 1:14–15, Jesus centered His ministry in and around Capernaum. He now returns to the place of His childhood and His family: Nazareth, some twenty-five miles to the southwest. Mark interestingly refrained from naming this village that rejected Him, and opted to call it His hometown (literally "fatherland").

When the Sabbath came, he began to teach in the synagogue (6:2). Undoubtedly, word of Jesus' ministry continued to reach Nazareth, so interest was at a high level. Mark's version of this Nazareth return is quite different from Luke's gospel (Luke 4:14–30), for Mark did not record anything Jesus taught. His primary interest was the negative response of the people who downplayed Jesus' acts and words into what might be called more domestic interests: **"Where did this man get these things?"** (6:2). It was not the question of wisdom or the previous miracles that draws their ire; it was His heritage! To the people in Nazareth, nothing in Jesus' youth would have given rise to such a man. His life was relegated to a craft—carpenter, to a lineage—Mary's son, and to a location—"with us." It is worth noting that Joseph, Jesus' father, is conspicuously absent in Mark. Many scholars believe he may have already died, and since Jesus was the eldest son, He would have taken over the family name and business (**"Isn't this the carpenter?"** 6:3). However, this may be theologically strategic for Mark. Jesus was not the son of Joseph; He is God the Father's Son, especially affirmed by the voice from heaven (1:11; 9:7). The people of Nazareth would not accept that Jesus might be "from God." In the first century, there was no such thing as being upwardly mobile. If you were born into a farming family, you were and always would be a farmer. So too with carpenters.[1] Humble beginnings meant a humble life and a humble end. In Jesus' day, it was scandalous to think that God would condescend to come to humans in a lowly family and ordinary trade.

This passage, therefore, is another scene where humans employed empirical criteria to identify Jesus. Those who should have known Him best did not know Him at all. The conclusion of the people is housed in an emotive response: **they took offense at him** (6:3). This is a powerful statement, for to take offense means to fall away. Thus, the reaction of Nazareth was not merely a failure to appreciate Jesus but an outright denial and rejection of His ministry.

Jesus responded proverbially: **"Only in his hometown, among his relatives and in his own house is a prophet without honor"** (6:4). This confirms that Jesus' earlier decision to reshape His family based on faith and obedience (3:31–35) was accurate. He has been rejected by family, country, and the religious leaders. Sadly, this rejection resulted in powerlessness: **He could not do any miracles there** (6:5). As brought to light in the last chapter, the miracles of Jesus were done in the context of faith, and it appears as if faith was nonexistent in the town of Nazareth: **And he was amazed at their lack of faith** (6:6).

2. MISSION OF THE TWELVE 6:7–13, 30

The sending out of the Twelve to preach repentance (6:7–13) and their returning to report the results of the mission (6:30) frame Mark's account of John the Baptist's death. Just as Jesus' ministry began with a proclamation of repentance and forgiveness (1:14–15), so the disciples' ministry paralleled His own.

Calling the Twelve to him, he sent them out (6:7). The "calling" of this verse is reminiscent of the disciples' original call in 3:13, when Jesus appointed them to be apostles (3:14–15). Jesus promises them that He would send them out to preach and to have authority to drive out demons. Up to this point in the story, only Jesus preached (1:14–15, 27, 38–39; 2:2, 13) and had authority over demons (1:21–28, 32–34, 39; 3:11–12). Now, their time had come. The practice of sending them out two by two will be one repeated in the rest of the book (11:1; 14:3) and in the life of the early Church (Acts 8:14; 11:30; 12:2; 15:39–40).

Jesus provided a careful set of directives for this mission, yet it surprisingly involves what not to take rather than a list of provisions. **"Take nothing for the journey except a staff—no bread, no bag, no money in your belts"** (6:8). Simply put, they were to travel upon the good graces and resources of the people they ministered among and to rely solely upon their hospitality. Sandals and staff are basic traveling equipment, thus the disciples were on a journey, similar to their teacher.

"Whenever you enter a house, stay there until you leave that town" (6:10). Hospitality was a necessity in the world of Jesus, and the reception of the disciples would be an indicator of the openness of a home or village to the gospel message. It is worth noting how the mission of the disciples and their impending ministry of miracles is placed next to Jesus' failure in His hometown (6:1–6). Jesus created a direct correlation between the hospitality of the people and their reception of the Kingdom message being preached by the disciples. If people in any

LIFE CHANGE

HOSPITALITY

Receiving a guest or stranger with gracious attitudes and actions was common in Old and New Testament times. From biblical texts, we begin to understand the virtuous nature of hospitality. It should not come as a surprise to see Jesus refer to it in Luke's parable of the Good Samaritan, Jesus' table fellowship with "sinners," and the analogy of the great banquet (Matt. 8:11; 22:1–4; Luke 14:16–24). Though the needs of travelers today aren't the same as in biblical days, the command for us to practice hospitality (Rom. 12:13) in our churches and homes is still valid. How will you welcome strangers?

place[2] refused to listen, He told the disciples, **"shake the dust off your feet when you leave"** (6:11). Rabbis performed this social shrug when they left Gentile territory to avoid carrying ceremonial defilement home with them. In this passage, Jesus used it as **a testimony against them** (6:11). Most likely Jesus was indicating that the townspeople's refusal to listen cut them off from the Kingdom promises that were initiated in and through Jesus. Rejection of Jesus' message of repentance as offered by His representatives was a rejection of their only hope. However, the gospel message often leaves room for one to listen anew. Thankfully, just because people were once inhospitable outsiders, they are not doomed to that fate.

In typical Markan fashion, the mission is summarized in an abrupt closing summary: **They went out and preached that people should repent** (6:12). The disciples followed Jesus' command. Outside of repentance, Mark did not report the content of the preaching. However, its efficacy is clear: demons were defeated and people with illnesses were healed. Yet, the results will not be reported back to Jesus until after the discussion regarding John the Baptist.

3. DEATH OF JOHN THE BAPTIST 6:14–29

The description of John the Baptist's death is chronologically out of sequence with the rest of the narrative. In actuality, it is a flashback to the beginning of Jesus' ministry, "after John was put in prison" (1:14). Yet the reader will find that John's death is revisited here because of the question raised by Herod Antipas regarding the identity of Jesus. Even more subtly, John's death foreshadowed the demise and death of Jesus.[3] **King Herod heard about this, for Jesus' name had become well known** (6:14). Herod was in fact not king but the son of Herod the Great and tetrarch of Galilee from 4 B.C. to A.D. 39. He was

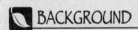

BACKGROUND

HEROD ANTIPAS

The son of Herod the Great, Herod Antipas, was born around 4 C.E., was raised in Rome, and lived until circa 39 C.E. He was responsible for massive building projects throughout the region of Galilee, which appealed to Rome. "King" Herod tried to appeal to the Jews by attending Jewish religious feasts. He married Herodias and had John the Baptist executed. In spite of all his political efforts, Herod was removed from leadership and exiled as a result of a political conspiracy.

reacting to the popular rumors of the day pertaining to the identity of Jesus and where He received the power to perform miracles.

The reader should note the introduction of the range of popular opinion about Jesus' identity: Some, including Herod, thought He was John the Baptist; some thought He was Elijah; and others thought He was one of the prophets (6:14–16). These same three options rose again when Jesus pointedly asked His disciples about His identity (8:27–30). The connection of Elijah coming at the end of time, based on Malachi 4:5–6, is historically cogent to this discussion. Were Jesus' miracles a sign of the impending "Day of the Lord"? Amazingly here, Herod's response to the discussion was closer to the truth than that of the synagogue leaders in Nazareth, for he agreed with the assumption that Jesus was **"John . . . raised from the dead!"** (6:16). It is interesting that the topic of resurrection was being associated with Jesus prior to His bringing up the subject.

For Herod himself had given orders to have John arrested, and he had him bound and put in prison (6:17). This story describes the injustice of life within the royal court. The hold Herodias had on Herod reminds the reader of the influence of another evil woman, Jezebel (1 Kings 21). The rationale for the arrest and beheading was **because of Herodias** (6:17). The disgrace John reacted to was not Herod's divorcing his first wife and marrying Herodias, but that Herodias was already the wife of Herod Antipas's half-brother Philip. John the Baptist seemingly was objecting to the marriage based on the prohibitions outlined in Leviticus 18:16 and 20:21. From Herodias's perspective, under Jewish law, it was unlawful for her to divorce her first husband. She took a different avenue to accomplish what she desired. Her Roman citizenship gave her access to Roman law, which gave her the right to divorce her first husband.[4] One can see how Jewish moral attitude would condemn their marriage. **So Herodias nursed a grudge against John** (6:19). The stage was set for conflict, and court intrigue sadly took precedence over the words of a righteous and holy man.

Finally the opportune time came (6:21). The occasion of Herod's birthday banquet was one during which Herodias could destroy John. She would do it at the expense of all around her. First, the attendees were all the important individuals in Herod's kingdom. Thus, Herod's reaction would be based on maintaining his honor rather than on truth or what is right, and Herodias knew this. Second, she subjected her own daughter[5] to shame as she **danced** [and] **pleased Herod and his dinner guests** (6:22). Herod was so enthralled with the erotic dancing of his step-daughter that he bequeathed to her a reward of unparalleled proportions. **He promised her with an oath, "Whatever you ask I will give you, up to half my kingdom"** (6:23). The extravagant gift, followed by an oath, and finally linked with remorse (6:26), indicates that this may have been the result of foolhardy, drunken action.

She went out and said to her mother, "What shall I ask for?" (6:24). The quick exit of the girl to converse with her mother indicates that Herodias was not welcome at the birthday party. Thus, to accomplish her self-righteous goals, Herodias placed her daughter in a compromising situation with her husband and their dinner guests. Moreover, to manipulate Herod with an erotic dance bordered on an incestuous act. **"The head of John the Baptist," she answered** (6:24). Herodias knew exactly what she was doing. Herod was bound by his oath in the presence of many witnesses, and to preserve his honor before his dinner guests, he had to fulfill the request. "John is treated as a political puppet instead of a prophet of God."[6] This clearly parallels the trial and death of Jesus before Pilate (15:1–15); those in charge manipulated the situations with a lust for power and against truth and righteousness. In the end, **John's disciples came and took his body and laid it in a tomb** (6:29). This event was certainly a precursor for the rejection, betrayal, death, and burial of Jesus.

At the end of the two-by-two mission of the Twelve, they **gathered around Jesus and reported to him all they had done and taught** (6:30). Thus, the story of John the Baptist's death is a digression, disconnecting 6:1–13 from this closing verse. Why? Profoundly, it interjects the theme of suffering and rejection as a real part of service in the Kingdom. Moreover, John's rejection and death foreshadowed Jesus' future journey. But the linking of the mission of the Twelve with John's death also intersects the life and ministry of the disciples with the possibility of their own deaths. What happened to John, and what would happen to Jesus, also became a probability for anyone who preached the message of truth.

Surprisingly, the only other time in the Gospel that the disciples are referred to as **apostles** is in 3:14, when they are initially called by Jesus. During the mission of the Twelve is the only time in the Gospel that they were actually faithful to the task Jesus called them to do: preaching and casting out demons.

4. FEEDING OF THE FIVE THOUSAND 6:31–44

Being the only miracle all four Gospels recount, the importance of this miracle cannot be understated. This passage will cause the reader to look forward to the second miraculous feeding in the book (8:1–10) and to the Last Supper (14:22–25). In each of the "bread" narratives Jesus liturgically takes the bread, blesses it, and breaks it before it is distributed to the people. The feeding of the five thousand points forward to the messianic banquets and the times of plenty in the Kingdom.

Once again, Jesus' popularity overwhelmed Him and the disciples, and they needed a retreat to be replenished. The **quiet place** (6:31) is in actuality a "wilderness place" or an uninhabited place. Moreover, since this passage is linked with the preceding mission of the Twelve, the disciples have tasted the demands of ministry themselves for the first time. Not only did Jesus need to get away (1:35), but the disciples did as well. **So they went away by themselves in a boat to a solitary place** (6:32). Though no place names are given, this trip is reminiscent of the former boat trips of Jesus across the Sea of Galilee. Thus, this miracle may be associated in and around His Galilean ministry headquarters of Capernaum.[7]

When Jesus landed and saw a large crowd, he had compassion on them. . . . So he began teaching them many things (6:34). The crowd once again followed Him, but Mark did not reveal why. In the past, crowds had approached Jesus for healings or exorcisms. Jesus immediately discerned their need: instruction.[8] His teaching can be understood with reference to its content; the **many things** may hark back to His lakeshore parabolic instruction in 4:1–2. But it may be more appropriate in this context to understand the phrase more from a temporal perspective, that He began to teach them for an extended period.

His disciples then came to Him and made what they believed to be a request of concern: **"Send the people away so they can go to the surrounding countryside and villages and buy themselves something to eat"** (6:36). It was late and the people needed food and shelter. Jesus' response took the disciples by surprise: **"You give them something to eat"** (6:37). The disciples' retort seems to have set their value on the people who stand before them: **"That would take eight months of a man's wages! Are we to go and spend that much on bread and give it to them to eat?"** Inherent in their response is not simply what the tangible cost would be to feed such a huge group, but they ask why they should devote so much of their resources. Jesus' compassion compared to theirs reveals that they are nothing like Him. He saw the people as sheep without a shepherd, and the disciples saw them as mealtime nuisances.

Jesus called for an inventory of provisions: **"How many loaves do you have? . . . Go and see"** (6:38). The inventory was meager: **"Five [loaves]—and two fish."** Yet, no doubt surprising all, **Jesus directed them to have all the people sit down in groups on the green grass** (6:39). The setting for this feeding miracle has already been described as a **solitary place** (6:32) and a **remote place** (6:35). This is the same Greek word that elsewhere is translated by the NIV as desert (1:3–4, 12–13). Notice however, that in this remote wilderness, Jesus had them dining on a table of green grass. Recall Psalm 23—the shepherd imagery (Ps. 23:1; Mark 6:34) and the green grass beside still waters (Ps. 23:2; Mark 6:39).

Taking the five loaves and the two fish and looking up to heaven, he gave thanks and broke the loaves (6:41). The repetition of the number of loaves and fish (6:38, 41) only enhances the nature of the impending miracle because of the "ludicrously inadequate amount of food supplied."[9] Jesus was functioning as the typical head of household, who would pronounce a blessing on the meal. "Blessed art thou, Lord our God, King of the world, who brings forth bread from the earth" (from the Jewish Mishnah *Berakhot* 6:1). But these were more than mere mealtime prayers. One can hear the words of Jesus in the feeding miracles cascade into the Last Supper meal (14:22–23): "Jesus took bread, gave thanks and broke it, and gave it to his disciples."

Then he gave them to his disciples to set before the people (6:41). Technically speaking, Jesus did not feed the five thousand. His disciples did. Jesus initiated the miracle, but the disciples carried it out. This will become a vital piece of information when the reader comes to the next feeding miracle in 8:1–13. For in that instance, there seems to be almost no recollection of this event, even though they participate in a hands-on fashion.

Finally, Mark provided insight into how the participants in the story were affected by the miracle: five thousand **ate and were satisfied**, with one basket of leftovers for each disciple (6:42–43). Moreover, this dramatic event reflects both the Mosaic wilderness events[10] and the Last Supper.

Throughout this gospel, Mark communicates the reaction of the people in the story: amazement, fear, or faith. But here there is no "amazement language." The reader does not know how the participants reacted or if, since Jesus was somewhat disconnected from this event, they were unaware of the miracle. Interestingly, Mark interjected no description of how the disciples reacted to this event, no comment regarding fear, no awe, no ignorance, and no understanding. The answer to the question "what did this event do to the disciples?" will come in the next passage, as the boat becomes a teacher's lectern.

5. WALKING ON THE WATER 6:45–52

The narrative begins as Jesus' **disciples get into the boat and go on . . . while he dismissed the crowd** (6:45). Once the crowd dispersed, Jesus **went up on a mountainside to pray** (6:46). Major incidents in Jesus' life were surrounded by extended times of prayer.

After praying, Jesus looked over the water and saw that the disciples were struggling, **because the wind was against them** (6:48). Jesus made His way over the water toward the boat. Terrified, the disciples **thought he was a ghost** (6:49) when they saw Him. The disciples failed to recognize Jesus in that moment; they also failed to recognize who He is as God's Son and the Messiah. Jesus comforted them: **"Take courage! It is I. Don't be afraid"** (6:50). Jesus stepped into the boat, and **the wind died down** (6:51).

Multiple elements of the moment caused the disciples' amazement. Jesus walked out to them on the water. The wind died down when He stepped into the boat. Shortly before this, He had fed more than five thousand people with practically nothing. Mark interjected a shocking interpretation that explains much of the disciples' perception problems: **their hearts were hardened** (6:52). In this pronouncement, Mark used a carefully chosen and highly important Greek verb form for the word "hardened." It indicates that the problem was not bound up merely with this specific, frightening meeting with Jesus. Rather, the disciples' hardheartedness was a lingering problem, and the grammar projects that this would become an ongoing dilemma. Like the Pharisees in 3:5, the disciples floating with Jesus on the water were found on the "outside," with the same heart condition of Jesus' enemies.

6. SUMMARY OF HEALINGS 6:53–56

When they had crossed over, they landed at Gennesaret and anchored there (6:53), Jesus disembarked from the boat, and immediately the people recognized Him. People who lacked the insider information of the disciples recognized Jesus, while the disciples' misunderstanding seems to have been growing. The people's knowledge of Him possibly came from a report of His healing the woman with a hemorrhage, for they begged to touch His clothes, replicating the action of the woman (5:28). Further, Mark created a subtle word play with the word "hear" as he described the means for the Gennesaret people being healed. **They ran throughout that whole region and carried the sick on mats to wherever they heard he was** (6:55). These people responded positively to what they heard, and all who touched Jesus were healed! Mark seems to contrast these "listeners" who were all healed with the disciples, whose lack of hearing in the preceding passage resulted in the hardening of their hearts (6:52). These people are examples of the good soil that Jesus described: "Others, like seed sown on good soil *hear* the word, accept it and produce a crop" (4:20, italics added).

ENDNOTES

1. One might even say that Mark exacerbated the problem of Jesus' humble birth by not telling the reader anything about Jesus' noble background, Son of David, Son of Abraham (Matt. 1:1). We do not even read of Jesus being called Son of David until the name is used by blind Bartimaeus in 10:47–48. Mark never used the name Abraham to refer to Jesus.

2. It is quite hard to tell if Mark's use of place refers to a house or an entire village. It may be that both were on his mind, just as Jesus' own household rejected Him (3:21) as well as His hometown (6:3).

3. Both John and Jesus were put to death by rulers appointed by Rome who saw their goodness and innocence yet acquiesced to socio-political forces. In Herod's case, he was influenced by a woman; in Pilate's case, the Jewish leaders.

4. Jesus attacked this "easy-out" in a marriage directly in His divorce diatribe in 10:12.

5. It is likely that the daughter's name was Salome, Herodias's daughter by her previous marriage.

6. Morna Hooker, *The Gospel According to St. Mark* (Peabody, Mass.: Hendrickson, 1991), p. 161.

7. Luke specifically located the miracle in Bethsaida (Luke 9:10), placing this on the northeast shore of the lake.

8. Thus, Mark tells the reader that this material, just like the previous parabolic teaching, falls under the guise of instruction. This practice alerts the audience that an interpretation will be necessary for them to comprehend its significance.

9. R. T. France, *The Gospel of Mark: New International Commentary on the Greek Testament* (Grand Rapids, Mich.: William B. Eerdmans, 2002), p. 267.

10. Note the reference in 6:35: "This is a remote place" and the words in 6:40: "So they sat down in groups of hundreds and fifties," finding in this arrangement the Mosaic camp in the wilderness. Thus, Jesus was shown as the "eschatological Savior, the second Moses who transforms the leaderless flock into the people of God" (William Lane, *The Gospel of Mark*, [Grand Rapids, Mich.: William B. Eerdmans, 1974], p. 230).

8

EATING
AND HEARING

Mark 7:1–37

1. A MATTER OF PURITY 7:1–23

This passage of Mark breaks down into subsections: 7:1–13 and 7:14–23. The first paragraph depicts a direct confrontation between Jesus and His Jewish opponents. The question was how one defined "purity." The Jewish leaders wanted Jesus and His disciples to adhere to the **tradition of the elders** (7:5), which Jesus saw as undermining the authority of the Old Testament. In 7:14–23, the Jewish leaders disappear from the discussion as Jesus addressed the crowds (7:14–15) and then His disciples (7:17–23). Jesus called into question a fundamental principle of

 BACKGROUND

TRADITIONS OF THE ELDERS

The covenant between Israel and the Lord was *the* reality that defined the nation of Israel. Thus, obedience to the stipulations of this covenant was essential to the nation's relationship with their Lord. In order to prevent disobedience to the covenant, the religious leaders of Israel formulated a "buffer" of instructions to ensure covenantal faithfulness. If the "Tradition of the Elders" or "Oral Tradition" was obeyed, then the people would not break the covenant.

The Law

Tradition of the Elders/Oral Tradition

Jewishness: its food laws. But the theme of purity or what makes one clean versus unclean unites this larger section. The apparently disconnected miracle of the Gentile woman (7:24–30) ties the chapter into a carefully crafted mosaic. The earlier discussion with the Jewish leaders (7:1–13) and with the crowds and disciples (7:14–23) is the issue of purity in theory. The exorcism at the request of the Gentile woman is purity put into practice.

TRADITIONS THAT DISTRACT

The Pharisees and some of the teachers of the law . . . saw some of his disciples eating food with hands that were "unclean" (7:1–2). In the past, most of Jesus' opponents had been local Pharisees (2:16, 24; 3:6) and Galilean scribes (2:6, 16). But this delegation was from Jerusalem. This group appeared in 3:22, accusing Jesus of blasphemy. This time they came to observe and critique the teachings and actions of Jesus. Immediately they noted the lack of observance of ritual washings.

The next two verses are parenthetical insertions to explain to Mark's non-Jewish readers the significance of this offense. As in the earlier incident of 2:18, 23–24, it was the actions of Jesus' disciples that caught the eye of the Jewish leaders. The confrontation was not over matters of the Old Testament Law, but over traditions. In Jesus' day, these rabbinic traditions were passed down orally from the rabbi to the student, generation after generation. They were written down and codified in the Jewish Mishnah in the second and third centuries; they were expanded in the Talmud of the fourth and fifth centuries. With reference to this passage, **the traditions of men** (7:8) instructed Jewish believers in the proper way to wash their hands, the quantity of water required, the position of hands (fisted or cupped), and the type of vessel to use (John 2:6) to remove ritual impurity. Disregarding the purity laws was a serious matter for tradition-minded Jews, for it disqualified one from worship and stained the inner conscience, hindering one's relationship to God.[1]

The information is gathered and explained to Mark's audience in 7:1–4. Here a formal charge was voiced. Why did the disciples not follow the **tradition of the elders** (7:3)? Jesus' response was housed within the words of the prophet Isaiah. The charge of the Pharisees and the scribes was countered with Scripture as a precursor to the argument itself. Yet from a rhetorical perspective, Jesus labeled their condemning behavior as similar to the religious hypocrisy that existed during the eighth-century-B.C. days of Isaiah. The application of the quote is most appropriate for this setting, for **their teachings** were merely **rules taught by men** (7:7). Moreover, this scriptural argument reorients "worship" to internal matters rather than external ritual washings. This matter will become Jesus' center of attention in 7:14–23 as He (re)defines what makes a person unclean.

Jesus then further contrasted the difference of each position: **commands of God** versus **traditions of men** (7:8). Jesus then escalated the charge against them when He said, **"You have a fine way of setting aside the commands of God in order to observe your own traditions!"** (7:9). The implication was that God's commands were in some way an inconvenience or even a nuisance supplanted by human reasoning.

Jesus next provided an example of the effects of this practice. He used one of the Ten Commandments: **"Honor your father and your mother"** (7:10). The foundational text is the fifth commandment from Exodus 20:12 and Deuteronomy 5:16, and it is supported by the addition of Exodus 21:17 to bring out the serious consequences of neglecting this commandment.

Jesus then illustrated how scribal tradition found a way for adult children to circumvent their divinely ordered responsibility to their parents. His example was not in dishonoring speech but financial responsibility. **"But you say that if a man says to his father or mother: 'Whatever help you might otherwise have received from me is Corban' (that is, a gift devoted to God), then you no longer let him do anything for his father or mother"** (7:11–12). An explanation is in order. God commanded children to honor their parents, and in Jewish tradition this in part meant to care for their parents' physical needs. In Jesus' case study, a child could dedicate his monetary worth at the Temple by declaring it "Corban." It expressed an intention to give the property and not an actual disposal of the material. Furthermore, the act was irrevocable. Money or property that was declared Corban was said to be dedicated to God. Thus parents could not be supported from it.

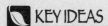

KEY IDEAS

CORBAN

This word developed into a term that referenced something of value that was dedicated for uses other than personal gain. Quite often this was used for religious purposes; hence Mark's parenthetical comments. The biblical witness suggests that some children who wanted to prevent their aging parents from accessing assets were using this idea maliciously. The dedication of something was often preformed by means of a vow, which in turn was irrevocable.

Jesus' conclusion was forceful: **"Thus you nullify the word of God by your tradition that you have handed down"** (7:13). One must not use a legal loophole to avoid God's commands. Many such cases were discussed in rabbinic literature of Jesus' time, making the thing dedicated unavailable for normal use, thus supporting Jesus' closing words: **"And you do many things like that."**

Jesus was not advocating the rejection of all traditions; He was thoroughly Jewish, steeped in the traditions of His ancestors. However, Jesus' argument was that traditions themselves may become corrupt when they run counter to the will and the purposes of God. Eminent church historian Jaroslav Pelikan wrote, "Tradition is the living faith of the dead, traditionalism is the dead faith of the living."[2] The covenant was not being jettisoned, merely the traditional trappings that hindered one's access to the word of God.

TRUE DEFILEMENT

After Jesus' rebuttal of the Pharisees and the scribes, He took this matter into the public forum: **"Listen to me, everyone, and understand this"** (7:14). This is another example of Jesus' parabolic instruction, and though the crowd became the direct recipient of His memorable words, the people most likely did not have a frame of reference in which to integrate them. This new teaching required interpretation. To understand it, one had to abandon tradition and adopt Jesus' kingdom principles.

"Nothing outside a man can make him 'unclean' by going into him. Rather, it is what comes out of a man that makes him 'unclean'"

(7:15). There were many ways one could become ceremonially unclean, such as touching a corpse or a contracting a skin disease. Taken at face value, **what comes out of a man** implied that emissions made one unclean (Lev. 15). That was not Jesus' point, as the disciples soon learn.

Jesus, per His normal routine, answered His disciples' questions privately (4:1–12, 33–34). Jesus knew the teaching had escaped the grasp of the crowds, but He expected understanding from His disciples. He asked them if they are **so dull** that they could not comprehend the message (7:18). Understanding and comprehending Jesus with specificity is not a prerequisite for discipleship; following is. And it was in their following that they were put in privileged places with Jesus to hear His teaching.

"Don't you see that nothing that enters a man from the outside can make him 'unclean'? For it doesn't go into his heart but into his stomach, and then out of his body" (7:18–19). This explanation provided the disciples with a perspective on the matter. Food in no way contaminates the heart; it is merely a source of nutrition. The radical nature of the parenthetical statement (**In saying this, Jesus declared all foods "clean,"** 7:19) should not be minimized, for the food laws of Israel combined together with the rite of circumcision and the observance of the Sabbath day epitomized what it meant to be Jewish. These religious practices kept followers of Judaism socially distinct from every other group of people. Moreover, in the first century, the sharing of meals was one of the main ways to interact socially. Thus the food laws made it impossible for a law-abiding Jew to share with a non-Jew.

In 7:18–19, Jesus only discussed what does not make a person unclean. In 7:20–23, he closed His parabolic explanation by detailing what does constitute impurity: **"evil thoughts, sexual immorality, theft, murder, adultery, greed, malice, deceit, lewdness, envy, slander, arrogance and folly."** The overall contrast illustrates that the things that go into the body (food) do not adversely affect the heart (7:19), but the litany of evil has its source already in the heart.[3] What is inside will come out. The term "evil thoughts" is positioned at the head of the list and is further particularized with the shameful list of sins comprising both actions and attitudes.[4] Each of these evils emanates from "within," describing the character of the person. Jesus defined impurity in a new light: as matters

143

of the heart not the washing of one's hands. The list is wide-ranging; twelve in all: the first six are plural, the second six singular. Additionally, the first half of the list may refer to several of the Ten Commandments: sexual immorality (7), theft (8), murder (6), adultery (7), and greed (10).[5]

The parabolic interpretation ends with the summary statement, **"All these evils come from inside and make a man 'unclean'"** (7:23). Though good may come out of such a person, it will be tainted by these matters of the heart. Human depravity is delineated in a frightening array of images, and the necessity of transformation is laid before all to hear. But the cure is not depicted; that will be saved for the cross and Easter.

2. GENTILE ENCOUNTER 7:24–30

Jesus journeyed near the Gentile city of Tyre, located in the ancient area of Phoenicia to the northwest of Galilee. In 7:24–8:10 Jesus focused His ministry in Gentile territory. **He entered a house and did not want anyone to know it; yet he could not keep his presence secret** (7:24). In the privacy of the home He was staying in, **a woman whose little daughter was possessed by an evil spirit came and fell at his feet** (7:25). Mark depicted a hopeless situation of a young girl possessed by an "unclean" (not "evil" as in the NIV) spirit. Her mother fell at Jesus' feet, similar to the Gerasene demoniac (5:6), the synagogue ruler Jairus (5:23), and the woman with the issue of blood (5:33). The woman **was a Greek, born in Syrian Phoenicia** (7:26). No one in the gospel of Mark has more strikes against him or her in approaching Jesus. She was a woman—a Gentile woman—living outside of Israel with a daughter who had an unclean spirit.

"First let the children eat all they want," he told her, **"for it is not right to take the children's bread and toss it to their dogs"** (7:27). Jesus used the word "first," which assumes that the Gentiles may be included at the meal even if they are served later. Paul made a similar statement in Romans 1:16: "I am not ashamed of the gospel, because it is the power of God for the salvation of everyone who believes: first for the Jew, then for the Gentile." This speaks not about the Gentiles' standing before God but about the progression of the Christian mission. Her response was equally cryptic but up to the verbal challenge: **"Yes, Lord,"**

she replied, "but even the dogs under the table eat the children's crumbs" (7:28). She seems to have granted at least in part Jesus' argument that the children (of Israel) had precedence over the (Gentile) dogs, but all had rights to be at or near to the banquet table. Did this woman in some fashion understand that Jesus' mission to Israel *first* was right and proper, but it must expand to all people?

As a climax to this discussion, Jesus said, **"For such a reply, you may go; the demon has left your daughter"** (7:29). It seems as if the conversation took precedence over the exorcism. Jesus, from a distance, cast out the demon, and the young Gentile girl was healed.

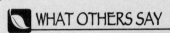

WHAT OTHERS SAY

PRETENSION

We separate ourselves from the people of God by pretentious attempts to differentiate those who are good from those who are evil.

—Augustine

3. A DEAF MAN HEARS 7:31–37

Then Jesus left the vicinity of Tyre and went through Sidon, down to the Sea of Galilee and into the region of the Decapolis (7:31). Jesus' travels seem a bit meandering. First He traveled from the city of Tyre north to Sidon. Next He took a circuitous route to the eastern side of the Sea of Galilee, visiting the region of the Decapolis. This was a largely non-Jewish territory where He ministered earlier with spectacular results (5:1–20).

The narrative has a couple prominent features. First, it continues the theme of Jesus' desire to avoid public attention and to keep His work a secret (1:34, 44; 3:12; 5:37, 43). Second, the technique employed by Jesus in the healing is described in a quite lengthy and earthy tone. He spit, touched the man's tongue, put His fingers in his ears, and used an Aramaic quotation.

At this, the man's ears were opened, his tongue was loosened and he began to speak plainly (7:35). It is difficult to tell what action actually brought about the healing. Was it the physical touch, the spiritual attitude, or the burdened sigh and the one-word prayer-command? Regardless, the effect was immediate,[6] and the crowd who brought him to Jesus was the first witness of His words. Thus, Jesus' command for

them not to tell anyone (7:36) is corporate in nature. Though the crowd is described with typical "amazement" language (1:27–28; 2:12; 4:41; 5:15, 20, 42; 6:51), for a rare moment the reader is informed of what they actually said: **"He has done everything well. . . . He even makes the deaf hear and the mute speak"** (7:37). This has a tenor of eschatological language as it seems to complete the prophecy of Isaiah 35:4–6.

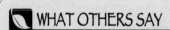

WHAT OTHERS SAY

TOUCHING EARS

By preaching the Word today, the minister is symbolically touching human ears that they may be opened to the living Word by the mystery of grace.

—Ambrose

As a final word on the passage, there is a close parallel with a similar episode that appears in 8:22–26: the healing of a blind man. In both, Jesus took the men away from the crowd for the healing (7:30; 8:23). He touched both men on the affected areas (7:33; 8:25). In both episodes, the people brought the men to Jesus (7:32; 8:22). Finally, His employment of spittle in healings is confined to these two healing stories.

ENDNOTES

1. Barnabas Lindars, "All Foods Clean: Thoughts on Jesus and the Law," *Law and Religion*, ed. Barnabas Lindars (Cambridge, England: James Clarke Company, 1988), p. 65.

2. Jaroslav Pelikan, *The Vindication of Tradition* (New Haven, Conn.: Yale University Press, 1984), p. 65.

3. The list is not exhaustive, for the New Testament contains several others (Gal. 5:19–21; Rom. 1:29–31; 1 Cor. 6:9–10).

4. The term "evil thoughts" is closely linked with the verb "comes," while the following nouns are in apposition to one another.

5. It should not be surprising to discover that Matthew, the most Jewish of the four Gospels, described the litany of evil much more in sync with the Ten Commandments: "For out of the heart come evil thoughts, murder (6), adultery (7), sexual immorality(7), theft (8), false testimony (9), slander (9)" (Matt. 15:19).

6. The common Markan word "immediately" is found in many of the ancient copies of Mark.

9

SUPPER, SIGNS, AND SIGHT

Mark 8:1–21

1. FEEDING OF THE FOUR THOUSAND 8:1–10

The transitional phrase **during those days** (8:1) keeps the story moving forward while carefully connecting it temporally and locally with the previous events. The time indicators become much more precise the closer Jesus got to Jerusalem and the last week of His life. Regarding location, we find Jesus and His disciples remaining in the Gentile territory of the Decapolis (7:31). The feeding of the four thousand in the Gentile land is a direct parallel with the previous feeding of the five thousand in Galilee (6:31–44). Mark reports that **another large crowd gathered** (8:1). Moreover, this second feeding of the four thousand, taking place in Gentile territory, assured that the Kingdom Jesus proclaimed would be ethnically diverse.

CHART		
	PARALLELS BETWEEN MARK 6–7 AND MARK 8	
Feeding Narratives	6:31–44	8:1–9
Boat Scene	6:45–56	8:10
Conflict with Pharisees	7:1–23	8:11–13
Discussion about Bread	7:24–30	8:14–21
Miracle Healing	7:31–36	8:22–26

These direct parallels in the blocks of material highlight the difficulty of Jesus' teaching ministry. The disciples were not merely intellectually deficient, nor did they simply need more information; they needed to be morally transformed. After each of the feeding miracles, the disciples failed to understand the significance of the bread (6:52; 8:14–21). Mark carefully repeated events—the feeding of the five thousand and feeding of the four thousand describe the disciples' *deafness* to the words of Jesus and their *blindness* to His miraculous deeds. Note carefully the miracles that occurred following each feeding: opening of the ears (7:31–37) and the healing of the blind man (8:22–26). No one will fully comprehend the person of Jesus unless first their deaf ears are opened and their blind eyes are healed. These events anticipate the work Jesus must do in the life of every disciple, then and now, before anyone can truly confess, **"You are the Christ"** (8:27–30).

SUPPER FOR THE CROWD

Following his normal practice, Mark provided the reader with insider information regarding Jesus' primary motivation behind the feeding miracle: He was responding to human need. The story begins with the note that **they** [the large crowd] **had nothing to eat** (8:1). Mark told much about the Christ by what moved Him to action. Jesus explained His motives to His disciples as He said, **"I have compassion for these people"** (8:2). The text implies that the crowd may have initially come with food, but their provisions had run out because they remained to hear His teaching beyond their original timetable. Moreover, Jesus says they demonstrated a desire to hear Him because **"some of them have come a long distance"** (8:3). This passage hints at a hunger that goes beyond the satisfaction derived from food (see also John 4:32–34).

The disciples responded to Jesus with words reminiscent of their previous feeding encounter (6:35–37): **"Where in this remote place can anyone get enough bread to feed them?"** (8:4). **This remote place** refers not only to the place of Jesus' prior feedings (6:32), but it echoes of the time and place of God's provision of food in the Exodus event. Thus, the words of the disciples might well have come from the lips of the complaining Israelites just before the Lord brought forth manna in the first wilderness experience (Exod. 16:1–5). Moreover, Mark employed a cognate of the word that is translated by the NIV as desert (see 1:3–4, 13, 35, 45). And it is here that we are to understand wilderness as a place of temptation. Thus, Mark proclaimed that what is about to transpire is a time of provision by Jesus and a place of proving by the people.

Jesus responded with exactly the same question He asked in the prior feeding narrative: **"How many loaves do you have?"** Surprisingly, the disciples seem to have had no recollection of a similar question to a similar need in a similar remote place. Yet they immediately knew that they had access to **seven** (8:5) loaves. As before (6:39), Jesus **told the crowd to sit down on the ground** (8:6), and His next actions are nearly identical to the previous feeding: He gave thanks, broke the loaves, and gave them to the disciples to distribute. Just as before, there were also **a few small fish as well** (8:7), for which He gave thanks and had the disciples distribute.

The people [once again] **ate and were satisfied. Afterward the disciples picked up seven basketfuls of broken pieces that were left over** (8:8). Scholars often find symbolic significance in the numbers recorded here: seven baskets left over as a sign of perfection and prefiguring the seven leaders of the Hellenistic church (Acts 6), or the four thousand men[1] present, which might represent Gentiles gathered from the four corners of the world. Mark may have recorded numbers given to him through the traditional material passed on to him or by eyewitnesses.

THE SIGNIFICANCE OF THIS MIRACLE

This passage incorporates several themes that Mark has been carrying along throughout the book. First is the denseness of the disciples. The disciples acted as if they had never witnessed the earlier feeding of the five thousand (6:35–44). Moreover, when Jesus asked the same question in the exact wording as before (6:38–8:5), they did not relate to the earlier conversation and miracle feeding. The disciples did not comprehend the Kingdom values outside their own worldview.

Second, Mark revealed that Jesus' compassion is not based on human response or human understanding. He satisfies the deepest needs of people and relieves their suffering, with abundance. Third, the context of this miracle is in the non-Jewish territory of the Decapolis. Jesus was most certainly feeding a Gentile crowd with the same bounty as His previous five thousand Jewish diners. Fourth, in these two feeding narratives (6:30–44 and 8:1–10), Mark showed no surprise or rebuke on the part of Jesus toward His disciples. In the midst of their blindness, Jesus did not isolate them as a means of reprimand. Rather, He instructed them by the miraculous object lesson, a memory they would recall during the Last Supper. This leads to the fifth lesson. This second miracle of the loaves not only looks back to an earlier scene, but it anticipates the eucharistic meal where Jesus would again take bread and bless and break it before graciously giving it to His disciples (14:22).

2. THE PHARISEES DEMAND A SIGN 8:11–13

In this short but terse encounter between Jesus and the Pharisees, Mark wanted the reader to understand that blindness was not a weakness limited to the disciples alone. The Jewish religious leaders **came and began to question Jesus. To test him, they asked him for a sign from heaven** (8:11). The NIV's translation of this passage may be just a bit tame. For the Pharisees were not *questioning* Jesus, but "disputing" (see RSV) or "arguing" (see NASB). Jesus' opponents were not *testing* Him to discover truth, but more appropriately were *tempting* Him (see Jesus' encounter with Satan 1:13). Finally they were not *asking* in any polite manner for the sign but "seeking" (see NASB), which takes on a severely negative connation based on Jesus' response. R. T. France said it best: "They [the Pharisees] do not come for dialogue, nor do they expect any sign to be given; their aim is simply to discredit Jesus."[2]

So, what was it that the Pharisees required from Jesus? They asked for **a sign from heaven**. For a first-century Jew, a sign by its very definition had its origin in heaven (see John 3:2). Thus, they were not asking for just another sign; they had in mind a particular sign distinct from the self-revelatory acts of Jesus. They were demanding Jesus to show or to say something that would verify His messianic status and signal Israel's deliverance from her enemy, Rome. Further, this would only be confirmed when the Gentile rulers who were polluting the land were cleansed from Israel. Jeffrey Gibson helpfully summarized that the sign from heaven they demanded was something that was "apocalyptic in tone, triumphalistic in character, and the embodiment of one of the 'mighty deeds of deliverance' that God had worked on Israel's behalf in rescuing it from slavery during its first exodus."[3] The irony of the situation is that this request from the Pharisees came immediately following a miraculous event that dramatically equated the works of Jesus (feeding four thousand in the wilderness) with the provision and deliverance of Moses during that Exodus (manna and water in the wilderness). These Pharisees were indeed deaf and blind, and Jesus would not be intimidated to take a plan of action different from God's purposes.

Mark interjected two other issues that added emotion to the already charged exchange. The first is the narrator's comment that Jesus **sighed deeply** (8:12) at the demand of His opponents. Mark painted Jesus as a real person in every way. Physically, He was hungry (3:20) and tired (6:31). Emotionally, He demonstrated the whole spectrum of human feelings. **This generation** is the second term of interest that Jesus attributed twice to the Pharisees in verse 12.[4] In Mark's gospel, miracles and parables have similar functions. For those with ears to hear, parables demonstrate the secret of the kingdom of God (4:11–12). For those with eyes to see, miracles demonstrate the power of the coming Kingdom. The reverse is just as true. Those without ears hear only parables, while those without eyes see only amazing acts. The ones without ears are considered "outsiders" (4:12), while the ones without eyes are referred to as "this adulterous and sinful generation" (8:38; see also 8:12; 9:19; 13:30).

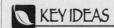

KEY IDEAS

SIGNS IN THE SYNOPTIC GOSPELS AND JOHN

The word "sign" was not used in Matthew, Mark, and Luke as it was in John.

In John, a sign (2:11; 4:54) was a divinely inspired event that pointed onlookers toward belief. In John, "miracle" does not occur.

In Matthew, Mark, and Luke, "miracle" was a wonder-working event that declared that the kingdom of God had come; a "sign" was seen negatively as a demand for proof of Jesus' identity (Mark 8:11–12; Matt. 12:38–40; Luke 11:29–32) beyond the evidence that God had already given.

At this Jesus **left them, got back into the boat and crossed to the other side** (8:13). It is difficult to determine if this verse is only transitional or a deliberate breaking of Jesus from the Pharisees. Though in English the phrase "left them" may appear neutral, in 12:12 and 14:50 Mark used the same words to describe a deliberate and permanent breaking of relationship. Mark might have wanted the reader to see these words as a clean and decisive break with the Pharisees and the "generation" they represent. From here on, Jesus invested in His disciples.

3. THE DISCIPLES' BLINDNESS 8:14–21

This passage stands at the end of the first half of Mark and may serve as a summary in describing the dullness of the disciples. The passage combines the literal theme of bread with the metaphorical theme of yeast, as it fully illuminates the disciples' blindness. Furthermore, Jesus seems to have been cautioning that the disciples' behavior borders on that of His most deceitful opponents. While the Pharisees faithlessly demanded a sign, the disciples did not seem any wiser, even though they personally participated in two feeding miracles.

The passage begins with a problem: **The disciples had forgotten to bring bread** (8:14). Being caught without proper provisions had happened two times previously, yet instead of trusting Jesus to multiply the one into many, they focused only on their meager holdings. The disciples had not only forgotten to restock their supply of bread, they had forgotten the feeding miracles. **"Be careful!" Jesus warned them. "Watch out for the yeast of the Pharisees and that of Herod"** (8:15). The word **warned** in the Greek is in the imperfect tense, likely indicating either an ongoing dialogue between Jesus and His disciples or that what followed was a summary of a more lengthy discussion.[5] The reference to **yeast** (leaven) is a familiar metaphor in the New Testament, usually referring to evil acts or intentions. Thus, Jesus may not have been warning about the ideological issues of the Pharisees and Herod, but warning them about the persons who fashioned a threat against the life of Jesus.

They discussed this with one another and said, "It is because we have no bread" (8:16). The disciples seem not to have acknowledged

Jesus' warning. Jesus was quite aware that the disciples and He were talking at cross-purposes. His first rebuke was "Why are you talking about literal bread while I am discussing something quite different?" And the implication of the NIV's choice of **talking** is far too safe (8:17). Jesus may have been using the word to indicate that the root of their "deliberations" was unbelief.

A series of accusations follows: **"Do you still not see or understand? Are your hearts hardened?"** (8:17). Then Jesus forced the disciples to respond to a succession of questions: **"When I broke the five loaves for the five thousand, how many basketfuls of pieces did you pick up?" "Twelve," they replied. "And when I broke the seven loaves for the four thousand, how many basketfuls of pieces did you pick up?" They answered, "Seven"** (8:19–20). These questions demanded the disciples to recall the most poignant parts of the two feeding narratives, primarily the parts of the miracles that they themselves participated in: the actual distribution of the food and the amazing leftover bounty. They should not have been able to forget the magnitude of the miracles, but as of yet, they only see them superficially.

Jesus' final words, though piercing, hinted at His hopefulness: **"Do you still not understand?"** (8:21). The NASB translates the word **still** as "not yet." Though it appears as if Jesus had given up on the Pharisees' being changed, He had not lost hope in the disciples. The implication is that eventually they will "see" and will "understand." As David Garland says, "Unlike the Pharisees, their problem is not that they refuse to see but that they *cannot* see until after Jesus' death and resurrection."[6]

ENDNOTES

1. There is no indication in the Greek wording to assume this number four thousand refers only to the men present. That implication comes from Mark's earlier use of the word *andros*—male in the numeric reporting of the feeding of the five thousand (6:44).

2. R. T. France, *The Gospel of Mark: A Commentary on the Greek Text* (Grand Rapids, Mich.: William B. Eerdmans, 2002), p. 311.

3. Jeffrey B. Gibson, "Jesus' Refusal to Produce a Sign (Mark 8:11–13)," *Journal for the Study of the New Testament* 38 (1990): 53.

4. The NIV, for the sake of readability, eliminates the second reference of the term. The NRSV has a more literal translation of the verse: "And he sighed deeply in his spirit and said, "Why does this generation ask for a sign? Truly I tell you, no sign will be given to this generation." Thus, Jesus' statement, as well as His demeanor, emphasized the moral inappropriateness of the question in its form: This generation . . . sign . . . sign . . . this generation.

5. Mark has placed summary statements at key junctures throughout the book.

6. David. E. Garland, *The NIV Application Commentary: Mark* (Grand Rapids, Mich.: Zondervan, 1996), p. 312.

Part Two

Jesus on the Way to Jerusalem— Discipleship Training

Mark 8:22–10:52

This section is framed by the healing of two blind men: the unnamed man in 8:22–26 and blind Bartimaeus in 10:46–52. Besides these two miracles and the exorcism in 9:14–29, there are no other miracles in this middle section of Mark. The "wonder-working Jesus" of Act 1 becomes the instructor of servanthood in Act 2.

One additional feature of 8:22–26 is noteworthy. Jesus never directly discussed His own death in Act 1. It was hinted at with the plotting of the Pharisees and the Herodians in 3:6. But Jesus' suffering and death take center stage in His discipleship training. And this only exacerbates the disciples' blindness, for a dying Messiah was an oxymoron in their worldview.

10

INSIGHT INTO THE MESSIAH'S TASK

Mark 8:22-33

1. THE FIRST HEALING OF A BLIND MAN 8:22-26

The two healings of blind men (8:22–26; 10:46–52) serve as bookends on this entire section; Mark wanted the reader to interpret Jesus' teaching in light of these two healings. One should not overlook the similarities of this first healing with that of the deaf mute in 7:31–37. Both took place in non-Galilean locations; Jesus was requested to touch the men; He responded to the request; and He demanded secrecy following the healings. Even the following phrases are nearly identical: **some people brought ... begged Jesus** ("begged him," 7:32) **... When he had spit** ("Then he spit," 7:33). The similarities in these two healings can also be seen in conjunction with the prophecy of Isaiah 35:5–6, which begins with the opening of the eyes of the blind and unstopping the ears of the deaf, work attributed to God in Psalm 146:8 and Isaiah 29:18. Thus, Mark's literary linking of these passages and his appeal to the Old Testament demonstrate a powerful witness for the person and work of Jesus.

This scene begins with Jesus and His disciples arriving in **Bethsaida, and some people brought a blind man and begged Jesus to touch him** (8:22). Bethsaida was a village outside of Galilee on the northeastern shore of the Sea of Galilee and was under the control of Philip, a son of Herod the Great. The expectation of the people was that Jesus could heal by merely touching the man, as He had done for others (1:41; 3:10; 5:27; 6:56; 7:33; 8:22; 10:13). Jesus **led him outside the village** (8:23), which was Jesus' normal practice, for miracles that engendered faith often were performed in privacy. After spitting on the man's eyes and putting His hands on him, Jesus asked, **"Do you see anything?"** (8:23). His question to the man parallels His later question to the disciples in 8:29: "Who do you say I am?" What the blind man saw is to be viewed as a precursor of what the disciples confess about Jesus.

The man's response seems odd: **"I see people; they look like trees walking around"** (8:24). Obviously the man had not been born blind, since he knew the appearance of trees. But his vision was only partially restored. **Once more Jesus put his hands on the man's eyes** (8:25). It was then that **his eyes were opened, his sight was restored, and he saw everything clearly** (8:25). Note the vivid description of the healing in rapid-fire succession. First, **his eyes were opened** is an intensified form of the verb "to see." Second, **his sight was restored** implies full restoration of health and sight (see 3:5; 9:12). Finally, **he saw everything clearly** leaves no doubt that this cure is complete. The last Greek verb is in the imperfect tense and might be translated "from this point forward, he *began* to see all things clearly," in contrast to the result of the first attempt.

Finally, **Jesus sent him home, saying, "Don't go into the village"** (8:26). It is uncertain if Mark wanted the reader to understand this as a command for secrecy similar to other miracles (see 1:44; 5:43; 7:36). But it seems as if knowledge of this miracle might have caused a newfound popularity for Jesus in this territory, thereby interrupting the private teaching He planned for His disciples.

The oddity of this healing story is the necessity of two touches by Jesus to heal the man. The larger Markan context reveals the pervasive effect of blindness and the gradual recovery of sight for Jesus' disciples. Markan scholar Morna Hooker closes her discussion of this passage with these words:

> The constant inability of the disciples in the chapters that follow this scene to understand Jesus' teaching about suffering—a failure which is remarkably similar to their inability beforehand to understand the significance of His words and deeds—suggests that Mark regards the disciples as semi-blind until the resurrection; until then

they are in the position of the half-cured man, who could barely distinguish between men and trees.[1]

As will be demonstrated in the next passage, it is quite possible to walk through life, even side-by-side with Jesus, having eyes only half open. Discipleship inside the church and formal education outside the church, though essential, are no substitute for the transforming power of the Cross. Spiritual blindness must be dealt with by Christ before we can stop thinking like humans and begin to think like God (8:33).

2. YOU ARE THE CHRIST 8:27–30

This paragraph has been called by many as the watershed of Mark's gospel. The character of the story changes dramatically following this short interchange between Jesus and His disciples. Nothing would ever be the same.

The town of Caesarea Philippi was at the northernmost point of Jesus' journeys, twenty-five miles north of Bethsaida. Caesarea Philippi was situated at the source of the Jordan River at the base of Mount Hermon. Caesar Augustus, to whom Herod dedicated a temple to the Greek god Pan, had originally given the land to Herod the Great. In 3 B.C. Herod's son Philip rebuilt the village and renamed it Caesarea Philippi to honor Caesar Augustus. Thus, the region was closely tied to Roman allegiances, making it theologically significant that Jesus was first declared the Christ in the land that proclaimed Caesar as lord.

It was while they were **on the way** that Jesus began His inquiry of the disciples. As mentioned previously, the phrase "on the way" (*hodos*) is more than a directional marker, for it became a metaphor for the direction God set before Jesus and the way Jesus called His disciples to follow by faith. Though this is the farthest distance Jesus would be from Jerusalem, it is the place of His clearest self-revelation. From there He turned and set His face toward the cross (see Luke 9:51).

Jesus' initial question was generic in nature: **"Who do people say I am?"** (8:27). The three options offered identify Him as a prophet-like figure. **"Some say John the Baptist"** (8:28). Herod Antipas's conjecture in 6:16 that Jesus was John the Baptist raised from the dead seems to have been on a par with popular opinion. **"Others say Elijah."** The belief that Jesus was John or Elijah implied that He was simply one in a line of prophets. Further, the general statement, **one of the prophets**, assigns to Jesus merely a preparatory function rather than a fulfillment or consummation role. Jesus' being discussed in the company of prophets demonstrates that the people failed to grasp the full significance of His person and, therefore, His mission.

Jesus' words **"But what about you?"** (8:29) have a strong contrasting tone in the original language, indicating that there was a better answer. The disciples had been entrusted with the "secret of the kingdom of God" (4:11), and they were being called to evaluate all the data they had accumulated about Jesus. **"Who do you say I am?"** In both clauses of 8:29, the pronoun **you** is second-person plural, making this a general question placed before the disciples as a group. **Peter answered.** Peter often functioned as the spokesperson for the entire group (see 9:5; 10:28; 11:21; 14:29). Yet the disciples were usually depicted as operating with one mind, even though only one spoke. In the gospel of Mark, the disciples operated as one like-minded unit rather than as twelve individuals. Unity is a fine thing, except that for the remainder of the Gospel the disciples were in discontinuity with the teaching and mission of Christ.

"You are the Christ" (8:29). The term **Christ,** meaning "anointed one" in Greek, is the equivalent of the Hebrew "Messiah." For the Jews of Jesus' day, "Christ" was not a title that contained a divine designation. In the Old Testament, it did not serve as a technical term for a coming deliverer. It was not until the intertestamental period (430 B.C.–6 B.C.) that there arose a range of eschatological hopes of a Davidic deliverer. By the time of Jesus, these seemed to coalesce into two major categories: (1) a popular hope for national liberation from the Roman rulers; and (2) a recognition of the need for the spiritual renewal of Israel herself. This confession of Peter represents a newfound sense of faith. The hopes of this small band of followers and the nation as a whole were pinned on their understanding of the term "Christ."

Up until this point in the narrative, the only title by which the disciples have addressed Jesus is "teacher" (4:38), and that term is used twice as often by others than by the disciples.[2] Even the term "Lord" was only spoken from the mouth of the Gentile woman (7:28) whose girl was healed.

The disciples had seen the demons cast out, assisted at the feeding of many people, and witnessed the sick healed. But it was not obvious to them that Jesus is the Messiah because Israel is not free from their Roman rulers. So, Peter, as the spokesman for the disciples, placed all their hopes in Jesus to perform this Messiah-based task. But Jesus refused to have this chief designation of His mission communicated to the crowds with such a restrictive, military-like agenda, so He **warned them not to tell anyone about him** (8:30). The second half of the Gospel defines the kind of Messiah Jesus truly is. The disciples were not to speak about Him as Messiah until they integrated His suffering, rejection, death, and vindicating resurrection into their message of the Messiah.

3. JESUS' FIRST PASSION PREDICTION 8:31–33

Coupled with the immediately preceding command to silence, the core of Jesus' self-revelation began with a redirection of the disciples' choice of titles. They chose Messiah; Jesus offered another, more enigmatic title: **the Son of Man** (8:31).[3] What Jesus was about to say regarding suffering and death might have been incomprehensible if He had retained the disciples' more victorious-sounding title: "Christ." Jesus would not allow himself to be categorized. For Jesus, the title "Christ" carried too much militaristic and nationalistic baggage; it had to be tempered with the less familiar "Son of Man" designation. He went on to teach His disciples the essential issues with reference to His identity.

The **"Son of Man must suffer many things"** (8:31). The disciples had seen nothing but power and victory in the acts of Jesus thus far. So these words had no place to take root. Moreover, the suffering and death of the Messiah raised huge theological problems. If Jesus was indeed the Messiah, why would God allow Him to **be rejected** and **be killed** (8:31)? Though the answer is not fully elucidated in the gospel of Mark, it is part of a plan found in the Old Testament. Mark reported that the Son of Man must suffer many things. The word **must** is often used of divine necessity as spelled out later in 9:12 and 14:21, 49. Thus, Jesus' rejection and death are to find their source in Scripture and the heart of the Father's will and not in the violence of Palestinian politics. Mark would not allow Jesus' death to be read as a sociological mistake but rather as an act of divine redemption.

CHART

THREE PASSION PREDICTIONS IN MARK

Mark 8:31	Mark 9:31	Mark 10:33–34
He then began to teach them that the Son of Man must suffer many things and be rejected by the elders, chief priests and teachers of the law, and that he must be killed and after three days rise again.	He said to them, "The Son of Man is going to be betrayed into the hands of men. They will kill him, and after three days he will rise."	"We are going up to Jerusalem," he said, "and the Son of Man will be betrayed to the chief priests and teachers of the law. They will condemn him to death and will hand him over to the Gentiles, who will mock him and spit on him, flog him and kill him. Three days later he will rise."

The wording of each of the three passion predictions is just a bit different. It is only in this passage that the reader of Mark sees the word **suffer**. But with **rejected**, Mark draws attention to Psalm 118:22, where Christians identify in Jesus' fate that the "stone the builders rejected has become the capstone" and His following vindication.[4] Each of the three passion predictions ends with the same climax: the resurrection of Jesus from the dead. The disciples were no more attentive to this aspect of Jesus' teaching than any other.

No matter how much explanation He provided, the disciples never achieved complete clarity. This unveiling of the messianic mission demanded a response from the disciples. And it came from Peter as **he took** [Jesus] **aside and began to rebuke him** (8:32). Peter displayed that he was at cross-purposes with Jesus' agenda. The word "rebuke" connotes a command by one taking authority over another. Jesus, without hesitation, **turned and looked at his disciples** (8:33), implicating them as coconspirators, as **he rebuked Peter.** The repetition of the same verb (8:31, command of Jesus to disciples; 8:32, Peter's rebuke of Jesus; 8:33, Jesus' rebuke to Peter) demonstrates irreconcilable perspectives. Jesus settled the issue when He ordered Peter to get behind Him. Note how this short statement is spatially as well as relationally oriented. First, Jesus said, **"Get behind me."** This is the same language used by Jesus in His initial call of His disciples in 1:17 and could be translated, "Come, behind Me." This might be understood as Jesus calling Peter to get back in step with Him. Further, there is another occurrence of the word in the next verse, where the phrase is translated, **"If anyone would come after me"** (8:34), cementing Peter's call to follower-ship based not on his notion of power or might, but on Jesus' revelation of rejection, shame, and death.

Relationally, Jesus called Peter **"Satan."** In short order, Jesus completed His own counter-rebuke of Peter. Peter's plan, which avoided the cross, placed him in league with Jesus' archenemy. This is partially why Jesus commanded (rebukes) the disciples to silence, for the proclamation of a Messiah without the cross is satanic in its message. This exchange was brought to a culmination with Jesus' closing reproof: **"You do not have in mind the things of God, but the things of men"** (8:33). The NIV makes this a separate sentence, while in actuality it is a dependent clause, specifically a result clause: "for you do not have in mind the things of God but the things of people." The plain teaching of Jesus (8:31) cannot be grasped on a merely human level.

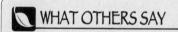

WHAT OTHERS SAY

VISION

The fact is this: we all need a vision. A vision is necessary because of the restless insistence of the mind to find answers to its questions and to organize reality into understandable patterns. A vision also gives us direction for behavior. It gives life predictability. Because of my vision . . . I know how to act. . . . To the extent that we are blind or have distorted reality our lives and happiness have been diminished. Consequently, if we are to change, if we are to grow there must be a change in the basic vision.

—John Powell

The vision for ministry that Jesus is teaching is irreconcilable with the vision Peter and the other disciples have for Him as the Messiah. The misguided vision of the disciples and their determined refusal to adopt

Jesus' revelation precludes them from full comprehension. Teaching, even from such a skilled educator as Jesus, would not adequately overcome humanity's blindness. Thus, Mark conveys a truth that became Christian doctrine: Men and women must not merely become educated (or catechized) in the Church; they must initially be transformed.

ENDNOTES

What Others Say Sidebar. John Powell, *Fully Human, Fully Alive: A New Life Through a New Vision* (Niles, Ill.: Argus Communication, 1976), p. 52.

1. Morna Hooker, *The Gospel According to St. Mark* (Peabody, Mass.: Hendrickson, 1991), p. 198.

2. Disciples use it in 4:38; 9:38; 10:35; 13:1. Others use it in 5:35; 9:17; 10:17, 20; 12:14, 19, 32; 14:14.

3. For a Son of Man discussion, see 2:10.

4. See also Matthew 21:42; Mark 12:10–11; Luke 20:17; Acts 4:11; Ephesians 2:20; and 1 Peter 2:7.

11

THE DEMANDS OF DISCIPLESHIP

Mark 8:34—9:1

This passage begins with an unusual comment about the recipients of Jesus' teaching. They included **the crowd** and **his disciples** (8:34). For the remainder of the second Gospel, Jesus instructed His disciples. However, as He described the true essence of a follower, His offer was universal in scope.[1] Previously (1:16–17) Jesus' call was undefined; it was "Come, follow Me," based on a promise to make His disciples "fishers of men." But here Jesus thematically linked the fate of His followers with His own mission: suffering and death. The call was not merely to acknowledge Jesus as the Messiah, but to become participants in the unfolding story as Jesus led His followers on the way to Jerusalem.

1. THE COST OF FOLLOWING JESUS 8:34-35

The call to discipleship is comprehensive in its reach (disciples and crowds), but it immediately takes on a conditional nature: **"If anyone would come after me"** (8:34). The phrase literally translated reads, "If someone wishes/wants after me to follow. . . ." Jesus demands a heartfelt choice, which eliminates other, possibly more appealing, choices.

Jesus set the agenda according to His spiritual compass; a follower must **"deny himself."** Powerfully, the insertion of the reflexive pronoun **himself** implies the first aspect of discipleship is to refuse to be guided by one's own interests. Moreover, self-denial is not to be confused with asceticism (the denial of things one desires) or even with self-discipline. Self-denial is the denial of the self itself (see Phil. 2:3–4). The second requirement of a follower is to **"take up his cross."** This is the first use of the word in the Gospel, certainly creating a link back to Jesus' earlier prediction of His own death. In the first century, a cross indicated punishment of a shamed criminal at the hands of the Romans. Moreover, this Roman form of execution might be heard by the listeners as a call to rebel against Rome and to risk their lives. Yet, the word will not reoccur until chapter 15. This provided Jesus with ample time to define the impact and meaning of His own death and the cross-bearing imagery associated with His followers. For in summary, the self-denial to which Jesus calls one is abandonment of one's autonomy and adoption of Jesus' leadership and lordship.

Finally, Jesus beckoned His disciples to **"follow me"** (8:34). Jesus' initial thrust into discipleship-making seems more directional than doctrinal. His call is bracketed with terms of motion. "Mark is rich in verbs of motion. Jesus is on the move; he summons disciples to come after him"[2] Each time Jesus called His disciples, He was in motion (1:16, 19; 2:14; 10:17). Further, His call was to get in step directly behind Him. Thus, for one to be a disciple, one must follow. The mark of a faithful disciple is to be seen not in fully comprehending all the theological nuances of the person of Jesus, but in setting one's sight unwaveringly on the path laid out by Jesus. The path to the cross is costly and counterintuitive, yet Jesus clearly laid out the directional markers for all who are willing to follow.

The demands of discipleship are further refined. **"For whoever wants to save his life will lose it, but whoever loses his life for me and for the gospel will save it"** (8:35). Jesus offered this paradoxical principle for savings one's life, using two meanings of "life." The word implies physical life in its first use (as opposed to death; see 3:4; 10:45). In this sense, people might think they can preserve their lives by avoiding conflict and persecution. However, Jesus' other meaning was that by losing one's physical life, one receives (saves) eternal life. More precisely, this call to a loss of life is not a morbid acceptance of death. Rather, it is an adoption of Jesus (**for me**) and His mission agenda (**for the gospel**) around which one reorients one's focus and through which one discovers true life. A disciple is to follow Jesus by publicly adhering to the gospel, proclaiming it to the world, and dying if necessary.

2. KEEPING AN ETERNAL PERSPECTIVE 8:36–9:1

"What good is it for a man to gain the whole world, yet forfeit his soul?" (8:36). Here the contrast between this **world** and the next (**soul**) is made more explicit. In this Gospel, "world" represents the created order in a neutral sense. **Gain** implies human ambition and drive for worldly success. Thus, one should not connote an evil intent on the part of the pursuer, but the explicit contrast as the loss of one's life or soul far exceeds any profit in terms of earthly gain.[3] This contrast is continued in the rhetorical question **"Or what can a man give in exchange for his soul?"** (8:37). This passage continues with the theme that we cannot grasp the priceless value of one life or soul, and that there is another way to categorize value apart from what we can see, hear, smell, touch, and taste.

Verse 38 repeats the conditional emphasis begun in 8:34: **"If anyone is ashamed of me and my words in this adulterous and sinful generation, the Son of Man will be ashamed of him when he comes in his Father's glory with the holy angels."** The contrast of honor and shame was a primary value of the first century. So, if anyone was ashamed of Jesus (**of me**) and His authoritative demands (**and my words**), she or he might have received worldly honor, but forfeited honor in the future, coming Kingdom. David Garland summarizes it this way:

> Jesus uses the threat of judgment to induce his followers to be faithful. To be put to shame is the opposite of vindication (Ps. 25:3; 119:6; Isa. 41:10–11; Jer. 17:18). Those who may be frightened by the edicts of earthly courts (represented in the Gospel by Herod Antipas, the high priest's Sanhedrin, and the Roman governor, Pilate) should fear even more the decision of the heavenly tribunal, which determines their eternal destiny.[4]

167

The use of the adjective **adulterous** reminds the reader of the frequent Old Testament charges against the nation of Israel as she constantly committed spiritual adultery and went out after other gods (Isa. 1:4, 21; Ezek. 16:32; Hos. 2:4).

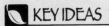

KEY IDEAS

HONOR AND SHAME

Social honoring and shaming were the methods of control used to encourage or discourage actions based on community accepted, standard rules. When more than one standard of rule presented itself as an option, one had to come to a conscious decision of which one to follow.

The traditional early church understanding of the **Son of Man** "coming" was that of the *parousia* or the second coming. Yet the imagery and background in this material comes from the visions of Daniel 7: ". . . one like a son of man, coming with the clouds of heaven."

He is presented before the throne of the Ancient of Days (Dan. 7:13–14), and "He was given authority, glory and sovereign power; all peoples, nations and men of every language worshiped him. His dominion is an everlasting dominion that will not pass away, and his kingdom is one that will never be destroyed." The scene is clearly set in heaven, and His "coming" is better described as an entrance into the throne room of God, not the "second coming" to earth. One must keep in mind that Jesus' teaching in 8:31 is an intricate series of contrasts between this world and the next, with the Son of Man prophecy as its climax. Thus, the shaming of the Son of Man on earth by people will result in their judgment in the heavenly realm.

There is an interesting combination of Son of Man language and the **Father's glory**. The voice at Jesus' baptism directly referred to Jesus as His Son (1:11). Jesus only referred to God as His Father again in 13:23 and in His prayer in Gethsemane (14:36). Yet the importance is not simply familial but theological. For here the Son of Man and Son of God concepts are closely linked with each other and with the messianic overtones of the entire passage. This would not happen again until Jesus' confession before the high priest in 14:62.

And he said to them, "I tell you the truth, some who are standing here will not taste death before they see the kingdom of God come

with power" (9:1). Seemingly, 9:1 assures the first-century disciples (and subsequent readers) that for all they abandon in this lifetime, they will indeed see the kingdom of God come and share in His exaltation. The implication is that the event being referred to is near enough that a privileged few will catch a glimpse of this unveiling. Numerous suggestions have been offered regarding the fulfillment of Jesus' prediction. The most prominent suggestions include (1) the death of Jesus and the resultant tearing of the Temple curtain, (2) victory over death in His resurrection, (3) His ascension and enthronement in heaven, (4) the coming of the Holy Spirit at Pentecost, and (5) the destruction of Jerusalem in A.D. 70. All of these would certainly be viable options within the lifetime of the original hearers. Yet nearly all except the first option fall outside the narrative of the gospel of Mark. Possibly the most text-centered line of interpretation would be to look forward to the Transfiguration (9:2–13). The events are linked temporally and precisely—after six days—a highly unusual practice for Mark outside of the passion narrative. Additionally, the Transfiguration narrative reports what the disciples saw, and the cloud appearing and enveloping the disciples is suggestive of the Mount Sinai theophany (Exod. 19), leaving the reader with the impression of Jesus coming in power. One could feel less than satisfied with seeing Jesus transfigured on a mountain being equated with seeing the kingdom of God come with power. Yet throughout the Gospel of Mark, the kingdom of God and the person of Jesus are inseparably linked. The Kingdom was brought near with the coming of Jesus and the proclaiming of the good news of God (1:14–15). Later, the secret of the Kingdom was revealed in Jesus' parabolic instruction (4:10–12). Thus, it seems appropriate for Mark to make known the joining of the Kingdom of God and the person of Jesus as a signal of the real, though not yet fully revealed, presence.

ENDNOTES

1. That Jesus would attribute the term "calling" to those outside of his discipleship circle is unusual, yet it alerts the reader that something emphatic is being revealed. (See 3:13, 23; 6:7; 7:14; 10:42; 12:43.)

2. Ernest Best, *Following Jesus: Discipleship in the Gospel of Mark*, Journal for the Study of the New Testament: Supplement Series (Sheffield, England: Sheffield Press, 1982), p. 36.

3. R. T. France, *The Gospel of Mark: New International Commentary on the Greek Testament* (Grand Rapids, Mich.: William B. Eerdmans, 2002), p. 341.

4. David Garland, *Mark: The NIV Application Commentary* (Grand Rapids, Mich.: Zondervan, 1996), pp. 328–29.

THE TRANSFIGURATION

Mark 9:2-13

C hapter 9 often begins with a verse that appears at first glance to be more closely connected with the initial discipleship speech of chapter 8 than with the material that follows. But in reality, Mark may have been artistically connecting two previously disconnected blocks of material.

1. THE DISCIPLES WATCH 9:2-4

The "some who are standing here" (9:1) could refer to an eschatological event, yet in this immediate context it is closely linked to the next event: **Jesus took Peter, James and John with him and led them up a high mountain** (9:2). The traditional site, Mount Tabor, could have been reached easily within the six-days time allotment. Yet it is not likely that a Jewish crowd would be this far north. Mount Hermon, much closer to Caesarea Philippi and to the next meeting place in Capernaum (9:33), is more likely. Possibly the vagueness of the exact location only increases the fact that it is to be understood as the new Sinai, the location of divine revelation.

The chronological marker, **after six days**, is so unusually precise[1] in the gospel of Mark that the attempt to fix this time accomplishes two goals. First, it links this story with the previous one. The reader must interpret the words of messianic suffering and the disciples' participation with Jesus in light of this radiant event. Second, a mountaintop experience reminds the biblically literate reader of Moses' six-day preparation before meeting God at Mount Sinai (Exod. 24:15–16). Further, Mark demonstrated that the suffering and death of the Son of Man is not irreconcilable with the glory of God seen on Mount Sinai. The disciples for the first time saw the reality of what Jesus told them in 8:31–9:1. Finally, Jewish tradition viewed Moses' ascent to Mount Sinai as a royal enthronement. Thus, the parallels with the Transfiguration would have the early readers of Mark understanding Jesus as King. Joel Marcus concisely says, "Like the Moses of the Jewish legend, Jesus is a king—indeed a king who participates in God's own rule."[2]

CHART

TRANSFIGURATION AND MT. SINAI

Jesus (Mark 9)	Moses (Exodus 24, 34)
9:2—Jesus took Peter, James and John with Him and led them up a high mountain	24:1, 9—Moses went with three men and seventy elders
9:2—Jesus was transfigured and His clothes became radiantly white	34:29—Moses' skin shone after being with God
9:7—God appeared in cloud and voice spoke.	24:15–18—God appeared in cloud and voice spoke
9:15—The people were astonished after Jesus descended from the mountain	35:30—People were afraid of Moses after he descended from the mountain

The event is told from the three disciples' vantage point: what they saw, what they said, and what they heard. First, what they saw: **His clothes became dazzling white. . . . And there appeared before them Elijah and Moses** (9:3–4). Mark reported that Jesus was transformed; Jesus' clothes became white beyond the capability of any earthly process.[3] The glowing clothes are the features of heavenly beings in both Old Testament references (Dan. 7:9; 10:4–11:1; Ps. 104:1–2) and in New Testament resurrection appearances (Mark 16:5; Acts 1:10; Rev. 3:4; 4:4; 7:9, 13–14).[4] Then the disciples saw **Elijah and Moses**.[5] These men represented the law (Moses) and the prophets (Elijah) in conversation with Jesus.

Moses and Elijah each had met God and heard His voice on Mount Sinai. These well-known Old Testament figures seemingly never died. Elijah was translated to heaven (2 Kings 2:11); Jewish tradition maintained that Moses' lack of a known grave on Mount Nebo (Deut. 34) pointed to his removal to heaven.[6] Thus, it seems Mark wanted the reader to combine the earlier remark by Jesus that "some who are standing here will not taste death before they see the kingdom of God come with power" (9:1) with the appearance of these two Old Testament figures who themselves had not experienced death. Together, they pointed toward Jesus' ultimate experience over death as a true sign of the coming Kingdom. Moreover, as the disciples descended the mountain with Jesus, their attention was not focused on the writings of the Old Testament but on the eschatological role Elijah (9:11–13) played in the time of Jesus. Additionally, the figure of Moses may not have simply been the receiver of the Law, but more closely aligned with the prophet hopes of first-century Jewish minds with promised "prophet like Moses" from Deuteronomy 18:15–19. Swiss New Testament scholar Eduard Schweizer wrote a most appropriate conclusion:

This story has united two expectations which were alive in Judaism: the coming of the prophet of the end-time who is like Moses and the appearing of Elijah at the dawning of the end-time. It has declared to every Jew that the fulfillment of the history of Israel and of every hope for the glorious end-time have already begun in the coming of Jesus.[7]

2. THE DISCIPLES SPEAK 9:5-6

"Rabbi, it is good for us to be here. Let us put up three shelters—one for you, one for Moses and one for Elijah" (9:5). Speaking for the disciples, Peter revealed that he did not fully comprehend the person of Jesus. His comment began with the name Rabbi, which he employed for the first time in dialogue with Jesus. Previously, he used the Greek equivalent "teacher" as the disciples encountered a storm on the Sea of Galilee (4:38).[8] He then offered up a human construction project as a response to the theophany: tents (tabernacles) for all three. One need not read into the response a desire on the part of the disciples to institutionalize Jesus, Moses, and Elijah. Rather, it may have simply been a human effort designed to honor the three. Yet the dilemma is that the disciples were either elevating the two prophets to a position equal with Jesus or demoting Jesus. Either choice was an error. For the narrator parenthetically interjected, **He did not know what to say, they were so frightened** (9:6). Again, their awe of Jesus demonstrates the disciples' ignorance and fear (4:41; 6:50).[9]

3. GOD SPEAKS 9:7-8

Then a cloud appeared and enveloped them (9:7). The cloud represents the shekinah glory of God. Reminiscent of imagery present in the giving of the Ten Commandments in Exodus 19, the cloud seems to have enveloped them. The text is a bit ambiguous regarding the precise antecedent to the word "them." Does it refer to all six of the men on the mountain or only Jesus, Elijah, and Moses? Yet the following verse reveals that **a voice came from the cloud,** which indicates the disciples were outside the cloud looking on as they heard the words.

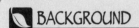

BACKGROUND

SHEKINAH GLORY

The word "Shekinah," though not used in the Bible, comes from the Hebrew verb *sakan*, "to dwell." It refers to the manifestation of God's presence in biblical references such as Exodus 13:2; 33:7–11; and Ezra 1:28; 11:23.

What is the meaning of the voice? First, for the reader it ties the event back to the baptismal scene and the Father's initiatory words of Sonship: "You are my Son, whom I love; with you I am well pleased" (1:11). Yet this one takes on a different role. The words at Jesus' baptism were a pronouncement to Jesus, while this time God spoke for the benefit of the individuals on the mountain. The heavenly voice contained more than an affirmation of Jesus' person; it had a command attached: **"Listen to him!"** Since these three disciples saw Jesus in all of His true glory and heard the command from God himself, the issue of "not listening" would no longer simply be a difference of opinion but outright disobedience and rejection of the Son of God.

Suddenly, when they looked around, they no longer saw anyone with them except Jesus (9:8). **Suddenly** indicates that without warning the dynamics of the situation changed. The phrase **looked around** also may imply that during part of the Transfiguration, the disciples listened but simultaneously hid their faces from the visual events of the theophany. The final clause literally reads, "Jesus alone with them," reflecting a change to normalcy (if there is such a thing in the presence of Jesus), returning to the way it was in 9:2, "where they were all alone." There seems to have been no lingering effect of the Transfiguration in the face of Jesus, unlike Moses, whose face continued to shine after coming down the mountain (Exod. 34:29–35).

4. JESUS EXPLAINS 9:9–13

The three disciples had caught a glimpse of the resurrected Jesus, but they were not to tell anyone until after it had become a full reality. This private preview would later become a public proclamation. The discussion of "rising from the dead" may seem out of place in the midst of the disciples overhearing a conversation between Jesus and two "deathless" men of God (Elijah and Moses). **They kept the matter to themselves discussing what "rising from the dead" meant** (9:10), implying direct obedience on the part of the disciples to Jesus' command. But throughout Mark, any discussion of Jesus' death and His ensuing resurrection fell on deaf ears (8:31–32; 9:30–32; 10:32–4). There was no established first-century paradigm for a dying and rising Messiah. Therefore, it is likely that their obedience was limited by their inability to grasp the concept well enough to engage in a discussion.

The logic of the ensuing question of the disciples' regarding the coming of Elijah arose directly from the mountaintop experience, which must have raised eschatological or end-times matters that required further explanation. For the Jews of Jesus' day assumed that the resurrection from the dead would be a corporate rising of Israel immediately preceding the final judgment, the great and terrible Day of the Lord (see Mal. 4:5). Besides, the scribes and teachers of the day did not espouse any understanding of a resurrection to take place as Jesus taught. Jesus

KEY IDEAS

DEVELOPMENT OF THE CONCEPT OF RESURRECTION

- Pre-exile, in Jewish literature there are no specific references to life post-mortem. Therefore, the term "sheol" should be understood as a gathering place for the dead. However, sheol was not a location absent of God's potential intervention.

- The concept of resurrection was intensely developed in intertestamental times. While some scholars attribute this development to the influence of foreign ideals, this is met with some doubt.

- What can be said regarding the evolution of this concept is that based on the fact that God is living, so too will the faithful.

- The absence of an explicit explanation regarding resurrection testifies that the New Testament witness, as influenced by the Old Testament, is more concerned with life in the present as the believer seeks to manifest Christ.

presented a completely new way of perceiving God at work, and the disciples had no mental paradigm in which to store the newly acquired resurrection timeline.

The initial part of Jesus' reply clearly agrees with the scribal traditions raised in 9:11. But Jesus rhetorically asked, **"Why then is it written that the Son of Man must suffer much and be rejected? But I tell you, Elijah has come, and they have done to him everything they wished, just as it is written about him"** (9:12–13). Jesus stated that Elijah had come. He had been powerfully portrayed in the form of John the Baptist, and he was mistreated and killed. The disciples were asking if the "end" was beginning with the appearance of Elijah on the mountain, since he had to come first. Though Jesus agreed, He forced the disciples to see that the "beginning of the end" was already in progress with the life and death of John the Baptist (1:1–3), and what took place on the mountain was not about Elijah or Moses but about the ensuing suffering of Jesus himself.

ENDNOTES

Key Ideas Sidebar: For further information, consult these sources: (1) Brown, Colin, *Resurrection* in Dictionary of New Testament Theology, edited by Colin Brown (Grand Rapids, Mich.: Zondervan, 1967), vol. 3, pp. 261–275; (2)

Merril, Eugene H., *New International Dictionary of Old Testament Theology and Exegesis*, edited by Willem A. Van Gemeren (Grand Rapids, Mich.: Zondervan, 1997), pp. 4:6–7.

1. Only other precise temporal reference is in 14:1. And the Passion narrative of chapters 14–16 is explicitly coordinated by the Passover week and the time references to Jesus' death.

2. Joel Marcus, *The Way of the Lord* (London: T & T Clark Publishers, Ltd., 2004), p. 92.

3. Interestingly, Matthew refers to Jesus' face shining like the sun, while Mark only comments upon His clothes.

4. Numerous other apocalyptic texts use similar descriptive elements (1 Enoch 14:20; 62:15–16; 2 Enoch 22:8–9; 3 Enoch 12:1).

5. Literally, the text reads, "Elijah *with* Moses." Some interpreters place the priority on Moses with Elijah playing a secondary role.

6. A lost apocryphal work, *Assumption of Moses*, referred to in several patristic writings, speaks of Moses' removal to heaven (see also Jude 9). For details on this matter, see Joachim Jeremias' entry in *Theological Dictionary of the New Testament*, 2.939 n. 92 (Gerhard Kittel and Gerhard Friedrich [editor], Geoffrey W. Bromiley [Translator], *Theological Dictionary of the New Testament* [Grand Rapids, Mich.: William B. Eerdmans, 1981]).

7. Eduard Schweizer, *The Good News According to Mark* (London: SPCK Publishing, 1971), p. 183.

8. In Mark, the Greek term "teacher" is used ten times to three for the Hebrew "Rabbi." R. T. France ponders if this "fits the strongly Old Testament feeling of the moment, particularly the presence of Moses the prototype teacher of the law" (R. T. France, *The Gospel of Mark: A Commentary on the Greek Text* [Grand Rapids, Mich.: William B. Eerdmans, 2002], p. 354).

9. Peter was not the sole mistaken disciple, but once again he serves as the mouthpiece of the group. Mark makes it clear: "*He* [Peter] did not know what to say, *they* [Peter, James, and John] were frightened" (italics added).

INEFFECTIVENESS AND MISUNDERSTANDINGS

Mark 9:14–50

1. THE DISCIPLES' FAILURE AT EXORCISM 9:14–29

Jesus, Peter, James, and John left the mountain and found the nine disciples and the scribes arguing over the disciples' inability to cast out an evil spirit from a boy. The large crowd and the teachers of the law only set this scene; they did not participate any further. But, their appearance served to heighten the public disappointment of the disciples. Additionally, it was Jesus whom the crowds really were seeking, for **as soon as all the people saw Jesus, they were overwhelmed with wonder and ran to greet him** (9:15). The nine disciples who were left out of the mountaintop experience remained behind to serve as the "second team." Then, when the star of the team came back onto the field, the fans rallied around Him. This is stated most emphatically by the father of the boy with the evil spirit who said, **Teacher, I brought *you* my son. . . . I asked *your* disciples to drive out the spirit, but *they* could not** (9:17–18, italics added). "In Your absence," the father said, "I relied on Your disciples, and they let me down." And his accusation literally worded says more than they were incapable; "they were not strong." The words of the passage reinforced the notion that though the disciples may have been chosen by the Teacher, they were not like Him.

Then, in one of Jesus' harshest rebukes, He said, **"O unbelieving generation . . . how long shall I stay with you? How long shall I put up with you?"** (9:19). Yet the recipient of the censure is the generic "you" (plural). Was Jesus directing it toward the father and son, the scribes, the crowd, or the disciples themselves? Matthew's gospel appears to clarify that Jesus' disappointment was directed toward the faithless disciples (Matt 17:20). But it may also be argued that the disciples did not make up what Jesus labeled as an unbelieving generation. Thus, Jesus may have been addressing himself toward all of humanity who were not demonstrating faithfulness in spite of His teaching and numerous miracles.

Jesus' answer for this generation was a clear demonstration that He is strong enough and that He has the authority to command and cast out the crippling spirits. **"Bring the boy to me"** (9:19). This is also almost the exact wording of the father's original request (9:17). What was seen as the disciples' failure and the unbelief of the crowd, and entire generation for that matter, would be corrected. **When the spirit saw Jesus, it immediately threw the boy into a convulsion. He fell to the ground and rolled around, foaming at the mouth** (9:20). The reaction of the demon in this exorcism was not dialog with Jesus (see 1:24; 5:7) but violence toward the victim. And the severity of the situation is that this had been taking place **from** [his] **childhood** (9:21). Notice Mark's threefold description of the symptoms: first the father initially came to Jesus (9:17–18), then the demon (literally: spirit) **threw the boy into a convulsion**, finally the father concluded with a plea to **take pity on us and help us** (9:22), as if this were his last hope. And the wording of the phrase sheds light on the explicit nature of the father's request: **if you can do anything.** He saw this as a difficult if not impossible case. The disciples had failed, though they had succeeded previously in casting out demons, so the father may have been implying, "Jesus, if You can offer even a small improvement in this destructive situation, it would be welcomed."

Jesus then retorted, **"'If you can'?" . . . "Everything is possible for him who believes"** (9:23). Here Jesus intimately linked faith with the appropriation of healing. Jesus demanded a public testimony of the man's faith. And at no other place in the New Testament is a more honest declaration made: **"I do believe; help me overcome my unbelief!"** (9:24). It seems as if the father was aware of his limitations, which had gone unacknowledged by the disciples. But they do have something in common: partial sight and faltering faith. Maybe the father was an image of the disciples. He knew that his failure to care for his son was due to his own faith (or unbelief) and not due to any limitation on the part of Jesus.

From this point forward, the father disappeared from the story. He was replaced with the **crowd . . . running to the scene** (9:25). Jesus **rebuked the evil spirit.** Previously the spirit had been euphemistically referred to as "a spirit which makes him mute" (9:17 NASB) or simply as "the spirit" (9:18, 20), but Jesus labeled him an unclean spirit. **"I command you, come out of him and never enter him again"** (9:25). The double-faceted command served two purposes. First, it reminded the readers of Matthew 12:43–45 where a demon could indeed return to an unprepared victim. But second, it declared the magnitude of this healing: a situation that had persisted from the boy's childhood was corrected for the rest of his life.

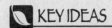

KEY IDEAS

FAITH IN MARK

Faith accepts a worldview that admits the potential for God, in His power, to affect the world in ways that supersede humanity's ability and the natural laws. Mark's overwhelming theological concept suggests that *faith is contingent on an expectation for God to move*, often against overwhelming evidence to the contrary.

BACKGROUND

EVIL OR UNCLEAN SPIRITS

The Greek word for "unclean" (*akathartos*) was initially used to describe an idea of ritual or cultic impurity. However, in His teaching, Jesus began to associate this concept with the Pharisees. By doing this, He began to disclose the divine desire for internal holiness in addition to external holiness. Understanding this, one can see why Jesus was so often positioned against the demonic forces of the world. These supernatural spirits prevented proper, godly intended, internal orientation, and, therefore, expulsion of these spirits was necessary.

The next two verses graphically describe the life and death struggle that transpired. **The spirit shrieked, convulsed him violently and came out. The boy looked so much like a corpse that many said, "He's dead"** (9:26). Death and all of its appearances was the goal of the demonic world and the fear of all humanity. Yet its destruction was only a touch away from Jesus. **Jesus took him by the hand and lifted**

him to his feet, and he stood up (9:27). This passage ends with clear resurrection language. Not as clear in the English are two Greek words that point the reader forward to Jesus' own death experience. The first word, "lifted," is most prominently used in 14:28 and 16:6, referring to Jesus' promise and post-resurrection appearance to the disciples in Galilee. The second word, "stood up," is employed in each of the passion predictions (8:31; 9:31; 10:34) and in the resurrection misunderstanding as Jesus and the three disciples were coming down from the mountain (9:9–10).

Assuming that 8:27–10:52 is a unit that describes Jesus' most intimate discipleship training, the next two verses must be understood as the climax of the story. **After Jesus had gone indoors, his disciples asked him privately, "Why couldn't we drive it out?"** (9:28). This "private questioning" after a difficult public teaching was common in Mark (4:10; 7:17; 10:10). But this time it was interrelated with a public humiliation on their part. After they seem to have done so well as they went out two by two, with specific authority to cast out evil spirits (6:7), and returned with a successful report (6:30), their real question might have been, "Lord, what has changed?" Jesus was emphatic in His response, yet vague in its meaning, when He said, **"This kind can come out only by prayer"**[1] (9:29). Did Jesus mean this kind of miracle, speaking generally, or this kind of evil spirit, speaking specifically? Possibly Jesus was asking them to evaluate the means of exorcisms. Who supplied the power or the authority? Did it come from within or without? Jesus himself, though self-authenticating in His speech, constantly looked to the Father in prayer for strength. He also found His power from the presence of the Spirit in His ministry. The disciples did not have access to the Spirit themselves (see 13:11 for the only reference of the Holy Spirit and the disciples), nor had Mark ever mentioned that they prayed.[2] Thus, Jesus may have been suggesting that not only did the disciples lack faith, but they were demonstrating spiritual arrogance for assuming they could cast out demons on their own. God is the only power on earth that can exorcise evil spirits, and prayer is the only means to appropriate His strength.

2. THE SECOND PASSION PREDICTION 9:30–32

The threefold series of passion predictions reinforced Jesus' desire to teach His disciples what "His Way" entailed. Yet at the same time, each pronouncement is coupled with a blunder in comprehension displayed in inappropriate behavior. This second prediction is a case in point. **They left that place and passed through Galilee. Jesus did not want anyone to know where they were, because he was teaching his disciples** (9:30–31). The previous episode was located at the base of Mount Transfiguration; the group moved from there through home territory for Jesus. His popularity had won Him massive and enthusiastic crowds, but it also precluded Him from personal mentoring of His disciples. It should be noted that the original Greek indicates that Jesus' teaching was ongoing in nature, not one isolated instructional event. That observation should be coupled with this being the second passion pronouncement, making this death-resurrection teaching the centerpiece of Jesus' instruction from the midpoint of the book to His death.

Of the three predictions, this one is the briefest. **"The Son of Man is going to be betrayed into the hands of men. They will kill him, and after three days he will rise"** (9:31). The verb tense changes are significant. First, the Son of Man is "going to be betrayed" (present tense in the Greek, though translated as future tense), giving the disciples the sense that it was occurring at the very moment of the teaching itself. The next two verbs, "kill" and "rise," are obviously future tense, indicating that the course was clearly set. The phrase "betrayed into the hands of men" did not occur in 8:31 and was particularized in 10:33 when Jesus further instructed that "the men" were the chief priests and the teachers of the law.

Two key Markan themes coalesce in the next verse: **they did not understand what he meant and were afraid to ask him about it** (9:32). Incomprehension was the normal reaction of the disciples, yet here they became fearful. Inquisitiveness had been a familiar discipleship custom (4:10; 7:17; 9:11, 28; 10:10; 13:3), yet they did not ask their questions out of fear. Was it because of Jesus' stinging rebuke of Peter in 8:33–38 and that they did not want a similar incident to be repeated? Or was it following the logic of some scholars who argue that "fear" would be better understood as "holy terror" or reverence, not simply an emotional, surface-level reaction? Either way, Jesus was teaching, but the disciples were not integrating His death and resurrection into their worldview.

3. WHO IS THE GREATEST 9:33–37

The essential element in this passage is its juxtaposition with Jesus' second passion prediction in 9:30–32. Jesus reiterated His plain teaching on sacrifice, and Mark told the readers of his gospel that the disciples did not understand. Now, this passage is a further elaboration about how far off track they really are from "thinking like Jesus" (8:33).

The setting of the previous passage was generally situated in Galilee, but here they specifically **came to Capernaum** (9:33). Additionally, as the previous section ended with the disciples afraid to ask questions of Jesus (9:32), Jesus turned the tables on the disciples as they entered a house. Then He asked, **"What were you arguing about on the road?"** (9:33). Jesus was aware of the disciples' disagreement as they traversed the Galilean countryside. Apparently, the nine other disciples were jealous of the status afforded to Peter, James, and John on Mount Transfiguration. Yet Jesus knew they were arguing about which of them was the greatest as they walked "on the road," which is also a Markan play on words for "on the way to the cross." This only heightened the sense of the disciples' shame and **they kept quiet because on the way they had argued about who was the greatest** (9:34). Both subject matter and timing were inappropriate. The disciples were seeking out personal honor while Jesus was teaching sacrifice.

The simple phrase, **sitting down**, adds to the air of formality and (4:1–2; more clearly Matt. 5:1). This type of discussion must be corrected, so **Jesus called the Twelve and said, "If anyone wants to be first, he must be the very last, and the servant of all"** (9:35). "If you truly want honor," He said, "you do so by lowering yourself to being a servant" (see 10:43–44). This teaching of status reversal was just as countercultural to the disciples as Jesus' previous instruction regarding himself as a dying Messiah. Honor was the most important sign of status in the first century, and Jesus relegated it to insignificance.

Jesus then moved from theory in the form of a pithy aphorism to practice in the form of an object lesson; **He took a little child and had him stand among them** (9:36). This acted-out parable employed a child, the lowest status in the first century, to draw application for the disciples. Note how this passage is slightly different from its Matthean parallel (18:1–6). There Jesus called the disciples to "become like little children" (18:3), while Mark demanded the disciples to overturn the status system of the day and "receive" the valueless as valuable. Jesus brought the child, one who had been on the fringes of the family, into the midst of the group. Then, dramatically, Jesus wrapped His arms around the child, attributing worth in a visual manner.

"Whoever welcomes one of these little children in my name welcomes me; and whoever welcomes me does not welcome me but the one who sent me" (9:37). The admonition is not just welcoming (receiving) one of these children, but welcoming **in my name**. This phrase is similar in kind to the authority Jesus bestowed on the disciples to cast out evil spirits in 6:7, and Mark linked this passage with the next with the phrase "in your name." Interestingly, Jesus saw "receiving a child" as the flip side of the coin for casting out evil spirits. Both were done in Jesus' name! Both took divine power to humble the proud.

4. DISCIPLESHIP EXCLUSIVENESS 9:38–41

The wonderful story fits perfectly with the previous passage, the disciples being called to welcome and receive someone they might at first glance have rejected. This thematic link is further reinforced with the phrase "in my name," used three times here.

"Teacher," said John, "we saw a man driving out demons in your name and we told him to stop, because he was not one of us" (9:38). The dialog began with the only solo appearance of John reported in Mark's gospel, addressing Jesus as "teacher." Not an uncommon designation ascribed by both the disciples and by outsiders, but this seems belittling since John himself was with Jesus on Mount Transfiguration just moments before. He told Jesus that they witnessed a man exorcising demons "in your name" without *our* permission. This report was not simply what they saw, but their response and their rationale. Their response was swift and continual. In the Greek, the wording is "we continually told him to stop," not simply a one-time rebuke.[3] They justified their behavior with the reason, **because he was not one of us**, literally, "he is not following us." First, he seemed to be doing "in Jesus' name" exactly what they were unable to do with the boy with the evil spirit in 9:14–29. Did this imply that the unknown and unnamed man working in Jesus' name had faith and was praying whereas the disciples did not and were not? Second, what does this imply about the nature of followership? Jesus had constantly called the disciples to "follow Him" according to His agenda, yet they consistently watered down Kingdom principles to fit their earthly thinking.

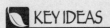

KEY IDEAS

"IN THE NAME"

The ancient notion that a name communicated something essential or characteristic of the bearer is apparent at certain places in the New Testament. Furthermore, in New Testament times a close connection existed between someone's or something's name and control over that person or thing. By proclaiming that person's or thing's name, the proclaimer would not only represent, but also exude, the authority of that person or thing (Mark 5:9 illustrates control over a demon). In light of this, the belief that invoking the name of Jesus would thereby exorcise a demon would not have been a far-fetched idea in the first century.

Finally, notice the pronoun chosen by John, "He is not following **us**." It's fair to say at this point in the Gospel that the disciples may have been in the same location as Jesus, but they were far from faithful followers.

Jesus' response was firm and cutting: **"Do not stop him . . . No one who does a miracle in my name can in the next moment say anything bad about me, for whoever is not against us is for us"** (9:39–40). Jesus was clarifying the nature of the Kingdom; it is inclusive not exclusive. It's not based on human status but on the value given to each man, woman, and child by Christ. Do not stop nor hinder anyone who offers even the most trivial gift in Jesus' name.

5. DISCIPLESHIP SAYINGS COLLECTION 9:42–50

This next section is a compendium of discipleship aphorisms, coming from both a positive and negative perspective. The phrase **one of these little ones** (9:42) links this section to the surrounding context. It points back to the receiving of the children in 9:33–37 and forward to the disciples' hindering of people bringing "little children" to Jesus in 10:13–16. The verbal connection in the passages is the phrase **cause to sin** (9:42, 43, 45, 47). "Cause to sin" appears in Mark 4:17; 6:3; 14:27, 29, the most prominent being in Jesus' prediction of all the disciples "falling away" in 14:27, 29. Since this immediate context is concerned with the subject of discipleship training and who should be welcomed into the Kingdom, maybe the best translation is "cause to fall" or "cause to lose one's faith." Jesus was condemning anyone who disabled the discipleship of another.

"If anyone causes one of these little ones who believe in me to sin, it would be better for him to be thrown into the sea with a large millstone tied around his neck" (9:42). The scholar R. T. France said, "To be the cause of another's spiritual shipwreck is so serious an offence that a quick drowning would be preferable to the fate it deserves."[4] But this begins with the real vision of a disciple. Whom will you welcome into the Kingdom? Children (9:36–37)? Additional believers (9:39–40)? What will be the limits? On whom do you place value? The consequence of overlooking and or devaluing even one of the children is worse than death.

The poetic structure of 9:43–47 is based on body imagery—hand, foot, and eyes—and the resultant deformity—maimed, crippled, and blind. The real punch to the threefold series is in the eternal consequence—hell. And the final statement draws the most descriptive depiction of hell; it's **where their worm does not die, and the fire is not quenched** (9:48), a quotation of Isaiah 66:24. And this last vision in Isaiah's book is the horrific scene of the destruction of God's enemies and their decomposing bodies left strewn on the ground. This is Mark's warning for today.

"Everyone will be salted with fire" (9:49). Though many scholars find the inclusion of these verses as out of place, Mark linked them with the previous paragraph via the word *fire*. But the difficulty arises with the next statement. **"Salt is good, but if it loses its saltiness, how can you**

make it salty again? Have salt in yourselves, and be at peace with each other" (9:50). How can salt lose its saltiness? This takes place when it ceases to function as salt, neither preserving what it comes into contact with nor adding additional flavor to what is being tasted. And Mark's point was to apply Jesus' metaphor to our own lives, "Have salt in yourselves." Simply put, "live and influence the world as God has designed you to be." Moreover, the Old Testament sacrificial laws found in Leviticus 2:13 state, "Do not leave the salt of the covenant of your God out of your grain offerings; add salt to all your offerings." In Mark's description of discipleship, he employed language of Temple sacrifice and offerings, pointing to the sacrificial and complete nature of following Jesus and in welcoming and preserving others.

ENDNOTES

Key Ideas Sidebar: Further consult Christopher D. Marshall, *Faith as a Theme in Mark's Narrative* (Cambridge: Cambridge University Press, 1989), pp. 116–118, and Sharon Echols Dowd, *Prayer, Power, and the Problem of Suffering: Mark 11:22–25 in the Context of Markan Theology* (Atlanta: Society of Biblical Literature, 1988), pp. 96–117.

1. The phrase "and fasting" appears to be a later addition reflecting the ascetic practices of the early Church rather than being in the original text of Mark 9:29. Some of the early manuscripts of Mark may be attempting to harmonize the account in Mark with Matthew's account of the same event. Matthew is certainly pro-fasting, and the early church had a preference to make Mark align with Matthew.

2. Matthew (6:5–15) and Luke (11:1–13) detail instructions regarding prayer, but in the Gospel narrative themselves, the disciples never pray. The first apostolic prayer in general is found in Acts 1:14, and the first recorded prayer is Acts 1:24–25 for the replacement of Judas.

3. The verb "told him to stop" is in the imperfect tense, indicating a continual sense, maybe reading "we kept telling him to stop."

4. R. T. France, *The Gospel of Mark: New International Commentary on the Greek Testament* (Grand Rapids, Mich.: Eerdmans Publishing Company), p. 380.

WHAT IT MEANS TO BE A DISCIPLE

Mark 10:1-31

1. DIVORCE AND REMARRIAGE 10:1-12

In the beginning of chapter 10, there are two setting changes. First, the geographic marker indicates a location change as Jesus and His disciples traversed from Galilee through Judea across the Jordan River into the region of Perea. Second, since **crowds of people came to him** (10:1), Jesus briefly returned to public ministry rather than His private teaching.

Some Pharisees came and tested him by asking, "Is it lawful for a man to divorce his wife?" (10:2). Back in chapter 7, Jesus was confronted by Jewish leaders (7:1) and questioned by them regarding an interpretation on Jewish tradition (7:5). He then provided an interpretation (7:6–16) and then explained its meaning to the disciples in private (7:17–23). This passage in chapter 10 is written in exactly the same form, only this time the discussion was not about Jewish tradition but the Law of Moses regarding divorce. Moreover, the Pharisees did not come merely to inquire or even to learn, but to test Jesus and to discredit Him.[1]

The only discussion of divorce in the Mosaic Law is found in Deuteronomy 24:1–4. There were two opposing views of the divorce options in Jesus' day. The first, more liberal, interpretation was from the Hillel school of rabbis. They said that divorce was legal for a multitude of reasons from almost any cause, even if the wife was a bad cook or if "he [the husband] found another fairer than she."[2] The more conservation school of Shammai only allowed divorce based on "unchasity." But in neither case was there an option for a woman to divorce her husband.

"What did Moses command you?" (10:3). Even before Jesus addressed the Law, He revealed His position, for Deuteronomy 24:1–4 is essentially about regulating the welfare of individuals after the divorce. Moses never commanded that people could divorce. **They** [Pharisees] **said, "Moses permitted a man to write a certificate of divorce and send her away"** (10:4). They were accurate in their rendering of the text, but Jesus presented a larger contextual view of the Pentateuch. All that God says regarding marriage is not found in Deuteronomy.

The Pharisees wanted to force Jesus into a conflict with the Law and with the teachings of the rabbis of His day. Rather, Jesus called upon the language of creation, relegating the Deuteronomy decree to mere concessionary regulations because of human sinfulness. Jesus forcefully interjected, **"It was because your hearts were hard that Moses wrote you this law . . . But at the beginning of creation God 'made them male and female.' '. . . A man will . . . be united to his wife . . .' Therefore what God has joined together, let man not separate"** (10:5–9). The divorce law, as Jesus saw it, was never God's will, but merely damage control to limit the fallout from relationships previously neglected and discarded due to hardness of hearts.

Mark shifted the story to Jesus' private classroom for the disciples, for His command about divorce has far-reaching implications. In what follows, Jesus described, at least in part, the value system of the Christian community. **He answered, "Anyone who divorces his wife and marries another woman commits adultery against her"** (10:11). Jesus shifted the talk from divorce to remarriage and what He attributed as its result: adultery. Some ponder today if Jesus would have allowed divorce without remarriage. But that was not part of the conversation in Jesus' time. In the first century, it was assumed that those who divorced would remarry. As a rule, marriage was not just a social option but a life necessity. The rigors of daily life could not be met alone. Unmarried women were easy prey for slavery or prostitution. In light of that, Jesus' charge to men is swift and harsh: divorce and remarriage makes one guilty of adultery. The phrase that is remarkable, given the male-oriented Jewish world of Jesus' day, is "against her." Jesus' argument was that divorce itself is an offense against God's creative will, but it is also an offense against the wife. Legally, a Jewish man only committed adultery against the husband of the wife he slept with (if she was married), certainly not against his own wife. This was a remarkable move toward an egalitarian view of the sexes. **"And if she divorces her husband and marries another man, she commits adultery"** (10:12). Jesus took this to the next level when He permitted the woman the right of divorce (unheard of in Jewish world), but she as well would be guilty of the same criminal offense as the husband.[3] Equality of the sexes in Jesus' eyes must include not just equal rights (divorce) but also equal justice for failure (adultery).

In a world where adultery and divorce are commonplace, the application of this passage should not be taken lightly. And as most modern-day readers know, the statistical numbers regarding divorce for those inside the church is no better than those outside. Thus, a few considerations may help us better understand Jesus. First, in this setting, Jesus was being confronted by His severest critics. This is not to be read as pastoral advice to grieving and hurting spouses. Second, Jesus was addressing the flippant way that the enforcement of the Law demeaned women as if they were property (see Exod. 20:17; Num. 30:10–14). Jesus values people equality. No longer were women to be treated as things. Third, Jesus was placing the highest value possible on the most intimate human relationship, marriage. It represents a covenant bond that cannot be broken. And He was clearly stating that divorces are human answers to sinful problems. Fourth, this passage may cause great anxiety for those who are divorced or remarried. They may be asking, "Am I committing adultery in the eyes of God?" And the church's response may inadvertently cause divorced persons to feel as if they are second-class Christians. But there is complete acceptance and forgiveness in Christ. In Jesus' encounters with the woman caught in adultery (John 7:53–8:11) and with the Samaritan woman at the well (John 4:4–29), today's readers find Jesus is compassionate and approachable.

2. LITTLE CHILDREN 10:13–16

In shaping the heart of a disciple, Jesus struck once again at the issue of status (a reminder of 9:33–37) and value: who is important in the world and who is valued in the kingdom of God. The story begins quite abruptly; **People were bringing little children to Jesus to have him touch them** (10:13). The text does not fully explain who the people were, most likely parents or related caregivers. The original wording indicates that these people were continually bringing their children to Jesus. Their desire to have Jesus **touch**[4] **them** to receive His blessing[5] is foremost on their minds. They may have been searching for a specific healing, for a blessing such as those received in the time of the patriarchs (Gen. 48:14), or for the traditional prayer and blessing offered by the rabbis on the Day of Atonement. Their coming is contrasted with the refusing attitude of the disciples; **the disciples rebuked**[6] **them** (10:13). Now the disciples found themselves sided against Jesus, and Mark states this with emotional emphasis, for [Jesus] **was indignant** (10:14). In part, this must encompass the disciples' failure to "welcome" the children as instructed in 9:33–37. Their hard-heartedness and blindness to the kingdom of God being a gift, not a commodity ascribed by status, is overwhelming. This gives rise to His wonderful pronouncement, **"Let the little children come to me, and do not hinder them, for the kingdom of God belongs to such as these"** (10:14). But one must carefully note Jesus' words. He demanded that no one hinder the children for the Kingdom belongs "to such as these." He did not say "to them." Jesus was widening the entrance, for it was not mainly about the children, but to all who share in their lack-of-status situation and by implication to all who share in Jesus' views. By contrast, His corollary verdict was equally narrowing: "If you do not adopt my agenda, you will have no part in my Kingdom." This has a refreshing echo of Jesus' beatitude in Matthew 5:3: "Blessed are the poor in spirit, for theirs is the kingdom of heaven."

Jesus closed the discussion with an appropriate reception into the Kingdom, and with an object lesson to the disciples' lack of receptivity; He warmly embraced the children.

3. THE POWER OF AFFLUENCE 10:17–31

This passage begins with Jesus' encounter with the man himself (10:17–22).[7] **As Jesus started on his way, a man ran up to him and fell on his knees before him** (10:17). The opening words "on his way" are not a neutral direction marker, as if Jesus was off on an afternoon stroll with His disciples. He was intentionally making His way to Jerusalem for rejection and death. But teaching the disciples His values was a key ingredient in the meaning of this Christian pilgrimage.

The approach of the man, his posture of honor, and Jesus' response imply that the man was utterly sincere in his request. **"Good teacher," he asked, "what must I do to inherit eternal life?"** (10:17). The end of the man's request is synonymous with Jesus' discussion of entering the kingdom of God, and in this passage the terms alternate (see 10:23–25, 30). However, the title by which he calls Jesus and Jesus' abrupt response cause problems. Perhaps Jesus heard unwarranted flattery in the man's words (heart?). By ascribing honor to the Teacher, was he assuming a reciprocal response from Jesus? The response was unexpected and certainly uncharacteristic to anything the man would have received elsewhere. **"Why do you call me good? . . . No one is good—except God alone"** (10:18).[8]

Jesus' direct answer began with the Ten Commandments; specifically the last six, numbers five through ten, with number five, honor your father and mother, placed at the end. An interesting observation is that the usual reading of the tenth commandment is "do not covet," yet here it is replaced with "do not defraud." It appears as if Jesus was presenting the commandments as a moral checklist of outward behavior rather than issues of inward action. The man's response was swift and somewhat overconfident in tone, **"Teacher," he declared, "all these I have kept since I was a boy"** (10:20). Though the man was claiming obedience and a sense of moral and legal cleanliness, he also seems to have been hungry for more than what had been offered to him through the legal code of the Jewish faith. This man's lifelong commitment to the Ten Commandments seems to have been respected by Jesus. Jesus was not seeing him as being hypocritical but simply missing the key ingredient of a fulfilled life, an unfettered relationship with Jesus. And since He

loved him (10:21), the offer of freedom from the cares of this world came without hesitation.

"One thing you lack . . . Go, sell everything you have and give to the poor, and you will have treasure in heaven. Then come, follow me" (10:21). The phrase "one thing you lack" must be emphasized as a present tense verb, "one thing you (are continually) lacking." Jesus' remedy for the man was divestment of his affluence and donation to those with no status. This was followed up with a present tense command, (continually) follow me. This is typical discipleship call language (see Mark 1:17, 2:14). Jesus was recruiting this man to be with Him in similar fashion to the previous twelve disciples already on board. In return, Jesus was promising him **treasure in heaven**. But the man declined the invitation, though the decision is expressed in stark terms, **at this the man's face fell. He went away sad, because he had great wealth** (10:22). The cost of following was too high.

Next Jesus spelled out the implications of the event for His disciples. Jesus said, **"How hard it is for the rich to enter the kingdom of God!"** (10:23). This statement should not be read as a barrier for the rich, but rather as a warning to all regarding the hold affluence has upon men and women; it can prevent them from seeing the true treasure of heaven.

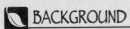

BACKGROUND

WEALTH AND STATUS

Wealth, referring to the amount of assets one possesses, often carried a specific connotation of God's blessing. While wealth was important, there were other factors that influenced one's social standing. Wealth was classified by length of heritage. A person who became wealthy did not hold as much social prestige as someone who inherited wealth. Wealth alone did not elevate a person in first-century Jewish society, but it was intertwined with status, power, and social privilege.

The disciples were amazed at his words (10:24). This should not be heard as "impressed by His wisdom," but they "were perplexed at these words" (NRSV). This did not fit into their worldview. For most Jews in Jesus' day, wealth was a sign of God's blessing, and if the wealthy could not get to heaven, who then had a chance? Jesus seems to have exacerbated the disciples' perception dilemma when He said, **"It is easier for a camel to go through the eye**

of a needle than for a rich man to enter the kingdom of God" (10:25). Not only would it be a hard task for the rich, from all outward appearances it would be impossible. And this is a standard way in the first century to state the impossible in a proverbial form (see Luke 16:17).[9] **The disciples were even more amazed, and said to each other, "Who then can be saved?"** (10:26). The disciples' misunderstanding increased all the more, for in a culture that saw wealth as a sign of God's blessing, who then can be saved? The word "saved" is to be understood in the fullest sense of entering into the kingdom of God. Throughout Mark, a declaration to be "saved" has been limited to the physical sphere, such as restoration of health (see 3:4; 5:23; 6:56; 10:52) or even life itself. But now, Jesus engaged the salvation conversation with clear eternal ramifications (see also 13:13 and 8:35).

Jesus' response to their question was on point, for they may have been thinking that salvation is thus impossible for anyone under any circumstance. **"With man this is impossible, but not with God; all things are possible**

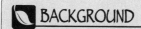

BACKGROUND
First Century Economy

First-century Palestine was an agrarian economy and relied heavily on a "kinship" system of exchange. Those with kinship ties did not expect exclusive commerce, but a reciprocal trade was expected within an acceptable timeframe from those not related.

The "patron/client" model was another important facet in first-century economics. A patron was a person who had resources available for someone less fortunate to use for his personal needs. In return, the client revisited loyalty and honor upon the patron. Because of ongoing obligations, it was this patron/client model that fed oppression and separation within the society.

with God" (10:27). Salvation from a human perspective must be on issues of social value and financial merit. But that only demonstrates that there are two opposing systems: people's and God's. With people, salvation is impossible; with God, even the rich can be saved. Peter's quick retort was a wonderful follow up of the wealthy man's question (10:17–22), for Peter said to Him, **"We have left everything to follow you!"** (10:28). His words, spoken for the group, carry some degree of self-righteousness, for he was contrasting their actions, leaving everything and following, with those of the rich man, who went away while retaining his wealth.

Jesus then pushed the conversation beyond the aspect of leaving "things" (**"no one who has left home or brothers or sisters or mother or father or children or fields,"** 10:29) to establishing the source of priceless Kingdom values; they are acting for Jesus **and the gospel.** Jesus wanted His disciples to move past "what" they were doing and examine the motives of "why" they were leaving them. Thus, Jesus' words should not be heard as a wholesale call to poverty and a complete renunciation of all worldly possessions. Ministry and discipleship need not begin with a massive liquidation sale, but with a reorientation of priorities. Nothing on earth should have a greater hold on a disciple than the values practiced by Jesus or contained in the gospel. It is all summarized in the final verse: **"But many who are first will be last, and the last first"** (10:31). A careful reader of the NIV notices that this verse begins with the contrasting conjunction "but." Peter's earlier words, "we have left everything and followed you," are true, but Jesus interjected that there was still a long way to go. "Things" may have been gone from their lives, but sin's residue of pride, self-centeredness, and hard-heartedness remained. The disciples may have been poor, but they had yet to achieve being poor in spirit.

ENDNOTES

1. In the original Greek, the word "test" is the same as the word "tempt." This implies that the same evil intentions of the Devil to tempt Jesus (1:13) were being equated with the "testing" of the Jewish leaders in the rest of Mark (8:11; 10:2; 12:15).

2. Quote by Rabbi Akiba in the Mishnah, *Gittin* 9:10.

3. Herodias's divorce of her husband referred to in Mark 6:17 was the exception that proves the rule.

4. For other places in Mark where touching became important, see 1:41; 3:10; 5:27–31; 6:56; 8:22.

5. This text reads like Genesis 48:14–18, people seeking a patriarchal blessing.

6. The word "rebuke" was constantly used in Mark for those in direct conflict with the way Jesus perceived of the kingdom of God; see 1:25; 3:12; 4:39; 8:30, 32f; 9:25; 10:13, 48.

7. Matthew told his readers the man was "young" (19:20); Luke informed his readers that he was a "ruler" (18:18). In Mark, he is simply called "a man."

8. Matthew softened the harshness of the wording: "Why do you ask me about what is good?" (Matt 19:17).

9. Preachers have popularized "the eye of the needle" to mean the small opening in the double-walled gate in the entrance of a city through which travelers must enter after the city gates are closed for the night. The image of camels bending down to get through the small opening raises a wonderful picture of difficulty and struggle. Yet there is no evidence to support this urban legend; in fact, it undermines Jesus' intention. He was stating not that it is hard, but that it is impossible for a wealthy person to enter on his own without God.

PARADOX OF GOD'S KINGDOM

Mark 10:32–52

1. THE THIRD PASSION PREDICTION 10:32–34

They were on their way up to Jerusalem, with Jesus leading the way, and the disciples were astonished, while those who followed were afraid (10:32). This verse, which depicts the setting for what follows, summarizes the situation in typical Markan language. First they were "on the way." This is not a directional marker, but a depiction of Jesus' mission in life; He was going to Jerusalem to die. Next the disciples were "astonished." This could be read to mean awe or wonder. But in the previous section, the similar word "amazed" (10:24, 26) shows the disciples were perplexed and confused, grasping for the meaning of Jesus' instruction. They also must be amazed that if what He has predicted will come true, why would one walk willingly, even purposefully, into the place of death? And there are others who are constantly following, yet fear keeps them at a distance, viewing the events but as yet uncommitted. **Again he took the Twelve aside and told them what was going to happen to him** (10:32). As in each of the previous passion predictions, He took the Twelve apart to speak plainly about the upcoming events; to them Jesus has consistently given insider information about His mission (4:10).

"We are going up to Jerusalem, . . . and the Son of Man will be betrayed to the chief priests and teachers of the law" (10:33). This third teaching is the most specific of the three, combining information from both of the prior two predictions. This is the first time that Jerusalem

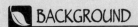

BACKGROUND

DEATH PENALTY

Provincial governors called "precepts" or "procurators" ruled Palestine. Major principal decisions were made by the governors, including the execution of criminals.

The Sanhedrin was given authority over minor governing issues, as long as those issues had no effect on Roman occupation. Furthermore, Jerusalem was given the status of a "holy city," because it housed the central worship center for Judaism. It was precisely this status that allowed opportunity for the Jewish ruling body to condemn someone to death. Only in issues pertaining to the Temple or religious matters could the death penalty be left up to the Sanhedrin.

was specifically mentioned. The betrayal is to be by the chief priests and the scribes, but surprisingly, the elders are not named.

Next, the death is described in two phases; first the Jews **will condemn him to death**, but then the death sentence will be carried out by the Gentiles, **who will mock him and spit on him, flog him and kill him** (10:34). The four verbal components (mock, spit, flog, and kill) of this Gentile abuse will come to fulfillment in the description in 15:15–25. The consistent portion of the three passion predictions is the resurrection language: **three days later he will rise** (10:34).

2. HUMAN SELF-INTEREST, DIVINE SERVICE 10:35–45

Then James and John, the sons of Zebedee, came to him (10:35). The juxtaposition of James and John's request with the previous sharing of the intimate details of Jesus' impending death is shameful. It is almost as if these two disciples (and the other ten who will soon become angry with them, 10:41) either did not hear His teaching or worse yet, treated it as if His words were irrelevant to the situation at hand. **"Teacher, . . . we want you to do for us whatever we ask"** (10:35). The title "teacher" is the most common designation of Jesus in Mark. Yet it further reveals the disciples' miscomprehension, since they failed to listen to Him in the role of teacher or rabbi. The arrogance of their request is almost deafening. They seem to have thought they had a right to positions of status in the Kingdom, all the more presumptuous following the teaching in 10:29–31, where Jesus explained the reward system "in this present age . . . and in the age to come." If James and John were defining the rewards of "eternal life" with the same values of power and status found in the present earthly age, they were sorely mistaken, thus further supporting the argument that they have not heard a word of the Teacher. Jesus responded with the question, **"What do you want me to do for you?"** (10:36).[1] Their answer was bold to say the least: **"Let one of us sit at your right and the other at your left in your glory"** (10:37). Most likely they were referring to a "messianic glory" expectation, Jesus reigning on the throne of David in Jerusalem. They thought Jesus was about to set up His kingdom on this final push to the Holy City. They had yet to incorporate the concept of suffering and death into the mission of the Christ. Their refusal to "think like God" (8:33) further alienated them from Jesus. The seats on the right and left, seats of power (see Luke 22:30), show they were understanding only in terms of honor.

"You don't know what you are asking" (10:38). Jesus reproved them; the way of the cup and baptism lay before them. In the Old Testament, the cup metaphor can be one of blessing (Ps. 16:5; 23:5; 116:13) or of judgment (Ps. 75:8; Jer. 25:15–29; Hab. 2:16). Yet assuming Mark's passion for Isaiah 51, there the metaphor is one of the suffering of God's people, specifically God's servant. Moreover, the modern reader will see eucharistic language pointing to the Last Supper (14:23) and to a vicarious suffering of Jesus for all (10:45). Water was another image of disaster in the Old Testament (Ps. 42:7; Isa. 43:2), so the image of baptism runs parallel with the cup of suffering.

Their misguided reply was brief: **"We can"** (10:39). Jesus, prophetically said, **"You will drink the cup I drink and be baptized with the baptism I am baptized with,"** but this is certainly looking further down the way, as James would die at the hands of Herod's sword (Acts 12:2) and John would be a political prisoner on the Isle of Patmos when he penned the book of Revelation. Jesus went on: **"but to sit at my right or left is not for me to grant. These places belong to those for whom they have been prepared"** (10:40). Simply put, Jesus was referring to positions of honor in His kingdom. Matthew 20:23 is more specific that this was the Father's decision, not His. Another possibility is that He was speaking of His coming crucifixion. Jesus' place of honor for all eternity will be the center cross; the places to His right and left there were ascribed to the criminals who were crucified with Him.

When the ten heard about this, they became indignant with James and John (10:41). The anger of the ten should not be understood as the rest of the group siding with Jesus over James and John. Rather, they were angry that these two had slipped in ahead of them in competition for the highest places of honor. This is made clear, since Jesus' next words of reprimand are spoken as He **called them** [all] **together** (10:42). Moreover, Mark showed that the disciples were constantly of one mind and heart, siding together against Jesus.

"You know that those who are regarded as rulers of the Gentiles lord it over them, and their high officials exercise authority over them" (10:41). Jesus once again was teaching Kingdom principles, for if one wanted to see examples of first-century power and authority, look to the Gentile model. Jesus was chastising the disciples for imitating the people who had done detestable things to them. Jesus called His disciples, and disciples of all ages, to a higher standard with the simple words **"Not so with you"** (10:43). The status and power of the world are to be overturned by the paradoxical precepts of the Kingdom—service and slavery—climaxing in the call that greatness is portrayed in one's being a **slave of all**.[2] Jesus then supplied the epitome of all examples for status reversal. **"For even the Son of Man did not come to be served, but to serve, and to give his life as a ransom for many"** (10:45). The earlier material about the Gentiles serves as a negative example. They exercised authority over their subjects because they could force it upon others. Jesus on the other hand, began with the Son of Man title from Daniel 7:14, which is a call to true authority, where the Ancient of Days was given all "authority, glory, and sovereign power." If anyone was rightfully due to be served, it was the Son of Man. "But" His mission was not about himself; it was about giving His **life as a ransom for many**. The phrase **ransom for many** has strong verbal connections to Isaiah 53, thus describing Jesus not only as the Son of Man but also as the Servant of the LORD. Jesus' "ransom" language is similar to the "sin offering" of Isaiah 53:10. The overall emphasis of Mark 10:45 resounds with the role of Isaiah's Servant who dies for the deliverance of His people.

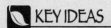

KEY IDEAS

UNDERSTANDING ATONEMENT

Atonement is necessary for humanity to exist in right relationship with God Almighty. Because of the consequence of sin, relationship between humanity and God has fallen short.

Atonement refers to the satisfaction of sin with its consequences concerning the relationship between humanity and God Almighty.

Therefore, the question becomes, "How is one to understand how atonement works?" Tradition has employed four explanations to help explain atonement.

Christus Victor Theory	Satisfaction Theory
Existing in the context of a supernatural war for humanity, it was the death of Christ that won the victory. Christ's death broke the bonds of sin, which humanity was powerless to break.	The effect of sin is an offense that violates the holiness of God Almighty. Therefore, a chasm, which is unbridgeable by human efforts, exists between God and humanity. Christ's atonement satisfies this offense.
Knowledge of Love Theory	Governance Theory
Sin has severed humanity from relationship with God, and it is sin that prevents humanity from understanding the depth of God's love. Concordantly, Christ's atonement reveals this divine love.	The existence of sin has progressed to destroy the moral fabric intrinsic to the cosmos. It is Christ's atonement that begins to reorder the intended moral standard of governance.

When isolated, the inadequacies of each theory arise. Therefore, each theory provides a different facet of atonement. All of these theories are intertwined and are to be consulted together in order to understand the action of atonement.

One should not overlook this passage for its soteriological (salvation) language. Mark is unusually silent regarding the mechanics of how one is saved. A few times, Jesus' purpose for coming has been brought front and center (1:38–39; 2:17). His means of salvation will be returned to again during Jesus' words at the Last Supper: "This is my blood of the covenant which is poured out for many" (14:24). Mark 10:45 uniquely coupled Jesus as the fulfillment of Old Testament prophecy with His own life mission. Here is a key to unlocking the question "Why did Jesus have to die?" The answer may not be given in how we are "actually" saved, but in what we are to do in response to Christ dying as a ransom for many (= all)?

3. THE SECOND HEALING OF A BLIND MAN: BLIND BARTIMAEUS 10:46–52

This healing of a blind man and the one in 8:22–26 serve as interpretative lenses through which to view the disciples' own spiritual blindness. It also should not be overlooked that the healing of the blind man Bartimaeus is the last miracle of Jesus in the gospel of Mark.

Then they came to Jericho (10:46). This passage not only summarizes the theological priority for Mark—spiritual sight to the blind—but it also sets the geographic setting for the remainder of the book. Jericho is the final town on the road to Jerusalem, located fifteen miles to the northwest. There is no description of activities in Jericho; it was not about the city but about the travels of the disciples, the large crowd, and their encounter with a blind man just outside of the city. They came upon **a blind man, Bartimaeus . . . sitting by the roadside begging** (10:46). His act of begging demonstrates that he was totally dependent upon society for his financial needs (Lev. 19:4). The crowd seems to have assumed Jesus would not want to waste His time on an individual such as this; yet the crowd, just as the disciples, got Jesus' agenda wrong. **Jesus stopped and said, "Call him"** (10:49). Note the implied subject of the imperative verb, "you (plural) call him." Jesus asked them to initiate Bartimaeus' healing process. The very man they had marginalized with their attitudes was now welcomed by means of their voices: **"Cheer up! On your feet! He's calling you"** (10:49).

Throwing his cloak aside, he jumped to his feet and came to Jesus (10:50). Common practice in ancient times was for the beggar's cloak to be spread on the ground beneath or beside him to accumulate the alms being thrown. This may indicate how much easier it is for a poor man to leave his garment and follow Jesus than it is for a rich man to sell all he has to enter the Kingdom (10:24–25). The answer to the question Jesus asked seems obvious: **"What do you want me to do for you?"** (10:51).

But his humble reply should be heard in contrast to the arrogant reply to the exact same question by James and John in 10:36. The blind man merely wanted to see; the disciples wanted self-glory in a Kingdom they were blind to comprehend. **"Go, your faith has healed you"** (10:52). There is no description of the means of the miracle or of the reaction of the large crowd or disciples, merely a pronouncement to go. Freedom from darkness had transpired and its source was found in the man's faith.[3] But this newfound freedom set Bartimaeus on a new path, and he **followed Jesus along the road** that led directly to Jerusalem.

ENDNOTES

Background Sidebar: Bruce, F.F. *Palestine, Administration of (Roman).* Anchor Bible Dictionary. Ed. David Noel Freedman. (New York: Double Day, 1992) v. 5 of 6.

1. See 10:51 for Jesus' exact same words to Bartimaeus. The contrasting answer is revealing of a true disciple.

2. Note the progression downward; in 10:43 you are to be a servant, and in 10:44 you lower yourself to be a slave.

3. Jesus previously has told people to go after a healing (1:44; 2:11; 5:19, 34; 7:29), and he also declared that faith has been the source (5:34).

Part Three

Jesus in Jerusalem—The Place of Suffering and Death

MARK 11:1—16:8

A s presented in the introduction of this book, the gospel of Mark falls naturally into a three-act story. In Act 1, Jesus enters the stage in Galilee, announcing the kingdom of God. Jesus assembles His disciples, and they witness His first evidentiary act of the coming Kingdom—the exorcism of an evil spirit in a synagogue in Capernaum. From there Jesus rarely rests as His declaration takes the form of healings, nature miracles, and a plethora of demonic encounters.

Act 2 of the divine drama springs on the scene with Peter's confession at Caesarea Philippi, the northernmost location in Jesus' mission. But Act 2 is best described as a walking classroom; Jesus "teaches plainly" for the first time the paradoxical truth of a suffering messiah. Jesus' disciples hear Him flesh out His kingdom values as they slowly traverse the back roads of Galilee, drawing closer to Jerusalem, where His mission will climax.

Act 3 can be broken into two distinct sections. Chapters 11–12 depict Jesus' final controversies with the Jewish leaders. Chapters 14–16 describe His passion and death. These two disparate movements are bridged by Jesus' eschatological discourse of Mark 13. This discussion helps to explain how the authoritative and popular Jesus of 11–12 fails to defend himself before His accusers.

16

ARRIVING IN JERUSALEM

Mark 11:1–33

1. THE ROYAL ENTRANCE 11:1–10

Mark brought Jesus' mission to a geographic climax. All of Jesus' teaching for the last three chapters has pointed in this direction, especially with the poignant third passion prediction (10:33), which for the first time explicitly equated Jerusalem with the place of betrayal and death.

Not only is Jerusalem seen as the geographic climax to the story, but in this location Jesus emphasized public proclamation and confrontation with the Jewish leaders. Correspondingly, the healing miracles that played such a prominent part in His earlier ministry cease all together. The only miracle-like event in the remainder of Mark is the cursing of the fig tree (11:12–14, 20–21). **Jesus sent two of his disciples, saying to them, "Go to the village ahead of you, and just as you enter it, you will find a colt tied there, which no one has ever ridden. Untie it and bring it here"** (11:1–2). From the passage's language, it is unclear if Mark wanted his readers to understand Jesus' words as those of a carefully orchestrated plan or knowledge arising from a supernatural source. Jesus did more than foretell the general events before they happen; He specifically rehearsed conversations with His disciples to avoid interference from others. **"If anyone asks you, 'Why are you doing this?' tell him, 'The Lord needs it and will send it back here shortly'"** (11:3). When the disciples were questioned

KEY IDEAS

EVENTS OF THE PASSION WEEK

Sunday—Day One:
  Triumphal Entry (11:1–10)
  Jesus visits the Temple briefly (11:11)
Monday—Day Two:
  Fig tree parable (11:12–14)
  Temple cleansing (11:15–19)
Tuesday—Day Three:
  Fig tree revisited (11:20–26)
  Jesus' authority questioned (11:27–33)
  Jesus teaches (12:1–13:37)
  Jesus at Bethany; anointing by woman
    (14:1–9)
  Judas's betrayal (14:10–11)
Thursday—Day Five:
  Passover meal (14:12–31)
  Garden of Gethsemane (14:32–42)
  Jesus arrested and Peter's denial
    (14:43–72)
Friday—Day Six:
  Before Pilate (15:1–15)
  Crucifixion (15:16–41)
  Burial (15:42–47)
Sunday—Day Eight:
  Resurrection (16:1–8)

about taking the colt, **they answered as Jesus had told them to, and the people let them go** (11:6).

If Jesus' words are being ascribed as prophetic, readers should not miss His actions as equally prophet-like. **When they brought the colt to Jesus and threw their cloaks over it, he sat on it** (11:7). The riding on a donkey is based on the words of Zechariah 9:9: "Rejoice greatly, O Daughter of Zion! Shout, Daughter of Jerusalem! See, your king comes to you, righteous and having salvation, gentle and riding on a donkey, on a colt, the foal of a donkey." This royal language is further enhanced by a never-ridden donkey;[1] by being welcomed with the messianic name, "Son of David," by a blind beggar; and by throngs of pilgrims on their way to the Passover festival who spread their clothes on the road as others and spread branches.[2]

"Hosanna! Blessed is he who comes in the name of the Lord!" (11:9). Hosanna is a transliteration of the Hebrew phrase "Save now." It is likely that in Jesus' day the phrase included the idea of salvation from foreign oppressors, specifically the Romans. Moreover, the second stanza sung in praise to Jesus is not part of Psalm 118.[3] It has been replaced with the political words, **"coming kingdom of our father David"** (11:10). Perhaps the crowd expected this king, riding on a donkey, to reestablish the long-lost glory of Israel's past. This grand arrival into Jerusalem was the equivalent of Jesus' drawing a line in the sand for the Jerusalem authorities, forcing a series of encounters.

2. THE FIG TREE AND THE TEMPLE 11:11–25

Though the NIV places 11:11 with the previous section, it seems to fit structurally with the following section, as the rest of chapter 11 is Temple-centered conflict.[4] At this point in the festival week, Jesus' entrance into Jerusalem was more Temple-centered than celebration-focused, since upon arrival in Jerusalem He immediately went to visit the Temple. The word "temple,"

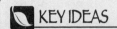

KEY IDEAS

MESSIAH

"Messiah" was used in the Old Testament to describe someone or something "anointed" by God for a specific purpose, and served as more of a description than a title. Over time, Israelites began to hope for the end of national trials, hardships, and oppressive rule. The messianic hope was that an ancestor of David would arise to liberate Israel and restore them back to national prominence (see 2 Sam. 7:12–16).

Jesus' entrance into Jerusalem, with no troops and on a symbol of humility (a donkey), struck a blow to the messianic assumptions of the Jews.

mentioned for the first time here in Mark and subsequently, refers to the whole Temple complex on the Temple mount. It is in the outer Court of the Gentiles in which the money changers' tables are erected. Jesus' teaching in chapters 11–12 transpired there, until the shift in 12:41, when He entered the Court of the Women to watch the widow put in her offering into the Temple treasury.

The city of Jerusalem was far too small to house all the tens of thousands of pilgrims, so many camped on nearby hills or stayed in neighboring villages such as Bethany.[5] This precipitated Jesus' move from Bethany after the Last Supper to camping on the Mount of Olives, specifically Gethsemane, following the Last Supper (14:26).

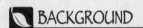

BACKGROUND

TEMPLE PRECINCT

Upon the Temple mount, the Temple's entire area was enclosed by an outer wall with various gates that led into the Court of the Gentiles. Both Jews and Gentiles were permitted within this area. Often teachers would address their crowds here, and it was in this court that Jesus' Temple cleansing occurred. Next was the Court of Women (Jewish only). Jewish men went on into the Court of Israel. Only priests and ritually pure men were permitted into the next area. Within the Court of Israel was the Temple, which had two divisions—the sanctuary and the Most Holy Place.

Much has been written on the next three troubling verses. This sign miracle must not be viewed as separate from the prophet-like action in the Temple. Mark wanted his readers to interpret Jesus' acts in the Temple (11:15–19) in light of the surrounding fig tree material (11:11–14; 20–25).[6] Thus, what was said about the failure of the fig tree to bear fruit should also be applied to the Temple.

Jesus focused on the leaves, for they were visible from a distance. Moreover, as He reached it, the fact that the tree had leaves *and* no fruit was what drew Jesus' rebuke. But the harshness for many comes from the supporting phrase **because it was not the season for figs** (11:13). As the leaves appear on the tree at the time of Passover, there are already small green figs, called *paggîm*, beginning to show. It may be that Jesus was searching for these preharvest signs of a coming bounty. But since Jesus did not see any "small green figs" at all, faith in the future harvest was dashed.

One should also remember that the "fig tree" metaphor is employed to denote Israel and her call to faithfulness.[7] Yet here in Mark, there was a real tree in full leaf, making a promise that it would not fulfill at the harvest. So too, Israel appeared outwardly beautiful yet was empty in her ability to fulfill the commitments of the covenant.

On reaching Jerusalem, Jesus entered the temple area (11:15). There are a number of events that can be described as contributing factors to the death of Jesus, but none is as clearly developed in Mark as this Temple action. The Temple and its destruction is the predominant theme in chapter 13. The cleansing act is revisited as the major charge against Jesus in the trial before the high priest (14:57–58); it was the source of the mocking of the bystanders while Jesus hung on the cross (15:29–30); and immediately following Jesus' death, the curtain in the Temple is torn (15:38).

The meaning of the Temple in the life of Israel cannot be emphasized enough. Spatially and functionally, it was the one place on earth where heaven and earth intersected and where God's presence dwelt. R. T. France said it this way:

The temple was not only the heart of Israel's religious life but also the symbol of its national identity. The rededication and purification of the temple in 164 B.C. after Antiochus Epiphanes had defiled it with the worship and the altar of Zeus and the restoration of temple worship were the high points of the Maccabean victory and were commemorated annually thereafter in the Feast of Dedication in December [modern Hanukkah]. The patriotic as well as religious symbolism of the temple was thus enormous, and the magnificence of Herod's rebuilding matched its symbolic significance.[8]

Jesus **began driving out those who were buying and selling there** (11:15). It is important to start with the understanding that at the Passover, tens of thousands of worshipers came streaming into Jerusalem to celebrate the feast. And coming long distances often precluded them from bringing their own sacrifice, especially a sacrifice that would be declared acceptable by the priests. Thus, it was normal practice to buy sacrifices upon arrival at the Temple. Moreover, the role of the "money changers" was not one of extortion, but pilgrims were expected to pay their required Temple tax (Exod. 30:11–16) in shekels, specifically Tyrian coins.[9] Therefore, from historical background and the fact that Jesus was casting out both those who were buying and selling, He was more concerned that these transactions were occurring in the wrong place—the Court of the Gentiles. Mark alone of the Gospels added the comment, **and [He] would not allow anyone to carry merchandise through the temple courts** (11:16). It appears as if the Temple courts were being used by the people of Jerusalem as a shortcut through town, taking animals or wares for selling elsewhere. Again, Jesus was not condemning tradesmen as such. Rather, Jesus condemned men trampling through the Temple irreverently.[10]

Now Jesus **taught them . . . "Is it not written: 'My house will be called a house of prayer for all nations'? But you have made it 'a den of robbers'"** (11:17). This "teaching" by Jesus is a conflation of two separate Old Testament passages, Isaiah 56:7 and Jeremiah 7:11. Here in Mark, the phrase, "for all nations" (missing from Matthew and Luke) stands as the key thought. Here in the Court of the Gentiles, Jesus was commanding, "Make this sacred space as well, for it is the call of Israel to be a 'kingdom of priests' and the original covenant to Abraham was that 'all peoples of the earth will be blessed through you'" (see Exod. 19:6;

Gen. 12:3). The nation of Israel was falling short, and it all began with their lack of reverence in the Temple.

Jesus' use of Jeremiah 7 went in a slightly different direction, upping the charges. For at that point the judgment was not just against crowding out worship and prayer in favor of trading and marketplace activity, but Jesus' use of the second quotation reminded His audience of the similar unacceptable Temple activity in Jeremiah's day. In the preexilic time of Jeremiah, as the Babylonian troops were approaching Jerusalem, the people were not concerned with personal faithfulness to the Lord but rather with the safety provided by the physical confines of Temple precincts against their pagan oppressors.[11]

One should not understand the word "robber" with the meaning of "a common criminal arrested for petty theft." Rather, in Jeremiah and in Mark, the word is better translated as rebel or insurrectionist, often attributed to one who was trying to overthrow the Roman oppressors.[12] The charge against Barabbas was similar in nature, who was arrested with the insurrectionists who had committed murder in a recent revolt or uprising (15:7). And this is explicitly the death sentence against the two robbers (better translated "rebels") who were crucified with Jesus at the cross (15:27). In both Temple speeches, Jeremiah's original and Jesus' reapplication, it is the Jewish leaders who are being condemned of insurrection. They are being portrayed as "rebels" against the Temple of the Lord.

These words were so inflammatory that **the chief priests and the teachers of the law heard this and began looking for a way to kill him** (11:18). Jesus was finally a danger to every aspect of Jewish leadership. Though the Sadducees, the Pharisees, and the Herodians rarely agreed on any tenant of the Law or its political implementation, they unanimously agreed that Jesus must die. **When evening came, they went out of the city** (11:19). Just as subtly as Jesus entered the city to come into the Temple, the Temple scene ends with Jesus once again departing the city.

In the morning, as they went along, they saw the fig tree withered from the roots (11:20). The fig tree was completely destroyed. Peter recalled the event from the previous day and thus saw this event as prophetic fulfillment. Two observations may be insightful at this point. First, Peter did not seem to understand that the fig tree and the Temple were to be intimately linked. He seems to have been commenting solely on the treatment of the fig tree. Yet in the presentation in Mark, both the leaf-filled tree and the Temple showed such promise. But upon careful inspection, they were actually lifeless. Jesus was describing what they were more than determining their fate. Second, this was not the end of the episode. Jesus reoriented the discussion around not "cursing" but "faith in God" (11:22) and in "prayer" (11:24).[13] This is Jesus' only true discourse teaching on prayer in the gospel of Mark.

"Have faith in God," Jesus answered (11:22). These words begin to put into context the events with the fig tree and the Temple as well as prepare for the next Temple confrontation (11:27–33); they set the scene for Jesus' return to the Temple and confrontation with the Jewish leaders regarding authority. Simply, Mark was exploring the connection between the loss of the Temple and prayer in the future of the Christian community as Jesus prophetically addressed the question, "How shall we worship without the house of God?" The Temple was to be replaced by a praying community.[14]

Moving a mountain (11:23) seems to have been a proverbial saying in Jesus' day equal to doing impossible tasks. In addition, the context of Mark implies Jesus' remarks may not be merely proverbially but cryptically prophetic; the "mountain" may specifically refer to the Temple mount.[15] Jesus was instructing His disciples to place trust in God and His power alone, not in the building. Prayer is not efficacious because it is offered at the Temple, as most Jews believed (1 Sam. 1:1–28, 1 Kings 8:27–30; Jonah 2:7). Rather, Jesus' death and resurrection create access to God through a Temple made "without hands" (14:58).

"Therefore I tell you, whatever you ask for in prayer, believe that you have received it, and it will be yours" (11:24). It is here that Jesus defined this faith issue in terms of prayer. However, this isolated verse is not Jesus' proclaiming power for its own sake. Rather, the next verse must be quickly incorporated: **"when you stand praying, if you hold anything against anyone, forgive him, so that your Father in heaven may forgive you your sins"** (11:25). Prayer is the power source that provides people with the real ability to forgive others for their deeds against others. Jesus explained that the Temple was no longer the place where the presence of God and His atoning act were exclusively available. Rather, communal prayer and corporate forgiveness could now be understood as the Holy of Holies in the community of faith. Jesus made this available at His death with the tearing of the curtain (15:38), and open access to God himself is a reality (see Heb. 10:19–22).

3. REACTION BY THE JEWISH LEADERS 11:27–33

The dialog recorded in 11:27–13:2 occurred within the Temple area. The controversies concern the very core of Jewish life and power—the Temple. And this all will climax with Jesus teaching the destruction of the "magnificent buildings" (13:1–2) that will soon no longer serve as the house of God.

Mark told his readers in 11:18 that the chief priests and the teachers of the law had issued a death warrant. Since Jesus' popularity with the crowd meant He could not be taken until there was a reversal of public opinion, the Jewish leaders had to discover or manufacture a way to turn opinion against Him. This leads to the series of face-to-face confrontations often described under the pretext of honest inquiry. First **the chief priests, the teachers of the law and the elders came to him** (11:27); soon the Pharisees and the Herodians (12:13) and, then, the Sadducees (12:18) would come. The Jewish leaders who could not agree on the basics of theology agreed that Jesus must be killed.

[W]hile Jesus was walking in the temple courts, the chief priests, the teachers of the law and the elders came to him. "By what authority are you doing these things?" they asked. "And who gave you authority to do this?" (11:27–28). In all likeliness, this encounter was in the Court of the Gentiles. The three Jewish groups named were the principal leaders of the Jewish Sanhedrin, or the Jewish ruling council, who ultimately put Jesus on trial and convicted Him of blasphemy (14:53–65). Their question was directed toward Jesus' activity in the Temple the previous day. Since the Jewish ruling council had not given their blessing, who had given Him permission to act?

In typical fashion for rabbinic debate, Jesus answered their question with another intimately linked question—the origin of John the Baptist's authority. **Jesus replied, "I will ask you one question. Answer me, and I will tell you by what authority I am doing these things. John's baptism—was it from**

heaven, or from men? Tell me!" (11:29–30). This refers to an earlier part of the Gospel; John was a fulfillment of Old Testament prophecy, especially Isaiah and Malachi. The Malachi 3:1 reference to John the Baptist quoted in Mark 1:2 says much more than "Behold I am sending my messenger before you." Malachi 3:1 goes on to say, "and the Lord whom you seek will suddenly come to His Temple." Thus, Jesus' question to the Jewish leaders reminds them and the readers of Mark that this was not merely a question of authority or leadership in the Temple, but of ownership. And with reference to John the Baptist, even in his greatness he knew his status, though divinely ordained, was of secondary importance to that of Jesus.

They discussed it among themselves (11:31). This "self-talk" among the Jewish leaders clearly depicts that they were concerned not with truth but with maintaining the status quo of the Temple and, therefore, their own position.

Jesus was protected on two levels: by the truth and by the crowds. The Jewish leaders knew of John's baptism and his popularity as a prophet. If they did not defame John, they would point out their own hypocrisy in not believing him. In what might have been quite a lengthy debate among themselves, they finally declare what they feel is the politically expedient middle ground, ignorance: **"We don't know"** (11:33). Jesus' final response and the passage as a whole testified against the words of the leaders. They did indeed know. They simply rejected the truth.

ENDNOTES

1. According to the Jewish writings in the Mishna *Sanhedrin* 2.5, no one else may ride a king's mount.

2. For additional royal overtones, see 2 Kings 9:13 as Jehu is anointed king of Israel.

3. These verses come from a section of the book of Psalms called the Hallel Psalms. The direct quotation comes from Psalm 118:25–26, the last of the psalms that was recited at all of the major feast pilgrimages to Jerusalem.

4. I am indebted to R. T. France (*The Gospel of Mark: New International Commentary on the Greek Testament* [Grand Rapids, Mich.: William B. Eerdmans, 2002], p. 436), who laid out the structure in the standard first-century chiastic pattern, uniting the passage into a cohesive whole:

    A. First visit to the Temple (11:11)

      B. Cursing of fig tree (11:12–14)

      A. Jesus takes action in Temple (11:15–19)

      B. Fig tree found dead (11:20–25)

      A. Jesus returns to Temple (11:27)

5. On Passover, the Law demanded for Jews to stay within the city limits (see Joachim Jeremias, *Jerusalem in the Time of Jesus: An Investigation into Economic & Social Conditions During the New Testament Period* [Minneapolis: Augsburg Fortress Publishers, June 1979], pp. 60–62 for insights into Passover arrangements).

6. This writing style is typical of Mark. He offered one story surrounded by another, asking readers to interpret them as a whole. This is affectionately called a Markan "sandwich" by scholars. Technically, the structure is labeled a chiasm.

7. William Telford, *Barren Temple and the Withered Tree, JSOT Supplement Series No. 1* (Sheffield, England: Sheffield Press, 1980), pp. 132–163. See Jeremiah 8:13; 24:1–10; Hosea 9:10, 16–17; Luke 13:6–9. This imagery is still true with reference to postbiblical and contemporary Judaism.

8. France, *Mark*, pp. 436–437.

9. France, *Mark*, pp. 436–437. In the time of Jesus, only one coin was acceptable to the Temple for the paying of the tax, the four-drachma silver piece minted at the city of Tyre (located on the coast of Lebanon). Throughout the region, people gave this coin its highest confidence due to the purity of its silver.

10. The traditions of Judaism are clear: actions that are inappropriate included using sacred space as a "short bypath" (m. *Berakhot* 9:5).

11. This trust in the Temple is called the inviolability of the Temple. Simply, Jewish people believed that pagans could never take the Temple because it was the "home of the Lord."

12. For the thorough definition of the concept of rebel, see throughout Martin Hengel, *The Zealots: Investigations into the Jewish Freedom Movement in the Period from Herod I Until 70 A.D* (London: T. & T. Clark Publishers, Ltd., July 1997), and R. A. Horsley, "Ancient Jewish Banditry and the Revolt Against Rome, A.D. 66–70," *Catholic Bible Quarterly* 43, pp. 409–432.

13. I thank Sharyn Dowd (*Prayer, Power, and the Problem of Suffering: Mark 11:22–25 in the Context of Markan Theology* (Society of Biblical Literature Dissertation Series 105) [Atlanta: Scholars Press, 1988], pp. 43–55) for the insights that connects this event not to cursing but to prayer.

14. Dowd, *Prayer*, pp. 45–55. Plus, take note that the communal aspect of prayer is highlighted as the pronouns in 11:22, 24–25 are plural; thus prayer is something the community does as a group, not a private transaction between humans and God (France, *Mark*, p. 448).

15. See Telford, *Temple*, pp. 56–59. The "holy mountain" is mentioned in Isaiah 2:2; 56:7; Psalm 78:54. The leveling of mountains is the sign of the eschatological

THE PARABLE OF THE VINEYARD

Mark 12:1–12

J esus **began to speak to them in parables** (12:1). The "them" in this passage is the same group who questioned Jesus' authority in 11:27–33—the chief priests, teachers of the law, and the elders.[1] This parabolic teaching is then to be read as Jesus' closing rebuke to this unyielding group. But this parable had a much different effect on the audience than Jesus' previous employment of parables in Mark 4. There, its meaning is only understood by a select few (4:11–12), while here in Mark 12, its meaning is so clear that it results in a death sentence, **Then they looked for a way to arrest him because they knew he had spoken the parable against them** (12:12).

A man planted a vineyard (12:1). The metaphor of a vineyard has a long history in the life of Israel. In each case, it illuminates God's disappointment with the faithlessness of His people. Mark 12 is no different. But the image in the parable, which is so closely based on the Isaiah 5 passage, moves in a slightly different direction. In Isaiah, the problem is the vineyard itself, and the vineyard will be abandoned and destroyed. In Jesus' parable it is the tenants who are culpable, and the owner of the vineyard will now entrust it to others. The Isaiah passage emits only judgment, while Mark resounds with hope for a completely new beginning.

The man **rented the vineyard to some farmers and went away on a journey** (12:1). In Jesus' time, an owner would establish an agreed-upon portion of the crops as payment for the renters. And in the establishment

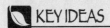

KEY IDEAS

Vineyard Motif in the Old Testament

Through these Old Testament passages (Ps. 80:8–18; Isa. 5:1–7; 27:2–6; Jer. 2:21; Ezek. 19:10–14), there are a few conclusions that can be drawn concerning Israel as the Lord's vineyard. First, the nation of Israel was one whom the Lord specifically chose to plant. Second, the Lord watched over His vineyard with loving care. Third, through the care of the Lord, this vineyard grew to be luscious and successful. Fourth, despite the care and success, the vineyard was uprooted and destroyed—retaining no resemblance of its former glory.

of a new vineyard, years might pass between the initial contract and the time when payment was due, allowing ample time for the grapevines to mature and for the renters to establish themselves.[2] **At harvest time he sent a servant. . . . But they seized him, beat him and sent him away empty-handed** (12:2–3). Though the owner sent a servant (literally, slave), this man was of some official standing, for he represented the interests of the owner. Refusing the slave means rejection of the owner. **Then he sent another servant to them; they struck this man on the head and treated him shamefully. He sent still another, and that one they killed. He sent many others; some of them they beat, others they killed** (12:4–5). Note the incremental mistreatment of the owner's representatives: first beating, then striking on the head,[3] and finally murder. The story resounds with the historical treatment of prophets who came to Jerusalem speaking for God (Jer. 7:25; 25:4; 26:20–23; 2 Chron. 24:20–22; Amos 3:7; Zech. 1:6). The latest of these was John the Baptist, beheaded for speaking the truth before Herod (6:24–29) and affirmed by Jesus and the people in 11:29–32.

"**He had one left to send, a son, whom he loved. He sent him last of all, saying, 'They will respect my son'**" (12:6). This is the climax of the parable and of the story of Mark as a whole,[4] the coming of the son as the official representative of the owner-Father. One might see this as an unrealistic expectation, that the tenants would treat the son with any more mercy or dignity than the slaves. Yet the parable reveals the very nature of God himself, patient with His own people, Israel. And at the same time this was His last attempt to establish ownership. The addition of the phrase "whom he loved" echoes the Father's voice from heaven

(1:11; 9:7) and increases the impact of the violence done to the son. In language similar to 11:31, the tenants conspired together against the son, this time to acquire full rights to the vineyard.[5] Irony shouts from the text, as if the owner would transfer His title to the property to the killers of His son. Can one extort the owner (God) out of anything by means of violent behavior? This linked the readers back to the previous Temple cleansing scene, when Jesus told the chief priests and scribes that they have made a house of prayer a "a den of robbers [rebels]" (11:17). First, they were accused of being in rebellion against God in His own house. Now they threatened to kill His Son for their own ill-gotten gain, and for a second time, the Jewish leaders have been accused of outright insurrection. The treatment of the son ends with these predictive words: **So they took him and killed him, and threw him out of the vineyard** (12:8). Death did not seem severe enough; he was not offered a proper burial, as if the son was a common criminal. Such treatment looked forward what Jesus would experience in just a few days.

Jesus then turned the tables on His interlocutors: **"What then will the owner of the vineyard do? He will come and kill those tenants and give the vineyard to others"** (12:9). Though "coming" is a common word in Greek and often is used in unpretentious ways, it also can be employed in an authoritative position, such as Jesus' "coming in the clouds with great power and glory" (see 13:26, 35, 36; 14:62). This should stand out as one of those uses. Moreover, the word "kill" is not representing the same Greek word in Jesus' passion predictions. Rather, this word is often translated as "destroy." It is used a total of nine times in Mark: twice referring to the violence the Jewish leaders were conspiring to do against Jesus (3:6; 11:18); twice describing what Jesus intended to do to unclean spirits who infect humanity (1:24; 9:22); most profoundly it is used twice in Jesus' call of self-denial to His disciples (8:35). Thus, this judgment-like passage shows the owner coming authoritatively to his own vineyard and treating the rebellious tenants as they have treated his son. Finally, the closing phrase [he will] **give the vineyard to others** looks beyond Israel herself forward in some degree to the new people of God.

Jesus' quotation of Psalm 118:22–23 connected the destruction of the Temple (11:12–27) and His impending death. Thus, the ancient ways of access to God through the Temple priests and its sacrificial practices was replaced with a new and living way. The religious leaders of Israel had rejected and slain the Son, in hopes of acquiring control of the vineyard, but they were obviously in conflict with the owner's will.

Then they looked for a way to arrest him because they knew he had spoken the parable against them. But they were afraid of the crowd; so they left him and went away (12:12). Just as in the previous controversy regarding the baptism of John the Baptist (11:32), the leaders were afraid of Jesus' popular base. So the chief priests, teachers of the law, and elders left Jesus with His following, all the while seeking an opportunity to arrest Him. They would not reappear again in the story until the passion narrative in chapter 14. Yet, they were the sending agents of the next group who was trying to trap Jesus.

ENDNOTES

1. For Mark, this tight-knit group arrived on the scene in the first passion prediction (8:31). They are also depicted as the constituents who comprise the Sanhedrin in the passion narrative (14:1; 15:1). It is certainly possible (probable?) that the Pharisees are to be seen as playing an influential role in Jesus' condemnation in the last three chapters of Mark, yet they are not named after 12:13.

2. J. Duncan M. Derrett, *Law in the New Testament* (London: Darton, Longman & Todd, 1970), pp. 289–290.

3. One can hear references to both John the Baptist (striking on the head = beheading; 6:24–29) and to Jesus (14:65; 15:19).

4. Maybe even the climax of God's work as a whole. Moreover, this can be viewed as a revelation of God's patience with His own people, Israel.

5. This is reminiscent of Genesis 37:20, with Jacob's sons plotting the murder of Joseph to get his inheritance.

CONFRONTATIONS, QUESTIONS, AND COMMANDMENTS

Mark 12:13-44

1. TO PAY OR NOT TO PAY 12:13-17

The chief priests, teachers of the law, and elders **sent some of the Pharisees and Herodians to Jesus to catch him in his words** (12:13). Mark depicted this day in the Temple as one of a continuous frontal assault from all parties of the Jewish leadership. Now the unlikely combination of the Pharisees and the Herodians is sent in. These two groups stood as polar opposites with reference to first-century Jewish life and practice. The Pharisees placed themselves with the people and the Torah. The Herodians situated their interests with the Herod, the aristocrats, and Roman occupation of the land. Yet now they were ignominiously united to try to disrupt the Temple teaching of Jesus.

"Catching" Jesus in His words was another way of attempting to invalidate His teaching. From the beginning He taught as one with authority (1:22, 27), and this confounded the Jewish leadership. Now this group would attempt to silence Him. The word "catch," though only used here in the New Testament, is often found in other Greek literature referring to the capture of wild animals and fish. Metaphorically, the Pharisees and the Herodians were on a hunting expedition to "trap" or "ensnare" Jesus. Readers must incorporate this devious intention as they read the seemingly complimentary words that follow: **"Teacher, we know you are a man of integrity. . . . you teach the way of God in accordance with the truth"** (12:14). These words are loaded and were intended to inflame the crowds in the Temple area. First, both the disciples and outsiders who seek His opinion called Jesus "Teacher" (5:35; 10:17; 12:14, 19, 32). Being a man of integrity who is not swayed by opinion was the Pharisees' way of painting Jesus into a corner with their question. They believed they would force Him into a "lose-lose" situation as Jesus would offend one influential group or another (Romans or Jews). Moreover, the best-case scenario would be to place Him in a position opposite the Romans. Thus, the compliment strategically positioned Jesus in the **way of God**.

Then they asked the question, **"Is it right to pay taxes to Caesar or not?"** (12:14). Every other time the word "right" has been used in Mark (2:24, 26; 3:4; 6:18; 10:2), it has referred to what is right or lawful according to divine law. This is no exception. Jesus either had to ascribe to paying mandated tribute to Rome, thereby alienating himself from the Jewish patriots and those who stood for the purity of Israel and against the foreign powers symbolized in the tax; or Jesus might have claimed a divine sanction against Rome, which would have put Him in the camp of the religious extremists or zealots and offended the puppet ruling family of the Herodians. But **Jesus knew their hypocrisy. "Why are you trying to trap me?"** (12:15). In the Gospel of Mark, Jesus is not often referred to as having knowledge of people's thoughts (see 2:8; 5:30), but here the implication is clear. They were out to get Him.

BACKGROUND

DENARII

A denarius was a silver coin, equivalent to approximately a day's wages. The problem with the coin was the inscription on it. "Tiberius Caesar, son of Divine Augustus" was on one side, and an inscription attributing high priesthood to someone on the other side. It was this claim of quasi-divinity that posed problems.

The head tax or poll tax in question was normally paid by a silver denarius, so Jesus then called for them to bring one to Him. Jesus himself did not have a coin, and thus His opponents produced the coin, setting them on the defensive already, for they were in the Temple precincts carrying a coin with an effigy of Caesar on the front, demonstrating the symbolic power of Rome. "It was a portable idol promulgating pagan ideology."[1]

Jesus asked them about the portrait. After they replied, he rendered His verdict: **"Give to Caesar what is Caesar's and to God what is God's"** (12:17). Their possession of the coin and their confession of what it bore foiled their plot. The Pharisees and the Herodians had no misgivings about doing business with Caesars' money, since they personally possessed "things that belong to Caesar." Jesus was also being quite clear on what

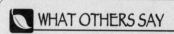

WHAT OTHERS SAY

WHAT WE OWE

One may owe Caesar what bears his image and name—money. One owes God what bears God's image and name. Since we are created in the image of God and bear His name as children of God, we owe Him our whole selves.

—David Garland

He was affirming. His choice of word was not simply "give," but "give back" or repay what already belongs to the Caesar. The Pharisees' use of the coin displayed some degree of dependence on Rome for services they provided as a governing body. The poll tax discharged that indebtedness.[2]

The second element of Jesus' pronouncement was much more open ended, literally, "[give] the things of God to God." Jesus was not speaking of these two entities, Caesar and God, as equals or even as competitors. Nor was He separating life into two distinct realms, the secular (the monetary or political arena) and the sacred (religious spheres); there is only one Lord. Furthermore, Caesar fell under the absolute authority of God. Thus, if Jesus expected His inquisitors to give what was financially due to Caesar, how much more should they carry out the same practice with what God claims as His? One rightfully owed Caesar what bears his image, money. Equally so, each person created in God's image owes their whole selves.[3]

2. SADDUCEES AND RESURRECTION 12:18–27

This passage is another in the long series of Jesus' confrontations in the Temple by different Jewish factions. Jesus was cast into a religious debate with the Sadducees regarding the resurrection.

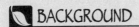

BACKGROUND

SADDUCEES

The Sadducees found their origin in David's priest Zadok (2 Sam. 8:17). This priestly line replaced the corrupt line from Eli and solidified its authority during the reign of Solomon. Therefore, the Sadducees, functioning since the monarchal period, possessed a more "conservative" perspective. Traditions of the forefathers and emphasis on the statutes found in the Torah were the cornerstones of covenantal life according to the Sadducees; they rejected the oral traditions. These aristocrats tended to be Roman sympathizers because an uprising would introduce Roman action and take precedence over their authority.

Then the Sadducees, who say there is no resurrection, came to him with a question (12:18). This is the first time in the Gospel of Mark that the name Sadducees has been used. They were from the more aristocratic elements from Jewish society, and this delegation may well have represented the prominent priestly families. Moreover, their theological perspective may have held the prevailing position in the Sanhedrin, the ruling Jewish council. As the pressure against Jesus mounted in the next few days, it was the Sadducees who formed the heart of the coalition that ultimately convicted Him of blasphemy and condemned Him to death (14:63–64). They are defined as Jesus' opponents, not only by being a part of the long litany of Temple accusers but also by being defined as being anti-resurrection. Three times thus far in the Gospel, Jesus has predicted His resurrection (8:31; 9:31; 10:34) and has clothed it in victorious language. Without the resurrection, Jesus' ministry would be deemed as a failure.

For the Sadducees, the heart of their faith lay in the Pentateuch, the first five books of the Old Testament. They rejected the theological development within Judaism of the afterlife. In actuality, there are only two Old Testament references that clearly express belief in the resurrection: Isaiah 26:19 and Deuteronomy 19:25–26.[4] For the most part, Judaism's hope of the resurrection arose from the apocalyptic writings of the intertestamental period between 300 B.C. and A.D. 100.

The questions they asked Jesus were based on the law of the levirate marriage (Deut. 25:5–10; Gen. 38:6–26; and the law as a guiding principle in the book of Ruth). The law is based on the outcome of a man who dies with no heirs. One of his surviving brothers was to take his widow in marriage, primarily for the purpose of keeping the brother's inheritance in the family. The contrived story unfolded about seven brothers who each married the same woman after each previous brother died without producing any heirs. The Sadducees asked, **"At the resurrection whose wife will she be, since the seven were married to her?"** (12:23).

The Sadducees did not believe in the resurrection. Their understanding of eternal life, based on the levirate law, was that a man's survival was through the continuity of his family line. Second, their understanding of the way others defined resurrection life was that it was identical to life on this earth, only lasting forever. This falsely assumes that the afterlife can be evaluated in terms of life as it is known here on earth.

Jesus' response was forceful; He detailed that their assumptions were wrong on two counts: Scripture and the power of God. He addressed the issue of God's power first. Jesus made a subtle yet substantial change in the discussion. In 12:23, 25, the discussion surrounded an active verb discussing the resurrection, **when the dead rise**. But in 12:26, Jesus employed a passive word that might be translated, "Now, as for the dead *being* raised . . . " Thus, first and foremost the resurrection is a demonstration of God's power. Next Jesus attacked their scriptural (mis)understanding. Jesus interpreted Moses and the burning bush through the lens of eternity. God remains God of the patriarchs Abraham, Isaac, and Jacob even though they died. Thus, they must still exist. For **"He is not the God of the dead, but of the living"** (12:27). Jesus closed His rebuke with the identical words in which He opened it: **"You are badly mistaken."**[5] So Jesus did not even attempt to describe what it will be like. He did however, tell what will be absent; there will be no marriage and no giving in marriage. What we might describe as the most important and the most intimate of all earthly relationships will not exist in eternity.

3. THE GREATEST COMMANDMENT 12:28–34

This next encounter is linked to the previous dialogue as **one of the teachers of the law came and heard them debating** (12:28). Yet this man did not represent an official delegation coming to trap Jesus in His words. Rather, he noticed **that Jesus had given them a good answer** (12:28). The word "good" should not be lowered to mean "clever" with reference to Jesus outwitting the trap. The scribe here and later in 12:34, ascribed to Jesus' words a positive moral sense that is so wholesome and satisfying that it led him to ask a more foundational question: **"Of all the commandments, which is the most important?"** (12:28). Rabbinic tradition has documented 613 commandments in the Law, 248 positive and 365 negative. This scribe was asking Jesus, "What is the overarching principle that unites this extensive legislation in a cohesive manner?

BACKGROUND

SHAMMAI VERSUS HILLEL

These individuals founded two rival Jewish schools that were responsible for the Jewish literature that deals with the religious obligations of Judaism and for transmitting the Oral Law.

Shammai (c. 50 B.C.E.–c. 30 C.E.)	Hillel (c. 70 B.C.E.–c. 10 C.E.)
Very conservative in approach and emphasized a literal and traditional translation of Scripture	• Became the head of the Sanhedrin • More liberal in approach, manifested by the presence of a Hellenistic influence • Developed seven rules of interpretation, which emphasized the purpose of the text that would later revolutionize Jewish tradition

"The most important one," answered Jesus, "is this: 'Hear, O Israel, the Lord our God, the Lord is one. Love the Lord your God with all your heart and with all your soul and with all your mind and with all your strength'" (12:29–30). Jesus was asked for one commandment but in actuality gave two. The first command comes with a preamble that securely grounded this command in Jewish monotheism and helped establishes Jesus' answer in the tradition of Moses. This passage Jesus was quoting comes from the *Shema* (Deut. 6:4), a prayer that encapsulates not only Jewish thought but also daily practice, since it is recited every morning and every night by pious Jews. The command to love God that follows (Deut 6:5) is defined with a series of four preposi-tional phrases, each with a different object that describes the whole person; heart, soul, mind, and strength.

But Jesus' second command was intimately linked to the first: **"Love your neighbor as yourself"** (12:31). One cannot love God in isolation from others. Here Jesus was quoting Leviticus 19:18, but in actuality, these two commands summarize the first and second part of the Decalogue (the Ten Commandments).[6] The difficult question from this quotation is what Jesus meant by neighbor. Is one's love to be limited to a fellow member of the Jewish covenant community or was Jesus extending love to encompass a larger definition? The law in Leviticus 19:34 expands the idea of neighbor to include resident aliens. But this issue was not explicitly explored here by Jesus. But in Luke's gospel, this passage is reshaped in Jesus' parable of the Good Samaritan (Luke 10:25–37).

Though Jesus has taken two distinctly separate commands, He spoke of them in singular form when He closed with this statement: **"There is no commandment greater than these"** (12:31). The scribe again referred to Jesus' teaching as positive: **"Well said, teacher,"** the man **replied. "You are right in saying that God is one and there is no other but him"** (12:32). He seems to have been restating Jesus' answer with His own Old Testament textual support, for he clothed it with a para-phrase of Isaiah 45:14: "and there is no other." Then the scribe reiterated Jesus' call to love God and love your neighbors. Finally the scribe divulged that he fully understood Jesus' teaching when he stated that obe-dience to this multifaceted love **is more important than all burnt offerings and sacrifices** (12:33). These words do have parallels from the Old Testament (see 1 Sam. 15:22; Isa. 1:11; Jer. 7:22–23), yet one must not forget where this dialogue was transpiring—inside the Temple precincts. Moreover, it seems as if for the first and only time in the second Gospel, Jesus' words were understood by a Jewish leader. The scribe's acceptance of Jesus' words shows **that he had answered wisely** (12:34). Jesus then ascribed to him one of the warmest affirmations found in Mark: **"You are not far from the kingdom of God."**

This section closes with Mark's summary statement: **from then on no one dared ask him any more questions** (12:34). From Jesus' triumphal entry into Jerusalem until now, the leaders of the Jews had been attempting to silence Jesus. In a succession of Temple mount encounters, the chief priests, the Pharisees, the Herodians, and finally the Sadducees all attempted to discredit Jesus. Yet Jesus silenced their diatribes.

4. THE QUESTION OF DAVID'S SON 12:35–37

Jesus then turned the tables on His earlier questioners. He posed His only question during His ongoing **teaching in the temple courts**[7] (12:35). The dilemma for Mark's readers is that not only is the question logically complex but also Jesus left it essentially unanswered. Jesus asked, **"How is it that the teachers of the law say that the Christ is the son of David?"** (12:35). The scribes had Jesus' lineage correct, coming from the line of David, yet they did not fully comprehend the plan of God for the Messiah. Jesus then exegeted Psalm 110:1 to show how they had misinterpreted Scripture: **"'The Lord said to my Lord: "Sit at my right hand until I put your enemies under your feet."'"** Jesus attributed these words of this psalm to David himself, **speaking by the Holy Spirit** (12:36). Thus was the impasse: if the Messiah is the son of David, why would David address him as my Lord? David must, by implication, have been referring to someone greater than himself.

Since Jesus did not explicitly answer the question, what might He have meant? First, Jesus should neither be understood to be devaluing the cry (confession) of Bartimaeus in 10:47–48 nor denying that Jesus is indeed not the Son of David. For that title remains a core value of the writers of the New Testament (Matt. 1:20; Luke 1:27, 32, 69; 2:4, 11; Rom. 1:3–4; 2 Tim. 2:8; Rev. 5:5; 22:16). Rather, Jesus was arguing that the title "Son of David" may have communicated His messianic mission as too firmly rooted in a nationalistic fervor. Simply, Jesus was saying, "It's true, I am the Son of David, but the title alone is insufficient."[8] **The large crowd listened to him with delight** (12:37). This delight was short lived, however, for the next time the crowd played a dominant role in the Gospel narrative, they were calling for Jesus' crucifixion (15:13).

5. THE SCRIBES AND THE WIDOWS 12:38–44

Logically breaking down the final verses in chapter 12 is a difficult task, since 12:38–40 is connected to the preceding passages by "teachers of the law" and to 12:41–44 because of the employment of the key word, "widow." For our purposes we will see the closing verses of chapter 12 as a summation of Jesus' Temple court teaching. In 12:38–40, Jesus *told* what religious hypocrisy looks like. In 12:41–44, Mark *showed* his readers an example of false piety, all taking place inside the Temple courts.

First, the telling. **"Watch out for the teachers of the law"** (12:38). Here Jesus was condemning the teachers of the law for parading themselves in public places and in houses of worship for the sole purpose of being seen and admired for their appearance of piety. Then Jesus reported the reality of their disregard for others, as **"they devour widows' houses and for a show make lengthy prayers"** (12:40). Knowing with precision what Jesus meant by "devouring" is difficult, but it seems to hinge on religious leaders who are serving as trustees or guardians of the estates of widows. They have appropriated much more than their proper share.[9] The caring for widows has a longstanding tradition throughout the Old Testament (Exod. 22:21–24; Deut. 24:17; Ps. 146:9; Isa. 1:17; Jer. 7:6), and a woman in the ancient world was particularly vulnerable. Surprisingly, teachers of the law were normally from the poorer classes,[10] and kindness shown to them was considered an act of personal piety. So, the hypocrisy of the scribes is most likely in the face of gracious acts of kindness from unsuspecting widows. Thus, Jesus' harsh words, **"Such men will be punished most severely."**

Now the showing part of Jesus' instruction. **Jesus sat down opposite the place where the offerings were put and watched the crowd putting their money into the temple treasury** (12:41). The exact location of this Temple treasury (box) is uncertain, but it is likely to be one of the thirteen trumpet-shaped collection chests placed throughout the court of the women. **Many rich people threw in large amounts**. This act is contrasted with a widow who threw in a miniscule amount. The coinage was the smallest denomination in use in Palestine. It was a copper coin worth less that 1/100th of a denarius. The two coins together formed less than 1/64th of a day's wages for a common worker.[11]

Most certainly there were many other people contributing to the Temple treasury, but Jesus interpreted the giving of the widow as an object lesson to His disciples. **Calling his disciples to him, Jesus said, "I tell you the truth, this poor widow has put more into the treasury than all the others. They all gave out of their wealth; but she, out of her poverty, put in everything—all she had to live on"** (12:43–44). Interestingly, the last time the disciples were named in the narrative was following the withering of the fig tree in 11:14. Ever since, though they most certainly were present, they have taken a back seat to Jesus' ongoing interchange with the Jewish leaders. Now, in what may be termed as the climactic instruction in the Temple, Jesus spoke to His disciples. Note Jesus' "calling of the disciples" (8:34; 10:42) and then Jesus' beginning His interpretation of the events with the phrase "I tell you the truth" (3:28; 8:12; 9:1, 41; 10:15, 29; 11:23; 12:43; 13:30; 14:9, 18, 25, 30). Mark's readers know that what follows is worthy of special note. Jesus called all those who follow Him to abandon the human way of bestowing honor and to adopt Kingdom principles; the first will be last and the last will be first. Furthermore, Jesus' private teaching to His disciples was in complete harmony with the previous rebuke of the teachers of the law (12:38–40), who only desire public honor from people, all the while rejecting the value system of God and the Scripture.

ENDNOTES

What Others Say Sidebar: David Garland, *Mark: The NIV Application Commentary* (Grand Rapids, Mich.: Zondervan, 1996), p. 463.

1. Garland, *Mark,* p. 462.

2. The tone of the passage causes one to question if Jesus may be taking it one step further. Not only is it permitted, but to withhold the tax may actually be equivalent to defrauding or stealing from Rome.

3. The early church father Tertullian said, "Render unto Caesar, the image of Caesar, which is money, and unto God, the image of God, which is in man" (*On Idolatry* 15; *Against Marcion* 4.38.3).

4. There are other references in the wisdom literature (Ps. 16:9–11; 49:15; 73:23–26; Job 19:25–26) that only took on the full sense of resurrection in hindsight of Jesus' raising from the dead.

5. The word for "error" (12:24) and "mistaken" (12:27) is the same in Greek.

6. Commandments 1–4 direct followers to worship God; commandments 5–10 call people to love one another. Philo, a first-century Jewish writer who called the Decalogue a summary of the Torah, described those who keep the first four commandments "God lovers" and the last six "men lovers." (*Decalogue* 108–110).

7. This sequence began with His entrance into the Temple mount in 11:15.

8. R. T. France said that it is "true but liable to misunderstanding" (R. T. France, *The Gospel of Mark: New International Commentary on the Greek Testament* (Grand Rapids, Mich.: William B. Eerdmans, 2002), p. 484.

10. See J. Derrett, "Eating Up the Houses of Widows: Jesus' Comment on Lawyers." *Novum Testamentum* 14 (Boston: Brill, 1972): pp. 1–9. See also William Lane, *The Gospel of Mark* (Grand Rapids, Mich.: William B. Eerdmans, 1974), pp. 440–441.

11. Lane, *Mark*, pp. 440–441; Joachim Jeremias, *Jerusalem in the Time of Jesus: An Investigation into Economic & Social Conditions During the New Testament Period* (Minneapolis: Augsburg Fortress, June 1979), pp. 111–16.

12. For the discussion of coinage, see Emil Schürer, *A History of the Jewish People in the Time of Jesus Christ* (London: T. & T. Clark, 1987), pp. 2:62–66.

19

PROPHETS AND PROPHECIES

Mark 13:1-37

1. JESUS' PREDICTION AND THE DISCIPLES' QUESTION 13:1-4

C hapter 13 begins with the words of an unnamed disciple: **"Look, Teacher! What massive stones! What magnificent buildings!"** The Temple had become a mere tourist attraction rather than a place of worship and sacrifice. Readers should not be surprised that Jesus predicted its destruction. Following the initial questions of the four disciples, the rest of chapter 13 are the words of Jesus. This is quite unusual for Mark, for only the parabolic instruction of 4:1–34 rivals chapter 13 for uninterrupted dialogue by Jesus.

The unnamed disciple seems awestruck by the magnificence of the buildings outer appearances. Yet this demonstrates that the disciples were still slow to grasp the instructions of Jesus declaring the moral and religious bankruptcy of the Temple practices. Jesus responded to the comment: **"Do you see all these great buildings? . . . Not one stone here will be left on another; every one will be thrown down"** (13:2). Though 13:1–2 creates the setting for the forthcoming question of the disciples regarding the destruction of the Temple, it also functions as the concluding remarks to the previous section of Jesus' ongoing confrontation with the Temple authorities. "Jesus' reply was to dismiss the magnificent display as—in the context of his ministry and mission—a massive irrelevance."[1]

Jesus was sitting on the Mount of Olives[2] **opposite the temple** (13:3). It is in this setting, with a clear view of the Temple mount, **Peter,**

James, John and Andrew asked him privately the question that arose as they were leaving the Temple earlier: **"Tell us, when will these things happen? And what will be the sign that they are all about to be fulfilled?"** (13:4). The rest of the chapter is Jesus' answer to these two questions. The answer to the question "when will these things happen?" (i.e., the destruction of Jerusalem and the Temple) is laid out by Jesus in 13:5–23. It begins and ends with recurrence of the word "watch."

The second question is answered in 13:24–37, and it begins with the words **"But in those days, following that distress."** These events build on the answer to the first question, but now Jesus elaborated beyond what they may even have been asking. He began with Old Testament apocalyptic-like language, "in those days," and then detailed the "signs" requested by the disciples (esp. 13:24–31) and warnings that pointed to the fulfillment of these things (esp. 13:32–37).

2. FALSE PROPHETS AND WARS 13:5–8

The literary structure of Jesus' description of the destruction of Jerusalem breaks down into a wonderful chiasm that points to the center as a means of emphasizing its importance.

A 13:5–6	False prophets	
B 13:7–8	Wars and rumors of war	
C	**13:9–13**	**Watch: Persecution**
[**B**] 13:14–20	Wars and rumors of war	
[**A**] 13:21–23	False prophets	

The section begins with the warning **"Watch out that no one deceives you."** The tone for the entire passage is set with this word "watch"[3] (used also in 13:9, 23, 33) and its synonyms (13:33, 35, 37). Without question, Jesus' agenda in this section (13:5–23) was not to set a timetable but to alert His followers what events should *not* be read as a sign. For example, **"Many will come in my name, claiming, 'I am he,' and will deceive many"** (13:6). Jesus stated that they will perform "signs and miracles" to deceive the church (13:22). The very things that Jesus refused to give as verification of who He is (8:11–12) are the means by which the false messiahs will create a following.

"When you hear of wars and rumors of wars, do not be alarmed. Such things must happen, but the end is still to come" (12:7). It is possible that Mark wanted his readers to make a connection between the coming of false messiahs and wars, but this is not explicit. It may be that Jesus was simply saying that the presence of wars, though often featured in Old Testament prophecy of divine punishment, are poor indicators with which to predict the end. Jesus said not to be alarmed at such things. The word "alarmed" is a rare one in the New Testament, occurring only three times: here, in Matthew's parallel of the same passage, and in 2 Thessalonians 2:2 with Paul's warning to the church not to be deceived that the day of the Lord has seemingly passed them by.

"Nation will rise against nation, and kingdom against kingdom. There will be earthquakes in various places, and famines" (13:8). Wars and natural disasters are taking place at all times throughout the world do not themselves usher in the kingdom of God. **"These are the beginning of birth pains."** The word "these" (literally, these things) refers directly back to the question of the disciples in 13:4, "When will these things happen?" Thus, Jesus emphatically stated that the coming of false prophets and many being deceived, wars, earthquakes, and famines should not cause alarm. They are only the beginning of "birth-pangs."[4] The imagery of a woman's labor pains was a common metaphor in the Old Testament that "symbolized the agony which would lead to a new beginning"[5] (see Isa. 26:17; 66:8; Hos. 13:13; Mic. 4:9). Throughout the New Testament, the term is cast in a number of contexts (John 16:21; Acts 2:24; Gal. 4:19; 8:22; 1 Thess. 5:3), with a range of meaning from "pains of death" (Acts 2:24) to the travail of those facing final judgment (1 Thess. 5:3). Thus, again Jesus reiterated that this was only the beginning of the suffering that will denote the beginning of the end.

3. THE PROMISE OF PERSECUTION 13:9–13

This section describes persecutions that are pointed directly at people who follow Christ. It begins with the recurring word of caution in chapter 13:

"Watch." Readers should hear the emphasis from the original Greek this way: "but as for *you*, continually watch *yourselves*." Though the same word has introduced the previous section (13:5), this next section takes on a different tone, as it discusses not what will happen generally to the world but how Jesus' followers will be singled out for hatred of the worst kind. First, **"You will be handed over to the local councils and flogged in the synagogues"** (13:9). The phrase "handed over" has ominous overtones that what is being predicted about the fate of the disciples has direct parallels with Jesus' final treatment. For in His own passion predictions (9:31; 10:33), this is how He categorized His fate. Moreover, the word for "handed over" is used thirteen times in the last four chapters of Mark, summing up the betrayal of Judas (14:10–11, 18, 21, 41, 42), the abandonment of the disciples (14:30–31, 50), the rejection by the Jewish leaders (15:1, 10), and Jesus' fate at the hands of the Roman leader Pilate (15:15).

These first two acts of persecution have a tone of betrayal. It is clear that these have religious implications, as if the disciples' faith in Christ has caused the religious authorities to publicly punish them as heretics or blasphemers. Next, **"you will stand before governors and kings as witnesses to them."** Now the tone has a distinctively Roman feel. First on trial before the Jews, then the Romans; this is not only a prophecy to the times after the resurrection of Christ, it is also a precursor to the passion narrative of Christ himself. Two important phrases describe why this is taking place. The first is the qualifier **"on account of me."** Earlier in their discipleship training, the disciples were warned that their honor would be found in their giving their lives for Jesus and for the gospel (8:35; 10:29). The second qualifying phrase is **"as witnesses to them."** Certainly, their persecution would be on account of Jesus, but it may also be for the sake of their persecutors. The persecution of the disciples (and all future disciples) at trial will be an opportunity of evangelism. This may be a blessing to the Jews and Romans or a curse, depending on how they hear and respond to the message. The disciples witness out of love for the Lord and out of love for their enemies.

"And the gospel must first be preached to all nations" (13:10). The connection between persecution and proclamation was already made by

Mark (6:11; 8:35–38). But now there seems to be a rationale for the waiting of the consummation of the Kingdom; it is for the nations. And since this passage is predicting the destruction of Jerusalem and its Temple, the gospel must go outside of Israel before that can take place.[6] This is Mark's clearest call to global evangelization (see Matt. 28:19–20).

"Whenever you are arrested and brought to trial, do not worry beforehand about what to say. Just say whatever is given you at the time, for it is not you speaking, but the Holy Spirit" (13:11). Jesus had, in essence, completely ignored the disciples' question at this point. He was not concerned with detailing the timing of the end from "signs" but with what they would do *when* they were indeed arrested (literally: handed over). Verse 11 is the only reference to the Holy Spirit in this Gospel with relation to the disciples. The prophetic passage certainly assumes a date after the death and resurrection of Jesus. Further, it assumes the Pentecost event in Acts 2. It would be then that the Holy Spirit would empower the disciples. In the end, for Mark, testimony and proclamation is the means through which the church will usher in the Kingdom (1:14, 38; 6:11).

"Brother will betray brother to death, and a father his child. Children will rebel against their parents and have them put to death. All men will hate you because of me" (13:12–13). The persecution is now described in even more localized and personal terms, as families turn again one another. Reminiscent of Micah 7:6, all of this will come to be "because of me"[7] Jesus said. **"But he who stands firm to the end will be saved."** The disciples, after Jesus' death, were called to patient endurance (standing firm).

4. A "SIGN"? 13:14–20

In the earlier section of 13:5–8, Jesus described wars and natural disasters in a general, almost global way. But now He turned to a localized matter—Jerusalem and her Temple—and to a specific time—the days and events that lead up to its destruction in A.D. 70. And there will be a major shift. Up to this point, the Christian followers were commanded to wait and endure, but now the time for action has come. Their fleeing will be triggered by what the onlookers "see." This event may introduce a "sign" more specific than those described in 13:5–13 and indicate that there will be progress from a time of delay toward that of fulfillment.

How would the disciples know of the shift? **"When you see 'the abomination that causes desolation' standing where it does not belong . . . then let those who are in Judea flee to the mountains"** (13:14). The precise meaning of Jesus' words has been the topic of interpretive conversations for centuries. His quotation derives from Daniel 11:31 (see also Dan. 8:13; 9:27; 12:11; Jer. 7:30–34). The historical referent for the event is supplied in the intertestamental book of 1 Maccabees 1:54–59 (NRSV):

> Now on the fifteenth day of Chislev, in the one hundred forty-fifth year, they erected a desolating sacrilege on the altar of burnt offering. They also built altars in the surrounding towns of Judah, and offered incense at the doors of the houses and in the streets. The books of the law that they found they tore to pieces and burned with fire.

Regarding this event, Antiochus Epiphanes was returning to Syria from Egypt after a victorious military campaign in 168 B.C. He ordered that the Jewish ceremonial law be stopped. Furthermore, he ordered that a pagan altar to the god Zeus (a desolating sacrilege) be set up on top of the altar of the burnt offering in the Temple and that an unclean sacrifice be made.[8] Since the phrase "the abomination that causes desolation" is not used with reference to any other event, those who heard it most certainly would have understood it in that context. Thus, it seems most probable that what Jesus was referencing must now correspond to what Antiochus had done. Finally, there is a grammatical issue that can be easily missed in this passage. The word "standing" is a masculine participle that is modifying a neuter noun "abomination that causes desolation." This might suggest that Jesus was referring to a person not an inanimate idol. This grammatical irregularity may explain Mark's parenthetical addition of the words, **"let the reader understand."** Ernest Best equates this phenomenon to our modern *sic* that is positioned after a word that seems misspelled or strangely out of place. "But when you see the thing, the abomination of desolation, standing where he (*sic*) should not be . . ."[9] Yet, since this is a call for the reader to understand "the abomination of desolation" as an analogy from the past and to apply it to the events transpiring in the present, it also might be likened to the reader giving a nod or a wink to the listeners as they are now given insider information. The desolation is not to be seen as merely a "thing" or an idol being set up in the Temple, but it might end up in actuality being a man. Antiochus IV Epiphanes' desecration of the Temple with a pagan altar in 168 B.C. was not the only effort to do so. The Roman emperor Caligula unsuccessfully attempted to have a statue of himself set up in the Temple in A.D. 40.[10] The reference to "it [him?] standing where it does not belong" (14:13) may indeed refer to a person and not an inanimate object. Another person to whom this pronoun might refers to could be the Roman general (and later emperor) Titus who commanded the troops during the destruction of the Jewish Temple in Jerusalem in A.D. 70. Another possible "him" might be the mystifying figure of the Antichrist depicted by Paul in 2 Thessalonians 2:4.

"Then let those who are in Judea flee to the mountains" (13:14). Note the direction of the flight: to the mountains. During most times of attack, the Jews fled *to* Jerusalem, especially to the Temple, for it was assumed to be inviolable (Jer. 7:4). Jesus, however, here instructed them there will be no safety in the Temple and no refuge in the walled city (Jer. 6:1; Rev. 18:4). The effects of this tragedy are depicted in graphic detail: **"Let no one on the roof of his house go down or enter the house to take anything out"** (13:15). The cataclysm was impending but had not yet come. There would not be time to go back. **"Let no one in the field go back to get his cloak"** was a reminder of the false move that was disastrous to Lot's wife in Genesis 19:26 (see Luke 17:31). **"How dreadful it will be in those days for pregnant women and nursing mothers!"** (13:17). The joy of motherhood is transfixed to tragedy. **"Pray that this will not take place in winter"** (13:18), for in the winter months, the rivers often flooded and cross-country travel was often impossible.[11]

"If the Lord had not cut short those days, no one would survive. But for the sake of the elect, whom he has chosen, he has shortened them" (13:20). The implication by Jesus was that God has worked out a timetable for these events.[12] Moreover, this is a demonstration of grace to the church, since the coming of the Kingdom will be a time of testing and trial.

5. MORE ABOUT FALSE PROPHETS 13:21-23

This section about the final days leading up to the destruction of Jerusalem in A.D. 70 ends just as it begins, with warnings about false prophets. **"At that time if anyone says to you, 'Look, here is the Christ!' or, 'Look, there he is!' do not believe it"** (13:21). The role of the disciples in all of this turmoil was to be faithful witnesses (13:9–11). One should not be surprised that others will point in different directions. Moreover, these **"false Christs and false prophets will appear and perform signs and miracles"** (13:22). They will provide people with the very things that they cry out for in the time of chaos. And many will follow after them. But Jesus' words here were not directed to the persuasion of the people in general but that the false prophets are attempting to **"deceive the elect."** For the real Messiah had already come, and here the clear instruction is that He would not save Jerusalem nor the Temple from destruction. Any sign or miracle that pointed in that direction was a religious hoax meant to deceive.

"So be on your guard; I have told you everything ahead of time" (13:23). Jesus brought the conversation back to the present disciples and to the immediate moment. He emphatically said, "*You* be on your guard!" These words were spoken in about A.D. 30 by Jesus on the Mount of Olives, forty years before the Temple's destruction. This should have brought some degree of comfort to the people of Jerusalem that these events would not catch God by surprise.

6. THE END OF THE WORLD? 13:24-37

"But in those days" are the introductory words to this next section. The word "but" in the Greek is a strongly adversative choice, contrasting the events that just occurred with those that will follow. The next words, "in those days," are time-honored in apocalyptic writing that assumes an end-time force (see Jer. 3:16, 18; 31:29; 33:15; Joel 2:28; Zech. 8:23). Jesus appears to be describing the events that will come after the travails in the destruction of Jerusalem. But Jesus wanted to put a stop to anyone attempting an end-times prediction. "The ambiguity is deliberate and Jesus does not intend for us to unravel it."[13] The only certainty is that the end is coming, so be ready.

THE COMING OF THE SON OF MAN

"'The sun will be darkened, and the moon will not give its light; the stars will fall from the sky, and the heavenly bodies will be shaken'" (13:24–25). The language of 13:24–25 echoes many Old Testament passages (Ezek. 32:7; Joel 2:10, 31; 3:15; Amos 8:9) but most closely parallels Isaiah 13:10 and 34:4. Apart from its cataclysmic imagery, it most often appears in the context of the collapse of ruling world orders and the rise of a cosmic-like replacement in which God's plan will reign.

"At that time men will see the Son of Man coming in clouds with great power and glory. And he will send his angels and gather his elect from the four winds, from the ends of the earth to the ends of the heavens" (13:26–27). Jesus' words turned from the terror of cosmic destruction to these positive words of the new order ushering in salvation. Daniel 7:13–14 is heard as the backdrop to this clarion call. Jesus employed the "Son of Man" designation throughout the Gospel as one who has the authority to receive all glory and power from the Lord himself. Now, as the direct result of the destruction of the Temple in 13:5–23, Jesus and the elect are to be seen as the true Israel. The powerful growth of the church in the face of impossible odds is the visual manifestation that the Son of Man is coming.

PARABLE OF FIG TREE

The questions of the disciples, "When will these things happen? And what will be the sign that they are all about to be fulfilled?" had not been forgotten by Jesus. He had carefully crafted His answer in 13:5–23, outlining the destruction of Jerusalem and the devastation of the Temple. Now in 13:29–30, Jesus returned to "these things": **"this generation will certainly not pass away until all these things have happened."** Thus, this passage cannot refer to the cosmic mayhem of 13:24–25 or to the *parousia* (second coming) in 13:26–27.

The fig tree was often used in Jewish literature to symbolize the signs of the messianic age.[14] This parable called the disciples to reflect over Jesus' previous teaching; just as they anticipated summer by the signs of nature, so they were to wait to **"see these things happening."** The leaves are the harbinger of future fruit. **"Heaven and earth will pass away, but**

my words will never pass away" (13:31). Isaiah 40:7–8 closely parallels the words of Jesus. The trustworthiness of Jesus is equated with that of God himself. Further, in Matthew 5:18 and Luke 16:17 analogous metaphors are used for the permanent validity of the law. Thus, here in 13:31, Jesus' words are on an authoritative equivalence of Scripture.

UNKNOWN HOUR

This section begins, "but concerning that day or that hour, no one knows" (Mark 13:32 ESV). This kind of language alerts the readers to a change of subject matter.[15] While Jesus utilized the plural "those days" to describe the siege of Jerusalem (13:17, 19, 20, 24), He had never used the singular to clearly indicate what "day or hour" He was using as a reference point. Finally, Jesus stated that no one knows. Earlier, Jesus spoke with absolute certainty about timing, but now He addressed a temporal issue with seeming vagueness. It seems clear that Jesus has moved from a subject of a known commodity, Jerusalem and the Temple, to the subject of the unknown, the *parousia*. The parallel passage in Matthew 24 clearly refers to the *parousia*. But in Mark's account, none of this explicit direction is given. It is quite difficult to tell exactly what "time" Jesus was discussing.

The list of the heavenly creatures who are expected to be aware of the "temporal secret" seems to be in ascending order of importance: the angels, the Son, and ultimately the Father. Framed within one of the highest Christological proclamations of Jesus, the Coming End of Times Judge, readers also find a seemingly contradictory divine limitation. How can the Son, sharing in the divine attributes, not know the mind of the Father? In addressing this question, one must keep two issues in tension. First, this passage in Mark is not so much dealing with Christology[16] but with eschatology. Thus, Mark did not elaborate on the issue, since it is only tangential to the discussion. Second, Mark's readers (and Jesus' disciples) are being given insider information about Jesus that will have direct impact on their understanding of events that will happen within the near future.

The Christological importance of this subtle "knowledge limitation" cannot be overlooked. Jesus stood as a faithful man in the midst of betrayal and denial by His disciples, in the face of rejection by the religious authorities, and suffered the most shameful of all deaths, yet remained faithful to the end. Thus, He truly represented what a true human should be and then triumphantly died and rose for us (10:45; 14:24).

"Be on guard! Be alert! You do not know when that time will come" (13:33). If Jesus did not know this time, neither does anyone else. Each must be vigilant. Here Jesus used a synonym for "day or hour" when He said, "when the time will come." Further, the verbs "guard" and "alert" are present tense commands meaning "continually be on guard."

Then He related the charge to a parable-like account: **"It's like a man going away: He leaves his house and puts his servants in charge, each with his assigned task, and tells the one at the door to keep watch. Therefore keep watch because you do not know when the owner of the house will come back"** (13:34–35). This vividly holds together the dual eschatological tensions; the end will come suddenly and one must be ready today. The time when the owner may come home is stated: **"whether in the evening, or at midnight, or when the rooster crows, or at dawn."** This series are the four different evening watches of the night according to Roman timekeeping. But here Mark was deliberately tying in the close of chapter 13 with the approaching passion narrative, for three of the four watches are mentioned in the subsequent passages. **"If he comes suddenly, do not let him find you sleeping"** (13:36). In the course of the night in Gethsemane, three of the four disciples who originally posed the Temple question to Jesus (13:3–4) were once again commanded to watch (14:34, 37–38), and they were sternly rebuked for sleeping.

Finally, this warning was not limited to the four disciples alone, for **"what I say to you, I say to everyone: 'Watch!'"** While the Temple destruction may have had a restricted audience in mind, this ending certainly does not. All Christians of all ages are expected to be on watch, no matter what the hour.

ENDNOTES

1. Mann, *Mark: A New Translation with Introduction and Commentary* (New York: Doubleday, 1986), p. 495.

2. An astute reader of the Old Testament would remember that the very place where Jesus is seated is also where the glory of the Lord is said to have departed from a corrupt Jerusalem in Ezekiel 11:23.

3. The word *blepō* in Mark does not simply mean "be on guard," but it is a call for "discernment concerning realities which lie beyond the observations of the physical senses" (Timothy Geddert, *Watchwords: Mark 13 in Markan Eschatology*, Journal for the Study of the New Testament [Sheffield, England: Sheffield Academic Press, 1989], pp. 60, 146).

4. Evidence that the term "birth-pang" is a technical term for "birth pang of the Messiah" comes from material after the New Testament time.

5. Morna Hooker, *The Gospel According to St. Mark* (Peabody, Mass.: Hendrickson, 1991), p. 308.

6. Often, Christians read this passage as a precursor to the *parousia*, the second coming of Christ. But that issue is not under discussion by Christ, merely the destruction of the Temple.

7. Literally, "on account of my name," which is also stated earlier in 13:6, "many will come [falsely] in my name."

8. Historically, this same language was repeated when the Roman emperor Caligula threatened a similar defilement when he ordered a stone statue of himself to be erected within the Temple in A.D. 40.

9. Ernest Best, "The Gospel of Mark: Who is the Reader?" *Irish Biblical Studies* 11 (1989): 12–32, quoted in David Garland, *Mark: The NIV Application Commentary* (Grand Rapids, Mich.: Zondervan, 1996), p. 496.

11. Josephus tells the story of Gadarene refugees who were seeking refuge in Jericho, could not cross the flooded Jordan river, and were killed by the Romans (Josephus, *Works*, 4.7.5).

12. The theme of shortening the days appears often in the Apocrypha also: 1 Enoch 83:1 ("For the Most High will surely hasten His time") and 2 Baruch 20:2 ("I now took away Zion to visit the world in its own time more speedily").

13. Garland, *Mark*, p. 500.

14. William Telford, *Barren Temple and the Withered Tree*, JSOT Supplement Series No. 1. (Sheffield, England: Sheffield Press, 1980), pp. 128–204.

15. See 1 Corinthians 7:1, 25; 8:1; 12:1; and 16:1 for changes in the questions Paul was addressing to the Corinthian church. See also 1 Thessalonians 4:9; 5:1 and Acts 21:25. Previously, Mark used this grammatical construction in 12:26 when he transitioned from the topic of marriage in the resurrected life to the specific topic of the resurrection ("now about the dead rising.")

16. The exact issue is that of the divine *kenosis* or the limitation of the divine attributes because of the nature of the Incarnation. For example, Jesus had to submit himself to the natural limitations of time and space while on earth.

20

ANOINTING FOR BURIAL

Mark 14:1–31

M ark 14–16 is known as the passion narrative. It has distinct, logical, narrative breaks and can be read paragraph by paragraph with great spiritual reward. But the real power of this section of the Gospel comes from reading it as a single unit. In typical Markan fashion, separate stories are laid side by side and subtly woven into a whole cloth.

1. ANOINTING FOR BURIAL 14:1–11

The Markan tendency to intercalate[1] narrative material provides the interpretative framework of the anointing at Bethany episode. Just as the two anointing scenes of 14:3–9 and 16:1–8 bracket the passion narrative, the plot of the leaders (14:1–2) and their recruitment of Judas (14:10–11) establishes the perimeter of the anointing at Bethany (14:3–9) and sets the passage into a theological framework. In other words, Mark wanted his audience to experience the "beautiful" act of the unnamed woman in light of the heinous acts of betrayal that surround it. Additionally, the effect of the "Markan sandwich" is that it connects two events that beforehand had been temporally and spatially unrelated.

In 14:1 **the chief priests and the teachers of the law were looking** [literally, "seeking"] **for some sly way to arrest Jesus and kill him.** Then, following the anointing passage, Judas similarly watched (literally, "seeking") for an opportunity to hand him over (14:11). In a frightening manner Mark directly connected the acts of Jesus' enemies with His own circle of followers. Furthermore, he placed emphasis on the pleasure the chief priests and the scribes gained upon "hearing" (14:11) that one of Jesus' disciples was now their "insider." In the midst of this secretive plotting, Mark then inserted a passage where Jesus was concurrently having His body anointed beforehand for burial (14:8). Ironically, what the Jews thought they were initiating in secret was already well underway in Jesus' agenda.

The time element in the gospel of Mark now radically shifts. This story has progressed at breakneck speed. One of the most common words in Mark has been "immediately"; Jesus moved from one place to another almost without rest. As He did, He was constantly interrupted, and relentless demands were put upon His time and energies. In chapter 14, Mark slowed the story down and focused on chronology, first in terms of days, and then later in the passion narrative he described hours and even moments with precision. **Now the Passover and the Feast of Unleavened Bread were only two days away** (14:1). Assuming Mark was counting in a Jewish manner, the phrase **two days** means "the next day." Thus, the day was most likely Tuesday (possibly Wednesday) of the Passover week and the crowds of pilgrims were swelling.[2] Jews in Jesus' day came to Jerusalem to celebrate this festival with hope that the Messiah would do for them what Moses did for their forefathers in Egypt. The lambs for the Passover meal were slaughtered on this afternoon (fourteenth Nisan), and the Passover meal was to be eaten between sundown and midnight (fifteenth Nisan).

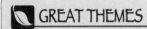

GREAT THEMES

PASSOVER

The Passover is the oldest and most important festival in Judaism, bringing hope for future redemption. It is a meal that commemorates the tenth plague, when the angel of death *passed over* the land of Egypt and killed all the firstborn males not protected by lamb's blood (Exod. 12). The Feast of Unleavened Bread was the weeklong festival following the Passover. Passover became representative of both celebrations.

The Jewish leaders did not want to kill Jesus during the Feast **"or the people may riot"** (14:2). The Jewish leaders were conveying their belief that at that time the people were willing to lash out against anyone who might threaten the safety of Jesus. Seemingly, they would sacrifice themselves, just as the disciples soon would do during the garden arrest (14:43–50). However, the fickleness of the crowd's position would be poignantly brought out later by Mark as they were stirred by the chief priests to shout out, "Crucify him!" not once but twice (15:13, 14). The people demanded that Pilate release the insurrectionist Barabbas (15:7) rather than Jesus. They chose one who had attempted to free Israel from Rome over against one who was attempting to free them from the bonds of sin. Mark reported that Jesus was a threat to the way people envision the world. The people in the story wanted to eliminate the enemy they saw, while Jesus desired to remove the greater threat that they could not even conceive.

While he was in Bethany, reclining at the table in the home of a man known as Simon the Leper, a woman came with an alabaster jar of very expensive perfume made, of pure nard (14:3). In the actual anointing passage (14:3–9), Mark identified three main actors: Jesus, the unnamed woman who poured expensive perfume over Jesus' head, and the disciples who reproached the woman for what they regarded as her frivolous act. The unnamed woman entered the scene unannounced. **She broke the jar and poured the perfume on his head. Some of those present were saying indignantly to one another, "Why this waste of perfume? It could have been sold for more than a year's wages and the money given to the poor." And they rebuked her harshly** (14:3–4). Mark then interjected intense emotion into the scene as the disciples[3] angrily pointed out the monetary waste of her act in comparison to the good it might accomplish in aiding the poor. The language moved from contemplation ("But there were some who said to themselves indignantly, 'Why was the ointment thus wasted? For this ointment might have been sold for more than three hundred denarii, and given to the poor'" 14:4–5 RSV) to condemnation ("And they reproached her" 14:5 RSV). Then Jesus spoke[4] to interpret the events properly. Surprisingly, He did not merely protect the woman; He memorialized her. **"I tell you the truth, wherever the gospel is preached throughout the world, what she has done will also be told, in memory of her"** (14:9). Jesus has spoken and the readers know how Jesus appraises the situation.

However, Mark did not make agreement with Jesus an easy proposition. In Jesus' day, it was proper to think in terms of provision for the poor. It was customary on the evening of the Passover to remember the destitute with gifts.[5] Furthermore, the disciples were acting in a manner appropriate to Jesus' previous instruction regarding the poor and the Kingdom's overall responsibility toward them.[6] Jesus' own ministry, particularly His miracles, had been focused upon relieving the misery of poverty, sickness, and the injustice of the social order upon the destitute. In an earlier episode in Mark, Jesus rebuked the disciples for their lack of compassion toward the children (10:13–16). In that incident, Mark reported that Jesus was angry (10:14) with the disciples for their improper response to the needs of one of society's lower classes. Now Mark tells his readers that the disciples were modeling Jesus' righteous indignation by being angry toward the woman's wasteful action. As a whole, Jesus taught the disciples that the coming kingdom would bring about a role reversal with the rich and poor, with the first becoming last and the last becoming first. It appears as if the disciples had adopted this new teaching, for in the anointing passage they quote Jesus' own command to the rich young ruler in their rebuke of the unnamed woman. The audience heard that the poor are the disciples' first priority.[7]

Further, first-century readers must have been surprised as Jesus defended the woman over the disciples' stern reproach of wastefulness. As they followed Him, they heard His teaching on the poor. Jesus had corrected them in the past, and now the disciples must have been convinced they stood in agreement with Jesus regarding the society's outcasts. Yet, they were still wrong as far as Jesus was concerned. Here, Jesus' point was not that the observers were involved in "bad work" since they desired to assist the poor. Rather, He was reinforcing the good work of the unnamed woman because she was involved in eternal matters of life that could only be performed at this one point in time.

Although modern readers know they should align themselves with Jesus and the woman, Mark has made that extremely difficult, since the disciples' response appears correct. Nevertheless, they were rebuked, unable to grasp the eschatological implications Jesus placed upon such an extravagant act. Furthermore, they were socially humiliated, since this rebuke took place in the house of a leper in front of a woman. David Rhodes demonstrates how the relationship of Jesus and the disciples is always troubling for Mark's readers.

> To the disciples, Jesus' actions and expectations occur without preparation or direction . . . they are expected to understand something about the rule of God but have never been told in a straightforward way what it is . . . they are simply not prepared for the unpredictable, overwhelming consequences of following Jesus.[8]

This became the readers' identification dilemma. They *must* choose Jesus, yet human logic and an innate sense of fairness made that difficult. The repetition of the second-person pronouns invites the audience to participate in the difficult decision: "**The poor *you* will always have with *you*, and *you* can help them any time *you* want. But *you* will not always have me**" (14:7, italics added).

Interestingly, there is no indication in the story that the woman comprehended the magnitude of what she had done. It is Jesus who elevated her actions to be seen as an anointing for burial. It is only through Jesus' perspective that the reader can comprehend His death as the quintessential act of giving, even above caring for the poor. Finally, Mark is conveying that unless readers integrate Jesus' death into their understanding of the gospel, they may find themselves doing "good work" (14:6) but in opposition to the agenda of God.

2. THE PREPARATION OF THE LORD'S (LAST) SUPPER 14:12–16

The introduction to the passion narrative has been artistically portrayed through Mark's sandwiching two discordant themes around another in 14:1–11. We found in the center of the sandwich the beautiful work of the woman as she sacrificially anointed Jesus for burial surrounded on both sides by the deceptive and traitorous acts of the chief priests and Judas. The issue of time is brought front and center, for the disciples seem to have been treating each moment as if it was of equal importance, not recognizing that His end was rapidly approaching.

Now, the story returns to the temporal aspects of the narrative: **On the first day of the Feast of Unleavened Bread** (14:12). Mark added his own cultural commentary onto its significance as he elaborated: **when it was customary to sacrifice the Passover lamb**. The heads of households brought their lambs to the Temple for sacrificial slaughter at midday on the fourteenth of Nisan (Thursday). The priests would offer the animal, sprinkle the blood on the altar, and return the dressed animal to the family for the Passover meal. The meal was to be eaten within the city limits, so for the time of the Passover, the city limits were expanded to accommodate all the pilgrims. This meal was to be eaten following sunset, thus making this day officially **the first day of the Feast of Unleavened Bread**.[9] Being from Galilee, Jesus and the disciples were pilgrims in Jerusalem at the time of Passover. According to first-century hospitality practices, it was the obligation of owners of homes in Jerusalem to assist them to carry out the Passover according to the Jewish law.

There was no meal more important in the lives of the Jews than Passover, for it was the memorial of a salvation event, was served within the safe confines of a family setting, and was the core of their understanding of being the people of God. Moreover, this setting accentuated the grace being offered by Jesus as the head of this discipleship household. He offered His life to this band of disingenuous children.

The disciples once again seem to have been blind to the discontinuity between their earlier earth-bound viewpoint (anger with the woman wasting perfume) and that of Jesus ("she has anointed me for burial"). Human eyesight saw the unfolding events in a dramatically different manner. Jesus predicted His death, and they saw business as usual. They were oblivious to the fact that unfolding before them was the most important series of events in the history of humankind; they saw it as just another Passover meal.

Jesus' disciples asked him, "Where do you want us to go and make preparations for you to eat the Passover?" (14:12). As mentioned above, since the disciples were pilgrims, the question "where" is quite sensible, assuming they must make arrangements to eat the meal within the city limits. A careful reader might note the strangeness that the disciples ask Jesus where they "might make preparations for you (singular) to eat." But that reinforces that even though this will be a family meal, it was to be seen as Jesus' meal, for He was the head of the household.

So he sent two of his disciples, telling them, "Go into the city, and a man carrying a jar of water will meet you. Follow him" (14:13). Jesus sent two disciples (Luke tells us it was Peter and John; Luke 22:8) with specific instruction of what to look for. It is difficult to tell from the text if this reflects preplanning on Jesus' part or if we are to understand that Jesus was in full control of every aspect of the subsequent events. Nevertheless, the command was to find a man carrying a jar of water (traditionally a woman's duty) and follow him. **"Say to the owner of the house he enters, 'The Teacher asks: Where is my guest room, where I may eat the Passover with my disciples?'"** (14:14). This certainly sounds to have been prearranged by Jesus, for we find that this man knew the title "Teacher" and had already made ready the room. Thus, maybe we as followers today should not be surprised that there are unknown followers in places, even before we arrive on a new scene. **"He will show you a large upper room, furnished and ready. Make preparations for us there"** (14:15). This large upper room (Greek *kataluma*) is the same word used in Luke's gospel at the beginning of Jesus' life when it is written that there was no room in the inn (Luke 2:7). The first-century connation is not of a hotel, for there was not such accommodation. Rather it was a guest room that might hold as many as thirty people. Jesus also described it as a large upper room, which seems to indicate that this man must have been a wealthy householder, not a standard one-room, peasant floor plan. Thus, the only part of the Passover that the disciples had to take care of was the meal itself. The room and the furnishings were already in place. The climactic remark is that **the disciples left, went into the city and found things just as Jesus had told them** (14:16). As had already transpired in 11:1–7 with the triumphal entry, when the disciples followed the instructions of Jesus, they found His words to be prophetic, and thus to be immediately fulfilled.

3. THE PREDICTION OF BETRAYAL 14:17–21

When evening came, Jesus arrived with the Twelve (14:17). There was certainly some time delay to allow for the preparation. The other ten disciples along with Jesus would have arrived, after sunset, for the meal had to be eaten at night (Exod. 12:8). The elaborate description of the furniture and the festive nature of the meal hint that this meal was not the norm for the disciples. It seems to have had the elegance of the wealthier class dinners, which was not unusual for this special meal of the year. **While they were reclining at the table eating, he said, "I tell you the truth, one of you will betray me—one who is eating with me"** (14:18). A Passover meal is lengthy and symbolic as it details the traditional blessings over multiple cups of wine, the reciting of the Exodus event, and the head of the household answers the prescribed questions raised by the children present.[10] Nevertheless, Mark did not report any table talk during the Passover meal, but moves directly into the prophecy of one who will betray Jesus. This is not new information to the disciples (9:31; 10:33), but to date, the agent of the "handing over" has not been identified, and nothing has been said to the disciples that would cause them to think it might be an insider job. The serious nature of the prediction can be heard in the "I tell you the truth" precursor statement. Scholars have noted the remarkable similarity of these words with the lament of David in Psalm 41:9: "Even my close friend, whom I trusted, he who shared my bread, has lifted up his heel against me." The horror of this setting was that **one who is eating with me** would be the one who handed Him over. Eating with one another in the first century was much more than a social act. Eating was seen as a act of acceptance, peace, trust, forgiveness, and even brotherhood.[11] The ominous scent of betrayal in the air would flavor the bread and the wine as it is consumed.

They were saddened, and one by one they said to him, "Surely not I?" (14:19). Interesting how Jesus was about to be betrayed by one of them, and they were the ones who were said to be emotionally affected by the situation. In the midst of the most self-sacrificing act of service in Mark, the disciples once again turned their attention inward to themselves. As Mark highlighted the emotions of the disciples, he was silent with how Jesus was affected by this situation. It would be inappropriate to assume that Jesus was not impacted by this. Rather, Mark saved much of the emotional impact of Jesus' passion and reported it in one cluster of phrases. It is housed in the penetrating insight into the humanity of Jesus as the burden of these betrayals is revealed as He prayed in Gethsemane (14:32–42).

"Surely not I?" is not the expected response from the disciples. More appropriate might be the more investigative "Who is it?" Rather, they were more concerned with proclaiming their own innocence. Moreover, the difficulty with the passage is to extract the vocal intonations of the disciples along with the literal words. Simply, since Mark was originally a spoken story, how would Mark have voiced these words? In Greek, the way a question is grammatically constructed can reveal the expected answer. In this case, the disciples, were confident that Jesus would give a cascading reply of "No" to each of them. Thus, it might be best to translate the question as, "It isn't I, surely!" with the emphasis placed on the word "surely" and an exclamation mark to seal the self-assured verdict of the disciples. Thus, the disciples, who in the preceding paragraph (14:13–16) were reminded that Jesus' words were prophetic, rejected His warning and instead stood on their own laurels.

In somewhat of a cryptic fashion, Jesus continued: **"It is one of the Twelve, . . . one who dips bread into the bowl with me"** (14:20). All of those present at the meal were possible betrayers. And as long as the disciples continued their self-absorbed pattern, they got no closer to discovering the criminal in their midst. Moreover, since they did not know the betrayer's identity, the meal did not take on Jesus' redemptive qualities. Rather it had a divisive effect, as everyone could be guilty of this high crime. **"The Son of Man will go just as it is written about him"** (14:21). The scripture that is referred to here is most likely Psalm 41:9. The disloyalty of those closest to Him did not surprise Jesus, yet it in no way absolved Judas from what he was about to do. Here we find the careful balance of divine sovereignty and human free will. Moreover, since the identity was unknown to the disciples, at this point they all stood equally capable and culpable of the same act. There was enough sin and stain to go around. As the story unfolded, Peter may not have been the betrayer, but he certainly denied Jesus and thoroughly shamed himself in the process. We must relent from looking at others and judgmentally condemning their sins as more grievous than our own. Their wrongs in no way eradicate the blackness from our own hearts. "All have sinned and fall short of the glory of God" (Rom. 3:23). **"But woe to** that man who betrays the Son of Man! It would be better for him if he had not been born" (14:21). The eventual fate of the "Betrayer" Judas was intentionally left vague by Mark, and will only be later disclosed by Matthew (27:3–5) and Luke (Acts 1:18–19).

4. THE INSTITUTION OF THE LAST SUPPER 14:22–25

While they were eating, Jesus took bread, gave thanks and broke it, and gave it to his disciples, saying, "Take it; this is my body" (14:22). In the Synoptic tradition, this is the briefest Last Supper account.[12] Nevertheless, it contains the four verbs that highlight the core of this sacrament: took, gave thanks, broke, and gave. These words echo those of the two earlier feeding miracles (6:31–44; 8:1–10), reminding the reader that in those times as well the disciples missed the divine perspective and the nature of their redemptive emphasis found in the "bread." Bread is the symbolic core of Jesus' ministry, and consistently the disciples seem to have choked on its significance.

In Mark's record, the emphasis may be focused in a slightly different manner than in the other accounts. There is no call to do this in "remembrance of me" as found in Luke and 1 Corinthians. Nor is there Matthew's direct command to "eat" (Matt. 26:26). Rather, Mark's liturgical center seems to fall, not surprisingly, on the death of Jesus "for many" and the eschatological function hinted at in 14:25.

As Jesus took the bread as the head of the meal, He was most likely offering the traditional Jewish Seder blessing upon the bread: "Praise be Thou, O Lord our God, King of the Universe, who causes bread to come forth from the earth" (*Berachoth* 6.1). However, Jesus' words, **this is my body**, will provide a new interpretation. First, they should not be taken literally, as if it was a cannibalistic meal. Rather, the symbolic act might be analogous to the action of Jeremiah (Jer. 19:1–20), when he smashed a jar against the gates of Jerusalem before the Jewish leaders.[13]

This was Jeremiah's way of holding the jar before the leaders and saying, "This is you." Thus, Jesus was holding the bread before the disciples and saying, "This is me." And the body for a Jew was not just the physical makeup, but comprised the whole being. Thus, the breaking of the bread was a symbolic act of what would in actuality take place in His own suffering and death. Moreover, it was a provision given to them just as God provides the very bread of life.

Then he took the cup, gave thanks and offered it to them, and they all drank from it (14:23). The second act of the Passover meal that Mark documents is the blessing of the cup. Apparently this was a common cup to be shared by all participants at the meal, including Judas. According to the later instructions given by the rabbinic writings, there were as many as four cups of wine shared at the meal.[14] It is difficult to determine if this would have been the second cup during the meal, offered prior to the full recounting of the Passover account from Exodus, certainly the appropriate place for Jesus to interject His redemptive interpretation to His forthcoming acts. Or this may be the third cup, which probably occurred when the main meal had been completed as the head of the house would rise from his reclining position with the final blessing saying, "Speak praises to our God, to whom belongs what we have eaten."[15]

"This is my blood of the covenant, which is poured out for many" (14:24). This is one of the few clear passages in Mark that directly discusses the issue of atonement (see also 10:45). It certainly has a sacrificial overtone linked with covenantal language. The best place to find the connection Jesus was making in this Passover meal is in Exodus 24, with Moses' covenant-making service at Mount Sinai that immediately followed the original Passover and Exodus event.

The verbal connections are unmistakable, as the first covenant was inaugurated with sacrifice and the pouring out of blood from bowls, so too, the new[16] covenant. The language of Jeremiah 31:31, 33 is also heard within the words of Jesus: "'The time is coming,' declares the LORD, 'when I will make a new covenant with the house of Israel and with the house of Judah. . . . I will put my law in their minds and write it on their hearts. I will be their God, and they will be my people.'"

The final phrase in 14:24, **for many**, must be treated in its original context, else misunderstanding might occur. One might imply that Jesus' death would only be effective for most but not all. But the word "many" (Greek *pollos*) linked with the earlier phrase "poured out" calls the reader to reflect upon the Suffering-Servant Song in Isaiah 53:5, 6, 7, 11–12. The connections between Isaiah 53 and Mark 14—the death of the lamb at Passover and the death of the Suffering Servant—collide with redemptive force.[17] And the words "for many" should not be seen as exclusive but available for all who choose to participate in the community of the redeemed.

There was an offensive nature to these words for any first-century Jew that we often lose because we have become so familiar to the ritualistic tone of them. Note how Jesus took the wine, blessed, offered, and they all drank from it. Only after it has been ingested did Jesus explain its significance: blood sacrifice! The Law of Moses forbids the consumption of blood (Gen. 9:4; Lev. 3:17; 7:26–27; Deut. 12:16). Food laws demand that the blood be poured as a sacrifice out before the meat can be consumed.[18] Yet, Jesus waited until after they had drunk the wine before He told them its meaning, **"This is my blood of the covenant."** These words must have been highly offensive to the disciples in their original meal. Forthcoming will be even more ominous words as Jesus will predict utter scandal in 14:27: "You will all fall away." It might be fair to say that if a person reads the eucharistic words of Jesus in Mark and feels comforted, it is just possible that he or she has misread His meaning. This is a scene depicting high treason against the King of the Universe. One of them will soon betray Him. Communion is a time for introspection and repentance, not celebration. His call is one of utter obedience to His agenda, His way, and simultaneously not to be ashamed.

"I tell you the truth, I will not drink again of the fruit of the vine until that day when I drink it anew in the kingdom of God" (14:25). Though most of the meal had a sinister tone of death and desertion, these closing words provided the hope of vindication. The word "until" is as important as any other word in the communion liturgy. This is not to be heard as the end but truly as the beginning. Additionally, the wine in that Kingdom will not be simply a restoration of the same, but it will be seen as "anew," the word noticeably absent from Mark's earlier comment on the "covenant." This will be the Kingdom worth waiting for.

5. THE PREDICTION OF DENIAL 14:26–31

When they had sung a hymn, they went out to the Mount of Olives (14:26). In many families, the dinner table at Thanksgiving or

Christmas may be one of lingering conversation long after the meal has been completed. Conversation may be lively and full of story telling. So too was table fellowship in the first century. It was common for participants to remain at the table for hours.[19] The meal would conclude with the antiphonal singing of the Hallel psalms (Ps. 113–118) as they were departing.[20] Psalm 118 is a beautiful climactic hymn of the Lord's faithfulness in the midst of wicked oppression. Scholars often point to 118:17 as shifting this psalm of praise to one with messianic overtones: "I will not die but live, and will proclaim what the LORD has done."

A careful reader would notice that Mark 14:27–31 appears to interrupt the temporal flow of the narrative. The singing of the hymn in 14:26 leads ideally to the group's arrival in Gethsemane in 14:32. Therefore, this paragraph, which describes the prediction of the disciples' desertion, may be viewed as the "travel conversation"[21] interspersed between the psalm singings. But its importance should also give insight as to the prediction of the betrayal of "one of the Twelve" (Judas, 14:10–11) is being compared to the corporate abandonment of all, "for you will all fall away." Therefore, it is worth noting that the Passover meal (more accurately, Mark did not narrate the meal itself but rather Jesus' interpretation of His death's enduring significance) is surrounded on both sides by predictions of betrayal. Furthermore, as the story unfolds, the fulfillment of Jesus' prophetic words becomes a subplot of Jesus' passion; as He faithfully walked to the Cross, the disciples correspondingly fell away.

Jesus wasted no words once they arrived at the Mount of Olives, across the Kidron valley directly opposite the Eastern Gate: **"You will all fall away," Jesus told them, "for it is written: 'I will strike the shepherd, and the sheep will be scattered'"** (14:27). The application of Zechariah 13:7 to this situation is interesting. Just as Judas' act of deceit was said to be "just as it was written" (14:21) so too Jesus told His remaining eleven disciples that the prophet Zechariah held another scriptural key, this time to their future behavior (14:27). This must have been disconcerting to them on this short journey in the dark of night. Moreover, if they were familiar with the larger context of the book of Zechariah, they would know that 13:7–9 describes the destruction of God's people on the heels of God's shepherd being struck down. The same would be true for Jesus' disciples. Through their rejection, desertion, and personal experience of suffering, they would become like Jesus.

Intermingled with the language of denial and failure, Jesus interjected a message of hope. **"But after I have risen, I will go ahead of you into Galilee"** (14:28). Galilee was not only the place of miracles and ministry in the first eight chapters of the Gospel, but it would also become the place of restoration and regathering of the scattered sheep. The importance of this message would be emphasized again as it is intimately linked to Jesus' resurrection by the "young man" (angel) in Jesus' empty tomb (Mark 16:7). This "good news" of Jesus appearing in Galilee was too much of a paradigm shift; the disciples could not comprehend it simply because they were fixated on what they perceived as the "bad news" of Jesus' impending death and their announcement of their willingness to die with Him.

The word for "fall away" (Greek *skandalizomai*, which is the basis for the English word "scandal") must be carefully incorporated into the understanding of this verse. It occurs eight times in the book as a whole (4:17; 9:42–47; 14:27, 29). The final two uses come in our immediate passage, 14:27 and 14:29. The first is Jesus' announcement of what would take place in the lives of each of His followers. Simply, their allegiance to Him would not be able to hold up under the pressure of the upcoming events. As of yet they did not have what it takes to deny oneself, take up their cross and follow (8:34). The second usage confirms the first by Jesus, because it is Peter's rejection of Jesus' prediction; for he said, **"Even if all fall away, I will not"** (14:29). Peter's remark, strikingly similar to his earlier rebuke and correction of Jesus in 8:32, was arrogant. He was rejecting the words of Jesus just as he had so many times previously in the Gospel. He would rather stand on his own bravado. Finally, we might understand "fall away" as Jesus placed it in parallel with the word "scattered" in the end of the quotation of 14:27, which is diametrically opposed to the attitude of a disciple—to follow. Also, Peter clarified its meaning in 14:31 when he said, **"Even if I have to die with you, I will never disown you."** Thus, "falling away," "being scattered," and "disowning" are all synonyms contradictory with the lifestyle of a disciple.

Jesus interjected another "I tell you the truth" saying;[22] its force is unmistakable and its fulfillment is nearly instantaneous—*this night.* **"I tell you the truth," Jesus answered, "today—yes, tonight—before the rooster crows twice you yourself will disown me three times"** (14:30). In spite of all Jesus' teaching and all the best intentions of Peter, he would find Jesus to be a stumbling block. As forceful as Peter's rejection of this idea—**Peter insisted emphatically, "Even if I have to die with you, I will never disown you"** (14:31)—in a few short hours Peter would summon the same intensity to support his oath that he did not know "that Nazarene, Jesus" (14:66–72). The other Gospels simply mention a single crow during the night. Why did Mark describe the rooster crowing twice? The simplest explanation, for those of us who take seriously the tradition that Peter related this story to Mark (see introduction) is that this is the most detailed account, preserved in all its vividness and repugnancy by the chief participant himself, Peter. Moreover, the fact that Peter reported that he heard the rooster crow the second time tells us that the first "hearing" served as a serious warning sign that the sin of denial was looming on his doorstep. Therefore, Peter's denial in 14:66–72 must not be read as mere moral failure or human weakness due to fear. Peter wanted his story to be read as outright denial of the person of Jesus or what the church would later call apostasy. Further, it becomes incomprehensible to say that Peter only "denied" the Lord, at least he did not "betray" Him like Judas. That reading does not do justice to the story that Peter himself portrayed to us. The blackness of the sin of his heart is found in that not only did he reject the prophetic words of Jesus, but he would also discard the warning sign of a rooster. Peter's failure was total and complete. And his own words, preserved by Mark, will not allow any room for justification. Peter's only hope after this disaster in Jerusalem would be the resurrection and reuniting in Galilee.

And all of the others said the same. But the real dilemma for Jesus is that all of the disciples were thinking just like Peter, not like Him. They had a self-confident sense of honor. They seem to have been more than willing to die with Jesus and even die for Jesus. However, if we examine their motives, the real question must be, "Will they die for the same reasons as Jesus?" Throughout the Gospel, the disciples seem to have comprehended the kingdom of God quite differently from Jesus, for theirs was from a human perspective (8:34). Moreover, they saw Jesus as the conquering Messiah-King, and when He comes into His place of glory (for the disciples, a Jerusalem-based throne), they would have liked to serve beside Him (10:37, 41). Jesus had commanded them not to act in this fashion, like the Gentiles who "lord it over them, and their high officials [who] exercise authority over them" (10:42). Jesus wanted them (and us) to adopt a countercultural lifestyle of service and humility (10:43–44), and His example is the core of our calling (10:45). For Jesus, this was a message worth dying for.

ENDNOTES

1. The narrative term intercalation means that Mark has inserted one story inside another to provide interpretive insight. Employing the sandwich metaphor, the bread is the plot of the leaders and Judas, while the meat is the anointing of Jesus by the unnamed woman.

2. Estimates of the number of people at the Passover are speculative at best. The normal population of Jerusalem was probably 30,000 (Joachim Jeremias, *Jerusalem in the Time of Jesus: An Investigation into Economic & Social Conditions During the New Testament Period* [Minneapolis: Augsburg Fortress Publishers, June 1979], p. 84). Scholars estimate that the Passover caused Jerusalem to swell to 44,000–180,000 pilgrims.

3. The passage is somewhat ambiguous in identifying the people present. For at best it only qualifies that a portion of the people were angry. Nevertheless, the larger context is about one disciple, Judas. Furthermore, Bethany has been a place where Jesus and the disciples have been together previously (11:1), as is the Mount of Olives (11:1; 13:3, 14:26). Mark has tied together several previous stories about the disciples and will follow with several more. It seems inconceivable that he would not want his audience to recognize these as the same men.

4. The words "and Jesus said" always serve as an introductory formula to a surprising response by Jesus (see 9:23, 39; 10:5, 18, 38, 39; 11:29; 12:17; 14:6, 62).

5. William Lane, *The Gospel of Mark* (Grand Rapids, Mich.: William B. Eerdmans, 1974), p. 493. Lane goes on to detail that it was also the practice to give as charity one part of the second tithe normally spent in Jerusalem during the feast.

6. See the feeding miracles (8:1–10); Syrophoenician woman (7:24–30); first will be last (9:35–37); cup of cold water (9:41); especially the rich young ruler

(10:21).

7. It is important to note that the other Gospels take a different slant on the moral aspect of this passage. Matthew attributes these reactions explicitly to the disciples. Luke places the words on the lips of a Pharisee, later addressed as Simon. John attributes this to Judas Iscariot. Mark omits all names along with John's side note about Judas's greedy motives. Mark takes this a step farther in that he has fashioned the story in a manner that does *not* give the readers any indication that the thinking of the disciples is morally inappropriate. He suggests that their perspective differs radically from Jesus' thinking.

8. Rhodes and Michie, *Mark as Story: An Introduction to the Narrative of a Gospel* (Philadelphia: Fortress Press, 1982), pp. 90–92.

9. For an elaborate explanation of the timeline and the possible discrepancy with John's chronology, see R. T. France, *The Gospel of Mark: New International Commentary on the Greek Testament.* (Grand Rapids, Mich.: William B. Eerdmans, 2002), pp. 559–63.

10. *Pesahim* 10:1–7 indicates that the traditions of the Seder meal were probably in place in some form in the days of Jesus.

11. One can look at covenants made over meals in the Old Testament: Abimelech and Isaac (Gen. 26:26–31); Laban and Jacob (Gen. 31:51–54). See David Garland, *Mark: The NIV Application Commentary* (Grand Rapids, Mich.: Zondervan, 1996), p. 526.

12. John does not contain the Communion ritual. It is instead subsumed beneath the foot-washing scene in John 13. The other New Testament account is found in 1 Corinthians 11:23–26.

13. This Old Testament citation was found in Garland, *Mark*, p. 526.

14. France, *Mark*, p. 569. See also Lane, *Mark*, pp. 505–507.

15. Paul, in the liturgical passage in 1 Corinthians 11:25, says, "After supper" and then refers to it as the cup of blessing.

16. Mark's gospel does not employ the language of "new" as explicitly found in Luke and Paul.

17. Jeremias says, "Without Isaiah 53, the Eucharistic words remain incomprehensible." See *New Testament Theology: The Proclamation of Jesus* (London: SCM Press, 1971), p. 291.

18. Morna Hooker, *The Gospel According to St. Mark* (Peabody, Mass.: Hendrickson, 1991), p. 342. Moreover, Acts 15:20, 29 seem to indicate that this principle is universal in scope, not simply limited to the people of Israel.

19. Lane, *Mark*, p. 509.

20. According to rabbinic sources, Psalms 113–118 form the *Hallel*, the Hymns of Praise, which were often sung at the Festivals of Passover, Pentecost, and Tabernacles. During the Passover meal, Psalms 113 and 114 would be sung

before the meal, and possibly Psalms 115–118 after it, when the fourth cup of wine had been filled. It is likely that Psalm 118 was the hymn sung by Jesus and His disciples referred to in Mark 14:26.

21. Jesus is often called by Gospel scholars a "peripatetic teacher." This is literally a Greek word meaning one who teaches as he "walks around." This might be a perfect example why Jesus in the gospel of Mark is called "teacher" or rabbi more than any other title.

22. This "amen" formulation saying occurs thirteen times in Mark: 3:28; 8:12; 9:1, 41; 10:15, 29; 11:13; 12:43; 13:30; 14:9, 18, 25, 30.

21

IN THE GARDEN

Mark 14:32–52

1. GETHSEMANE 14:32–42

Several issues converge in the Gethsemane passage. First, with the exception of His cry from the cross, this is the only time when Jesus discussed His suffering in a direct, personal manner.[1] Up to this point in the narrative, Jesus' emotions[2] have been expressed subtly through Mark's narrative commentary. Furthermore, Jesus has consistently referred to His mission in a personally detached, indirect sense by employing third-person "Son of Man" sayings.[3] Thus, in typical Markan fashion, **he began to be greatly distressed and troubled** (14:33). Then, shockingly, Mark interjected the first-person emotional expression of Jesus: **"My soul is overwhelmed with sorrow to the point of death"** (14:34).[4] Notice how Mark prefaced Jesus' words of direct discourse in 14:34 with indirect discourse in 14:33 to give the reader two doses of Jesus' deep anguish.[5] This is a new view of Jesus. The words are so descriptive and draw such emotion that one might envision Jesus hanging from the cross rather than kneeling before the Father in prayer.

Surprisingly, it is in the midst of prayer that the description of His pain is revealed. Again, Mark first provided his own commentary to the reader as Jesus **fell to the ground and prayed that if possible the hour might pass from him** (14:35). Thus, before the readers hear the actual prayer of Jesus, they are told how it is to be understood. Next readers witness Jesus' first-person soliloquy: **"Abba, Father, . . . everything is possible for you. Take this cup from me. Yet not what I will, but what you will"** (14:36). Up to this point, Mark has kept Jesus emotionally detached from His impending death. Now, it abruptly surfaces as the audience hears Jesus not just teaching about His death but actually experiencing His own suffering. This is even more profound when one notes that Mark concealed Jesus' physical pain at the cross from his readers. At no place in Jesus' death scene did Mark provide any commentary into Jesus' physical suffering.

Mark's words echo back to Peter's confession of Jesus as the Messiah. There is a common theme in Jesus' rebuke of Peter, "You do not have in mind the things of God, but the things of men" (8:33), and Jesus' prayer, **"not what I will, but what you will"** (14:36). In the first, Peter attempted to eliminate the tension between the mutually exclusive concepts of Messiah and suffering being put forth as the divine plan (8:32). Jesus firmly rebuked Peter for his appraisal of the situation and told him he was "thinking like men." Now, in the garden, a similar problem arose for Jesus. He would have to make a conscious decision to choose God's will over His own. We are not to mistake the importance of this event. "Thinking like God" is as much a matter of the will as it is a cognitive function. Jesus was being tempted to reject the divine plan and adopt His own. Jesus had to truly come to grips with the mystery of human suffering, and He was entering upon the decisive struggle with evil.

Mark has withheld the personal travail of Jesus until this moment in the story. With the themes of suffering and temptation coalescing in this passage, the readers are reminded of Jesus' original confrontation with Satan (1:12–13); this conflict is not to be interpreted as a one-time occurrence. Mark disclosed that Jesus' temptation to "think like men" had always been confronting Him, in every decision and every action from the initial demonic encounter in the wilderness to His death cry from the cross.[6] And here, at this point, Jesus was wholly approachable by the reader. His guard was down, so to speak, and readers are invited in to see Jesus "made like his brothers in every way. . . . Because he himself suffered when he was tempted, he is able to help those who are being tempted" (Heb. 2:17–18).

Jesus' experience of "grieving unto death" became a firsthand ordeal for not only Jesus but also for the reader. We see and hear Jesus as He separated himself from the disciples (14:35). We watch Him fall to the ground. And the words that He spoke express distress and trouble. We can sense His frustration with the sleeping disciples and hear Him speak words of warning (14:37–38) that go unheeded. We are told that this occurs not once, not twice, but three times with *the same words*. The adverbial repetition of **again** (14:39–40) and **still** (14:41) provides the reader with markers for emphasis, deepening the emotional response of the audience.

Finally, the response of the disciples to all of Jesus' travail comes in two forms. First, they slept. **Then he [Jesus] returned to his disciples and found them sleeping. "Simon," he said to Peter, "are you asleep? Could you not keep watch for one hour? Watch and pray so that you will not fall into temptation. The spirit is willing, but the body is weak"** (14:37–38). The second response is in verbal commentary: **They did not know what to say to him** (14:40). The disciples may have been present to witness this event, yet they provided no comfort and were perceptually ignorant of the real battle being waged.

2. JESUS' ARREST 14:43–52

Just as he was speaking, Judas, one of the Twelve, appeared (14:43). In Gethsemane, there was a plethora of first-person dialogue that essentially slowed down the story time. But in this section the pace escalated as Mark summarized the actions and spoke for all except Jesus and Judas. There will be little time for the reader to think and reflect during this encounter. One must react by instinct or by personal beliefs.

Earlier in the chapter the reader was tipped off that this was a carefully crafted plan on the part of Judas, as "he watched for an opportunity to hand him [Jesus] over" (14:11). He had consulted with the chief priests and obviously received their approval to bring with him **a crowd armed with swords and clubs, sent from the chief priests, the teachers of the law, and the elders** (14:43). Moreover Judas **had arranged a signal** for the troops to know Jesus (14:44). Thus, the disciples[7] stood toe-to-toe against an armed crowd.

Now, our concern is how Mark's presentation may affect the reader's understanding of the event. Though the disciples may not know the extent of Judas's involvement, the reader certainly recognizes his opposition to

Jesus' agenda. Mark introduced him as **one of the Twelve,** and then that name of honor was quickly contrasted with his descriptive name, **the betrayer.**[8] Furthermore, the crowd with swords and clubs came "with him," which throughout the story has been a euphemism for discipleship.[9] Thus, reader hears the ironic overtones; one of the Twelve was in league with the enemy.

Then one of those standing near drew his sword and struck the servant of the high priest, cutting off his ear (14:47). The unidentified swordsman's bold attempt to thwart the arrest would certainly be heard in an animated fashion. Moreover, one might audibly cheer for the disciples as they finally overcame their paralyzing fear and stood firmly for Jesus against His adversaries. They seem to have been more than willing to fulfill their death-pledge made to Jesus just moments before, ready to do battle for their leader.[10] Given the vividness and seriousness of the scene, the personal sacrifice of the disciple(s) must be taken as genuine.

Yet, with emotions strained for everyone in the story, Jesus made an abrupt break in the action. He ignored the swordplay and refrained from any comments on the severed ear or the possible retaliation by the mob. Rather, Jesus answered Judas' betrayal and the discples' counter-attack with a question: **"Am I leading a rebellion . . . that you have come out with swords and clubs to capture me?"** (14:48). These ideologically charged words refocus the attention from the disciples' bravado to the voice of Jesus.

The Greek text begins with the phrase "as against a robber." Jesus spoke directly to His accusers. The disciples simply overheard His show-

BACKGROUND

LĀSTĀS

Concerning this word, allusions can be made to brigands, which is a term given to represent individuals who plundered, often banding together to travel and to operate. These people used violence and guerilla tactics for economic or political gains. Therefore, it is no wonder that *lāstās* were often labeled "revolutionaries." This term mirrors more of a terroristic nuance than a criminal one.

stopping words leveled at the armed crowd, **"Am I leading a rebellion that you have come out with swords and clubs to capture me? Every day I was with you, teaching in the temple courts, and you did not**

arrest me" (14:48–49). The readers witness the powerful effect of the overheard word. In honesty, the question seems out of place in the midst of a chaotic situation. It forces all eyes away from the threefold use of the sword (14:43, 47–48) and onto Jesus' words. Jesus has returned to His didactic method, causing the disciples (and readers) to focus on His emphasis; He did *not* come as a revolutionary. The translation of the word "robber" (*lāstās*) is vital to comprehending what Jesus was conveying to the forces, but even more so to the disciples, who overheard these words. Jesus was not implying He was merely a common thief, but that they came to arrest Him for being an insurrectionist, a revolutionary who posed a threat to Rome. Jesus' use of "revolutionary" would be verbally linked to His earlier Temple action, "My house will be called a house of prayer for all nations. But you have made it a den of *robbers*" (*lāstās*, 11:17). As Jesus was driving out the money changers, He was pointing out the corrupt nature of Temple practice.

In Jesus' use of the quote from Jeremiah, He took it out of the realm of possibility and stated emphatically, "*You* have made it a den of revolutionaries (*lāstās*)." In both Temple speeches—Jeremiah's original and Jesus' reapplication—hearers were being condemned of insurrection (*lāstās*) against God.[11] Thus, one of the charges for which Jesus was crucified is the very crime that people have been guilty of throughout human history—dethroning God's agenda and crowning their own.[12]

Finally, these ominous words: **Then everyone deserted him and fled** (14:50). The predicted desertion became a reality, and in the midst of a crowd of armed soldiers, Jesus was alone. In the original Greek, the last two words are "fled all." The unprepared reader has no time to make a mental or emotional shift as he or she reads, "they all deserted him and fled."[13] Thus, Jesus' prediction of the disciples' desertion (14:27) and its fulfillment at His arrest (14:50) serve as excellent examples that those who cling to self-interests that clash with Jesus' agenda will ultimately find themselves guilty of rebellion; that is insurrection against God.

A young man, wearing nothing but a linen garment, was following Jesus. When they seized him, he fled naked, leaving his garment behind (14:51). After the tragedy of the corporate abandonment of the disciples, we read of this enigmatic boy who ran away, seemingly as an afterthought by Mark. We are uncertain whom this might be, possibly an eyewitness to the events known by the early readers of Mark, akin to Alexander and Rufus who are named as present at the crucifixion in 15:21. There has been throughout the ages a somewhat sacred suggestion that this is a narrative self-portrait of Mark himself in a cameo-like appearance, but we have little or no supporting evidence for this position. However, the passage should not be discarded simply because it may be troublesome for the interpreter, for it clearly teaches several subtle and sustainable truths. First, since this apparently is not one of the twelve disciples, we can draw the conclusion that there were other "followers" who were willing to go this far with Jesus. The call to discipleship though hard, is not reserved for only the spiritual elite, but for all willing to sacrifice for the Master.

Second, this passage of the young man may serve to further demonstrate the disciples' willingness to die for Jesus (14:31), especially if they might rise to the status of martyrs. This young man is said to be wearing a "linen cloth," and the only other place in Mark where this word occurs is in 15:46 in reference to a linen burial shroud purchased by Joseph of Arimathea and used to wrap the body of Jesus. If this detail is significant, it suggests that this young man (another term only used of the angel-like figure at the tomb; 16:5) may not be Mark's autobiographical note, but that he is being painted as the typical mind-set of Jesus' followers. Against all odds (two swords [14:47; Luke 22:38, 49] versus a cohort of soldiers), they came prepared to do battle against their Roman oppressors. They knew that Jesus could strike fear into those who opposed Him. Moreover, in their belief, power and miracles were the hallmark of Jesus' claim to His messianic reign. For His followers, there would be no better time for Him to overwhelm His opponents and take the throne by force. They came dressed for death, prepared for burial, with nothing on but a "linen burial garment."[14]

Now, the worst of all possible scenarios unfolded. Jesus, who wields all the power of heaven, allowed himself to be arrested and ultimately to be humiliated and die, just as He has predicted (8:31–32; 9:31–32; 10:32–34). His words, which earlier fell on the deaf ears of the disciples, were now becoming true.

ENDNOTES

1. S. E. Dowd, *Prayer, Power, and the Problem of Suffering* (Atlanta: Scholar's Press, 1988), p. 153.

2. Prior to 14:32, references to Jesus' emotional makeup have been limited to 1:41 (being filled with compassion and being angry); 3:5 (with anger, being grieved); 6:6 (amazed at their unbelief); 6:34 (having compassion); 8:2 (having compassion); 10:14 (angry); 10:21 (love). Thus, the narrator has related to the reader only how Jesus interacted with the situations of others, not His own situation! Furthermore, from this point on in the Gospel, both the narrator and Jesus are silent regarding Jesus' personal feelings, with the exception of 15:34.

3. See 8:31; 9:12, 31; 10:33–34, 45. This is not to detract from the Christological importance of the "Son of Man" saying, but they also structure the passion predictions with the absence of emotional involvement

4. Just a few verses prior to Gethsemane, in the Last Supper passage when Jesus predicted that "one of you will betray me," it was the disciples who became sorrowful (14:19), not the one being betrayed. Though the words are only cognates, they do express the irony of the disciples' unwarranted sorrow versus Jesus' Gethsemane experience.

5. H. B. Swete, *The Gospel According to St. Mark: The Greek text with introduction, notes and indices* (London: Macmillan and Co., 1920), p. 342. "His words recall Psalm 42:6, 11; 43:5, but his sorrow exceeds the Psalmist's; it is a sorrow which kills." See also Jonah 4:9.

6. The concept of the temptation pervading Jesus' entire ministry originates in the temptation of 1:12–13. Karl Kuhn, "New Light on Temptation, Sin, and Flesh in the New Testament" in *Scrolls and the New Testament: An Introduction and a Perspective*," ed. Krister Stendahl (New York: Crossroad, 1992), p. 112. "When the Markan account of the temptation of Jesus limits his exposure to *peirasmos* to forty days, it is due to an intentional limitation. That which can be truly said of Jesus' entire life on earth is here changed into a vignette."

7. As in previous passages (see 4:35–41), the participants in the arrest are not named as the disciples. They are called "one of those standing near." The perfect participle of "standing" becomes almost a technical term for bystander in the rest of the book (see 14:69–70 referring to Peter's jury in his courtyard trial; 15:35, 39 referring respectively to the mockers at the cross and the centurion).

8. The verbal linking of Judas the person with Judas the betrayer is made with every occurrence of his name in the gospel of Mark. His introduction in 3:19 appears in the initial list of the Twelve. The next time his name is mentioned, just following the anointing passage (14:10), it reads, "Then Judas Iscariot, one of the Twelve, went to the chief priests to betray Jesus to them."

9. See 2:25; 3:14; 4:36; 5:18, 24, 37, 40; 14:33.

10. Peter's pledge to the death (14:31) begins with an emotional marker indicating the reader should understand the words "vehemently." It then contains a first-person dialogue between Peter and Jesus of a promise of faithfulness until death and ends with the other eleven making a similar pledge.

11. The same idol-like worship practice was condemned with the early Israelite trust in the magical power of the Ark (1 Samuel). M. Hengel, *The Zealots*; R. A. Horsley, "Ancient Jewish Banditry and the Revolt Against Rome, A.D. 66–70," *Catholic Bible Quarterly* 43, "Josephus and the Bandits," *Journal for the Study of Judaism* 10 [1979].

12. Note the depiction of His death scene: "They crucified two robbers (*lāstās*) with him, one on his right and one on his left" (15:27).

13. The use of the phrase "deserted him" carries such a wide range of meanings with a Markan focus upon following rather than forsakenness. Moreover, the first two uses of the word in Mark involving the disciples are found in the calling of Andrew and Peter (1:18) and James and John (1:20). In the first we find they *left* their nets and followed Him. In the second call to discipleship, James and John *left* their father Zebedee in the boat with the hired men and followed Him. The clear verbal ties to discipleship are overwhelming. And just the opposite can be said for their desertion. Now they have discovered His messianic intentions and categorically reject Him.

14. R. C. Tannehill, *The Disciples in Mark: The Function of a Narrative Role*, Journal of Religion, 57 (1977), p. 403 n. 38.

ON TRIAL

Mark 14:53—15:15

O nce again, the Markan method of bracketing material highlights the
irony as these trials are structured to take place concurrently. Jesus
first stood alone before the highest Jewish tribunal (14:53–65) and later
before Pilate, the ultimate Roman authority in Jerusalem (15:1–15). Nestled
in the midst of these two life-threatening trials, Peter was cross-examined by
a powerless servant girl (14:66–72).

1. JESUS' TRIAL BEFORE THE HIGH PRIEST 14:53–65

The chief priests finally had
Jesus, since Judas found the
"opportunity to hand him over"
(14:11). **They took Jesus to
the high priest, and all the
chief priests, elders and
teachers of the law came
together** for a meeting of the
Jewish judicial body (14:53).
Yet, **Peter followed him at a
distance, right into the
courtyard of the high priest**

 **KEY IDEAS**

SANHEDRIN

The Sanhedrin was the religious ruling
body of Israel. Originally consisting only of
Sadducees, the Pharisees were added to this
group for political reasons. This elite group
was given the responsibility to conduct the
"internal affairs" in Judea. These affairs
were issues that did not directly affect
Rome or Roman policies. However, if these
"internal affairs" posed a threat to Roman
policy, Rome was quick to assume control.

(14:54). The original Greek reads, "Peter at a distance followed." The
separation of subject and verb with the spatially oriented prepositional phrase
gives the reader an opportunity to perceive Peter's declining follower-ship
as a hint to his questionable discipleship. **There he sat with the guards**

and warmed himself at the fire (14:54). Mark further focused upon Peter's precise location within the courtyard—sitting and warming himself. Peter's action must include a sense of puzzlement as the disciple now rested in the company of Jesus' enemy, the guards.

Then Jesus' trial began. Mark pushed it forward as he explained: **The chief priests and the whole Sanhedrin were looking for evidence against Jesus so that they could put him to death, but they did not find any** (14:55). These human efforts to trap Jesus failed miserably as **many testified falsely against him, but their statements did not agree** (14:56). The failed attempt of the Sanhedrin to convict Jesus in 14:53–65 is portrayed as a comedy of errors, especially since the conspiracy against Jesus had been progressing since the early collusion of the Pharisees and the Herodians (3:6). With years of pretrial preparation, prearranged testimony, and predetermined verdict, these men did not seem capable of carrying out an orchestrated lie. Laboriously, Mark informed his audience of the deceptive acts at work. The threefold repetition of failure to find testimony (14:55–56, 59) reverberated in the ears of first-century readers when their leaders' real agenda was described as false witness (literally, pseudo-testimony).

This judicial travesty continued with an interjection by the high priest: **"What is this testimony that these men are bringing against you?"** (14:60). In the face of witnesses failing to corroborate one another's testimonies, the high priest asked Jesus to respond in this courtroom caricature. As a fitting response, **Jesus remained silent and gave no answer** to the tribunal (14:61). The reader may feel a momentary sense of relief, as another desperate attempt by Jesus' opponents to kill Him (3:6; 11:18; 12:12; 14:1) has been avoided; for according to Jewish law He would have to

KEY IDEAS

BLASPHEMY

The concept behind the term "blasphemy" can be understood generically as exhibiting a contemptuous manifestation toward God exuded through word or deed. While the biblical text institutes death by stoning for this offense (Lev. 24:13–16), only a flagrant profanation of the name of the Lord constituted death by the time that the Mishnah was constructed. For the rest, flogging became the normal means of punishment.

be released for lack of evidence since at least two witnesses must agree on the charges. Then the high priest placed his question in a form to which Jesus was willing to respond: **"Are you the Christ, the Son of the Blessed One?"** For the first time in the Gospel, Jesus answered a question about His messianic identity unambiguously, **"I am"** (14:62).[1]

This mockery of a trial closed as the high priest called upon the council: **"Why do we need any more witnesses?" he asked. "You have heard the blasphemy. What do you think?"** (14:63–64). However, the wording is quite revealing. Note two issues. First, their verdict was to be based upon what they had heard. This of course precluded them from using their own pseudo-testimony as a part of their verdict. To convict Jesus, they could only consider His own words. Second, Mark subtly reinforced his human perception dilemma as the high priest asked, **"What do you think?"** The word "think" (the Greek is *phino*; literally the question should read, "How does this appear or seem to you?") only occurs here in Mark. Though the high priest was asking the jury for a decision, it may be that Mark was simultaneously asking his readers, "How does this appear to you, humanly speaking of course, based on what you have heard?" The verdict: **They all condemned him as worthy of death** (14:64).

The decision was sealed with the shameful attack against the person of Jesus: **Then some began to spit at him; they blindfolded him, struck him with their fists, and said, "Prophesy!"** (14:65). Ironically, again in the midst of Jesus' silent defense, the readers recall the prophetic words from Jesus' thrice-repeated passion prediction (8:31, 9:31, and especially 10:33–34). The opponents demanded prophecy, and the readers hear fulfillment.

2. PETER'S TRIAL BEFORE THE SERVANT GIRL 14:66–72

Immediately, without reprieve, Mark placed before his readers another episode that solidified Jesus' role as prophet: Peter's threefold denial (14:66–72). Placing it between Jesus' twin trial scenes before the Sanhedrin (14:53–65) and Pilate (15:1–15) revealed Peter's denial beyond the mere surface level meaning of the words. First, since we are in the midst of trial scenes, Peter's words should be heard as his own legal deposition entered into these proceedings. Second, it might be fair to say this is the trial of the chief disciple, who throughout the Gospel had been the voice representing the other eleven. As Jesus stood trial before the most influential religious entity in the land and the most powerful political force, Peter was asked to bear witness to what he knows before a powerless servant girl.

While Peter was below in the courtyard (14:66). The transitional word "while" temporally connects these events with Jesus' trial (14:53–65). Simply, what Jesus went through as He faced the Sanhedrin

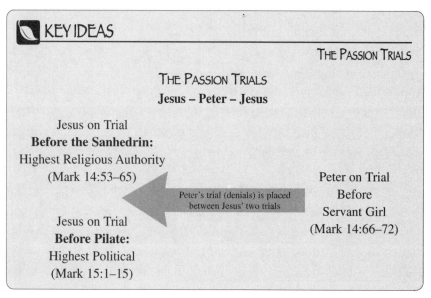

KEY IDEAS

THE PASSION TRIALS

THE PASSION TRIALS
Jesus – Peter – Jesus

Jesus on Trial
Before the Sanhedrin:
Highest Religious Authority
(Mark 14:53–65)

Peter's trial (denials) is placed
between Jesus' two trials

Peter on Trial
Before
Servant Girl
(Mark 14:66–72)

Jesus on Trial
Before Pilate:
Highest Political
(Mark 15:1–15)

was taking place at the same time as what was about to take place with Peter. Moreover, Peter's trial before the servant girl occurred in the courtyard of the high priest's house. This inquisitor is described as the least powerful in the entire story. Earlier, it was her master who accused Jesus of blasphemy, and he and his cohorts had the power to carry out their divisive plans. She, on the other hand, could do nothing but point and speak.

When she saw Peter warming himself, she looked closely at him (14:67). The Greek contains two different verbs for "looking," implying that she initially noticed him and then made a closer examination to make certain that she recognized him. The careful identification of Peter by the woman might cause the reader to overlook the position of Peter: "warming himself." Two items are worth noting. First, this one-word phrase in the original Greek links this passage to the earlier trial of Jesus (14:54), where we found Peter situated near the fire. Now Peter was in the light, most likely centrally located in the high priest's courtyard. Second, Peter found himself in the company of other servants or guards under the control of the Sanhedrin. Peter moved into the enemy's camp, and he followed closer to Jesus than any other disciple, thereby once again showing his willingness to risk all for Jesus. Nevertheless, he is still described as following "at a distance" (14:54) and warming himself with the guards (14:54, 67), placing him in a position ready to fall. **"You also were with that Nazarene, Jesus,"** **she said** (14:67). Jesus was possibly being cast as a quasi-foreigner, which would again be emphasized by the bystanders in the third and final challenge (14:70). There may also have been a note of sarcasm, since Galileans were held in contempt by the inhabitants of Jerusalem. Moreover, the accusation also had a note of association tied to it. Peter was being accused of being "with Jesus," a label of the followers of Jesus (see 3:14, 32, 34; 4:10).

But he denied it. **"I don't know or understand what you're talking** **about," he said, and went out into the entryway** (14:68). The word "deny" occurs in this form only here and in 14:70. But a compound form of the same word has resonated throughout the second half of the Gospel, almost as a predictive forewarning (8:34; 14:30, 31, 72). The direct quote from Peter simply clarifies and intensifies the denial. Peter's denial sidestepped the question; his answer implied a lack of knowledge about an issue rather than a deliberate dissociation from Jesus. That will not surface until the climactic third denial (14:71). Once again, Peter's location was called to the forefront as he left the light and comfort of the fire to draw away from the accusing words and stares of the servant girl. Some early manuscripts include the notation "and the rooster crowed." However, the best historical records available do not include this comment. If the rooster did crow, Peter seems to have been oblivious to the sound.

When the servant girl saw him there, she said again to those **standing around, "This fellow is one of them"** (14:69). Mark seems to indicate that this same servant girl followed Peter to the entryway, and it is there that her second confrontation ensued. She did not address Peter, but the other people present. Possibly from this group were some who participated in the actual arrest of Jesus in Gethsemane.[2] They may have been better suited to substantiate her allegation of Peter's relationship to the band of disciples dispersed during the arrest. **Again he denied it** (14:70).

Peter's second denial failed to convince the bystanders who overheard him. **After a little while**, possibly for consultation among themselves, they posed the final accusation, quite similar in context to the first, but the charge took on a corporate stance. Mark did not indicate how they knew Peter was a Galilean, but Matthew's gospel clarifies that his "accent gives him away" (Matt. 26:73). **He began to call down curses on himself** (14:71). The wording "he began" is not new for a reader of Mark, as it has already introduced an element of change twenty-seven times into the story of Mark (see for example, 1:45; 4:1; 8:11; 8:31; 12:1; 14:33). At this point, Peter's denial took on its new descriptive and verbal actions. This denial employed two synonyms for a twofold oath, thereby intensifying its meaning. Another colloquial way to express it might be, "May God do to me . . . if I am not telling the truth."

Immediately the rooster crowed the second time. Then Peter remembered the word Jesus had spoken to him: "Before the rooster crows twice you will disown me three times" (14:72). As mentioned above, most ancient manuscripts do not have the passage that states the rooster crows the first time (see 14:68). That makes this the first reference to the fulfillment of Jesus' prophetic words (14:30). However, it is vital to remember that the apostolic source of Mark's material came from Peter. Thus, he is the originator of this shameful story about his denials. Moreover, for him to report that the rooster crowed a second time, he must have heard it the first time somewhere in the midst of the first two denials. If that is true, the nature of Peter's denial takes on a completely new character. The rooster's first crow was a divine warning signal given specifically for Peter's ears that he was disregarding the words of Jesus. However, this was not new to Peter, and his hardheartedness (6:52; 8:17) came to fruition as he attempted to save his life, and thus lose it as he testified of his shame for Jesus and all He stood for (8:35–38).

The final statement about Peter may seem simple, but it caries profound overtones. Just above we discovered the blackness of a sinful heart as he intentionally ignored Jesus' predicted sign and rejected knowing

Him in any fashion (14:71). But now Peter remembered the words from Jesus. In Mark's gospel, this was the beginning point of redemption, for deafness and blindness to Jesus are characteristic of a fallen person. Thus, Peter having ears to hear and eyes to see (4:10–12; 8:17–19) was a byproduct of the wonder-working miracles of Jesus throughout the second Gospel (see also Eph. 1:13–14, 18–23). In the end, Peter **broke down and wept** (14:72). His reactions are difficult to pinpoint. The term "broke down" may imply "throw oneself down" but it also carries a wide variety of additional meanings, such as "covering his head," "beating himself," and "thinking about it."[3] But its meaning prepares the reader for the final word about Peter—he wept. The verb in the Greek imperfect tense implies either the beginning of the event "he began to weep," or that the moment of Peter's self-discovery was filled with continual and intense remorse, thus, "he wept uncontrollably." One may pose an interesting question: "What is the difference between the denial of Peter and the betrayal of Judas?" None of the Gospels clearly delineate why Peter's actions were seen as temporary while Judas's were final. But in part, the answer may be found the last phrase, "he wept" (14:72). Peter's failure seems to be a direct result of his attempt to follow Jesus (14:53), albeit "from a distance." In other words, Peter failed under the pressure of following. Judas's actions on the other hand, are presented as a calculated change of allegiance. This is good news for ancient and modern readers alike because it is a gospel of second chances. The warmest words Peter ever heard may have come from the women who returned from the tomb on that first Sunday morning with the message from the angel, "Go tell his disciples *and* Peter . . ." (16:7, italics added).

In summary, some of the chilling effects from Peter's denials come from the narrative sequence itself, for each denial seems to escalate in force as the story progresses. Initially, Peter only rejected the words of the servant girl. Peter's response to the second challenge was a public denial. Finally, when the third question was posed by the entire group of bystanders, Peter called down a curse on himself. In the end, Peter was never directly challenged about his faith, only his associations. But the two are intimately linked throughout the Gospel. Peter never cursed Jesus by name, but the damage was done nonetheless. If Mark's ancient audience was listening carefully, they would have heard that not even the boldest and strongest disciple is immune from failure. One may not be impervious to spiritual collapse, but one cannot escape the grace of the risen Lord Jesus.

3. JESUS' TRIAL BEFORE PILATE 15:1–15

Very early in the morning, the chief priests, with the elders, the teachers of the law and the whole Sanhedrin, reached a decision (15:1). It is possible that the earlier trial (14:53–65) was not the official meeting of the Sanhedrin, but a preliminary "fact-finding" body from which charges would be brought to the official gathering. However, the jury was most certainly rigged in the first trial, and the only reason Jesus was charged was due to His own testimony that He was "the Christ, the Son of the Blessed One" (14:61–62). **They bound Jesus, led him away** and formally handed Jesus over[4] to Pilate with charges that held the death penalty.

"Are you the king of the Jews?" asked Pilate (15:2). The question being asked by Pilate was slightly nuanced: "Are your claims limited to a religious agenda, or do you harbor political ambitions that are a threat to Rome herself?" Jesus' reply was somewhat ambiguous: **"Yes, it is as you say."** The English seems a bit more certain than the Greek, which literally reads, "You say so." Throughout Mark, every human evaluation of Jesus fell short of the truth. Here is no exception. The title "King of the Jews" employed by Pilate is somewhat synonymous with the term "Christ" as it has been used by the disciples (8:29) and by the high priest (14:61). It is a politically and religiously

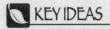
KEY IDEAS

PONTIUS PILATE

Information about this historical figure comes primarily from the Gospel accounts, Josephus, and Philo. Tacitus, an independent Latin historian, makes a brief reference. Based in Caesarea and ruling Palestine, Pilate was a subordinate to the authority in Syria, the commander of the East. Pilate's duty was to control the province by means of Roman policies. However as history reveals, this was no easy task. Eusebius (ii.7) chronicles that Pilate killed himself after he was tried and convicted for the slaughter of the Samaritans, which is chronicled by Josephus (Ant. xvii.4.1.).

loaded term that implies an ambassador of God who is empowered to overthrow the pagan Roman rulers who are possessing the land that was God's gift to the Jews. As used by Pilate, "King of the Jews" implies at the least the possibility of political turmoil, at the most, revolution. But Jesus' less-than-direct answer to Pilate's question left him unconvinced that Jesus was the threat to Rome that the Jewish leaders implied. On the heels of this opening question, another salvo of charges comes from **the chief priests** [who] **accused him of many things** (15:3). Initially, the Jews brought to Pilate the charge of "King of the Jews," but then they brought additional evidence to support the original crime or even entirely new charges to inflame the already tense situation. From this point further, **Jesus . . . made no reply, and Pilate was amazed** (15:5). The word "amazed" (see 5:20; 6:6) carries with it a positive quality coupled with a sense of pondering the meaning of the events. Pilate's amazement appears to arise from the Jews' unbridled hatred for Jesus contrasted with His unquenchable humbleness and lack of self-defense in the face of lies. This may explain why in the ensuing verses, Pilate attempted to set Jesus free.

At this point Mark took his readers on a minor narrative digression regarding the practice of setting a prisoner free during the Passover feast. Though there do not seem to be any extant documents that provide direct historical evidence to this practice in Judea under Roman times, scholars have created a large body of data that documents that this custom is well known throughout the world in many ancient cultures.[5] A man called Barabbas was in prison with the insurrectionists who had committed murder in the uprising. Additionally, Barabbas was an obvious threat to Rome, for his crime of murder was most certainly against a Roman soldier or a Roman citizen. The offense of insurrection was common during the early years of the first century until the Jewish war in A.D. 66–70, since Jews were trying to throw out their pagan rulers from the land and reestablish self-rule under the house of King David. It is possible that the two "robbers"[6] who were crucified beside Jesus (15:27) were from the religious-political party aligned with Barabbas.

"Do you want me to release to you the king of the Jews?" asked Pilate (15:9). The question was posed to the crowd, as will become apparent in 15:11. Yet Pilate knew it was **out of envy that the chief**

priests had handed Jesus over to him (15:9). A cunning politician, Pilate recognized that he faced severe problems. Passover was the time of the year when talk of rebellion saturated the conversation in Jerusalem. His only desire was to survive the feast days without a riot. With tens of thousands of pilgrims in and around Jerusalem and not enough soldiers to fend them off, Pilate chose the path of least resistance from the Jewish leaders. Yet, he was also astute enough to recognize from the many and varied accusations made against Jesus (15:3) that the Jewish leaders' motives were far from pure. Maybe Pilate noticed the contrasting attitudes displayed by the Jewish leaders and Jesus during His interrogation (15:2–5). Perhaps Pilate's political savvy made him alert to the malevolent aspirations of the Jewish leaders. Yet Mark may have been hinting at a larger, long-term issue. The term "envy" summarizes the thread of "rival claims of authority" that has run between Jesus and the Jewish leaders through the preceding chapters. From the time Jesus entered the Temple in Mark 11, Jesus' teaching and the people's popular response (11:18; 12:12, 37) had overshadowed, if not publicly humiliated, the Jewish leaders. But the chief priests stirred up the crowd to have Pilate release Barabbas instead. The man recently arrived from Galilee did not garner enough popularity to counteract the inciting of the crowd by the chief priests.

So, Pilate asked them for a verdict: **"What shall I do, then, with the one you call the king of the Jews?"** (15:12). Pilate's historical role in the narrative may be that of Roman judge, but a more subtle function in the passage is that of an interrogator who enhances the hypocrisy of the Jewish leaders (15:10–11) rather than assigning guilt to Jesus. This was finalized as Pilate declared Jesus innocent of the charge(s) brought against Him. This passage is focused, much like the trial of the Sanhedrin, on Pilate's question and the title ascribed to Jesus: "Are you the King of the Jews?" "One could point out that Jesus' answer to Pilate's question is ambiguous when compared to his affirmative reply before the high priest."[7] Though His reply is in the affirmative, Jesus' response indicated there was a difference in how He and Pilate each defined the term. Jesus was indeed "King of the Jews" (Israel) neither as one who incited rebellion against Rome or as one who will restore Israel to its national splendor, but as one who paradoxically exercised His royal authority by willingly enduring the mockery of His enemies and obediently choosing the way that led to death (14:35–36; 15:25–26).

Mark carefully crafted the narrative to show that in spite of Jesus' answer, Pilate did not believe that Jesus was an insurrectionist.[8] As a matter of fact, since Jesus remained silent (with the exception of His cryptic reply in 15:2), Pilate spoke as Jesus' only advocate. The disciples had abdicated that role. At this point in the passion narrative, no one stood beside Jesus, with the exception of the unnamed woman who anointed Jesus in 14:3–9. Jesus' actions and words had offended His disciples (14:4–5, 27, 37, 50) and enraged the Jewish leaders (14:43, 53–65). Thus, Jesus stood alone. Adding to the sense of Jesus' humiliation, the Roman governor of Judea was the lone spokesman interceding on His behalf.

"Crucify him!" they shouted (16:13). Crucifixion was the normal punishment in the provinces of Rome for insurrectionists and was certainly consistent with the charges being brought against Jesus. But Pilate forced them one last time to make their position clear as he asked, **"Why? What crime has he committed?"** (16:14). The question rang with religious overtones as it literally reads, "What 'evil' has he done?" Consistently throughout Mark, Jesus was accused of "doing evil," and now with the opportunity to recapitulate all the data in this last official trial before Pilate, not one scrap of evidence could be brought forth to convict Him. Ironically, Jesus the Judge has told us that the real reason for humanity's accusation against Him is the evil thoughts in our own hearts (6:52; 7:21; 8:17) or even the enigmatic accusation that an unredeemed mind is under the influence of Satan himself (8:33).

Wanting to satisfy the crowd, Pilate . . . had Jesus flogged, and handed him over to be crucified (16:15). Earlier, Judas Iscariot handed Jesus over to the Jewish leaders (14:10–11; 42, 44). Next the Jewish leaders handed Jesus over to Pilate (15:1) for the furtherance of their own agenda. Now Jesus was being handed over by Pilate to the soldiers for flogging and crucifixion, in order to quell any possible uprising of the crowds.

Though Pilate never wavered in his belief that Jesus was not an insurrectionist ("King of the Jews"), he acquiesced to the pressure of the Jews and sentenced Jesus to death for this crime. The Jews, knowing Pilate would not give Jesus the death sentence for blasphemy, had to unrelentingly push for this trumped-up charge of sedition. The charges brought by the Sanhedrin to Pilate were vastly different from the verdict handed down the night before. The duplicity of the Jewish leaders is commented on by William Lane:

> It must be considered highly ironical that having branded Jesus as a blasphemer because he failed to correspond to the nationalistic ideal, the council now wanted him condemned by the pagan tribunal on the allegation that he made claims of a distinctively political nature.[9]

Pilate had to condemn Jesus for fear that he himself might have appeared to his superiors as a pseudo-insurrectionist in collusion with Jesus against Rome. Likewise, the Jews threatened an insurrection of their own if Jesus was not found guilty. In the midst of the appearance of insurrection (Pilate), the threat of insurrection (Jews), and the pardon of a convicted insurrectionist (Barabbas), Jesus was condemned of a crime of which no one believed Him to be guilty. In this scramble to maintain the religious and political status quo, the passion narrative handed down verdicts on two levels. Read at the surface level, the Jewish leaders and Pilate found Jesus guilty of the charges of blasphemy (religious) and sedition (political), seemingly as an act of their own self-preservation. The second-level verdict is handed down in each reader's personal mental courtroom as he or she overrules Jesus' human judges and vindicates Him of all charges.

ENDNOTES

1. Mark 14:62 reads, "I am." Matthew 27:11 reads, "You have said so" and Luke 22:70 states, "You say that I am." Both seem to soften the messianic claim

Mark is making. This presents the interpreter with an interesting set of problems. Reading Mark 14:62 as "you say I am" certainly explains the other synoptic renderings of this passage. On the other hand, Jesus' stark answer, "I am," would be the more difficult reading, commonplace in the Markan material. Additionally, in these hard readings, the usual pattern of both Matthew and Luke is to soften the words of Jesus. In conclusion, the stronger textual evidence that points to "I AM" cannot be discounted. This makes the passage even more important for Markan Christology. For the first time in Mark, the "Son of Man" phrase does not serve as a qualification or corrective to mistaken messianic perception. Rather, it is a clarification that the Messiah is in fact the Son of Man standing in their presence.

2. The gospel of John supports this thesis (John 18:26).

3. Raymond E. Brown, *Death of the Messiah* (New York: Doubleday, 1994), vol. 1, pp. 609–610, gives nine different possibilities for the meaning of this word.

4. This word in the Greek is *paradidōmi* and occurs twenty times in Mark with a wide range of meanings. But when used within the passion narrative, it takes on the meaning of "betray" (in association with Judas; 14:10–11, 18, 21, 41, 42, 44) or "hand over" (with reference to the Jews 15:1, 10 or to Pilate 15:15).

5. See Josef Blinzler, *The Trial of Jesus: The Jewish and Roman proceedings against Jesus Christ described and assessed from the oldest accounts* (Westminster, Md.: Newman Press, 1959), pp. 205–208; Raymond Brown, *The Death of the Messiah* (New York: Doubleday, 1994), vol. 2, pp. 814–19. Assyrians, Babylonians, Greeks, and Romans outside of Judea practiced this custom; there is no reason to believe that this is a contrived practice in this setting.

6. The term "robber" in 15:27 could mean thief. But the best definition of the term, both historically and within the context of Mark 15, is that of "insurrectionist" or zealot. Thus the robbers and Barabbas were from the same mold.

7. Frank Matera, *The Kingship of Jesus: Composition Theology in Mark 15* (Atlanta: Scholars Press, 1982), pp. 63–64.

8. Jack Kingsbury, *The Christology of Mark* (Philadelphia: Fortress Press, 1983), pp. 126–27, Kingsbury's evidence that Pilate does not see Jesus as an insurrectionist is persuasive, especially when he exposes a third definition for the term, "King of the Jews" as it is employed by the Jews (15:26). Mark and his readers now are juggling three uses of the same phrase.

9. William Lane, *The Gospel of Mark* (Grand Rapids, Mich.: William B. Eerdmans, 1974), p. 550.

FROM THE CROSS TO THE GRAVE

Mark 15:16-47

1. SOLDIERS MOCKING JESUS 15:16-20

The mocking of the soldiers is bracketed by two similar phrases: "to be crucified" (15:15) and "to crucify him" (15:20) Thus, this cruel exhibition is a delay that will accentuate the shame and humiliation just prior to Jesus' death.

The soldiers led Jesus away into the palace (15:16). Just as the judgment of the Sanhedrin led to the mocking of Jesus as a "prophet" (14:65), Pilate's ruling placed Jesus at the will of the Roman soldiers for their time to humiliate Him as a pseudo-king. The soldiers[1] took Jesus into what may have been part of Herod's palace that might today be called the barracks or sleeping quarters. The **whole company of soldiers** (15:16) is a Roman military technical term for the tenth part of a legion, normally containing six hundred troops. It is not likely that that many soldiers were off duty during the feast. However, Mark was certainly relaying that all the soldiers who were available became part of this corporate mocking.

The mocking of the soldiers in 15:16–20 is so blatant that it causes the reader to stumble. The purple cloak, the crown of thorns, the sardonic homage; it is a mock coronation culminating with the words **"Hail, king of the Jews!" Again and again they struck him on the head with a staff and spit on him.**(15:18–19). Matthew reported that Jesus was given a mock scepter (27:29), and this may be the weapon they struck Him with. The spitting served two purposes; first it is fulfillment language of the Suffering Servant from Isaiah 50:6. Second, in the Greek, the word "spit" is onomatopoeic (*em-putuō*). A careful reader can almost feel the soldiers spit in cartoon style: "pthooy."

Furthermore, as this demonstration continued to unfold, Mark has conveyed that no one in the story believed Jesus was a king by Roman standards or a messianic ruler according to Jewish law. Therefore, the reader draws another conclusion—He is a king, but not one by any human designation. His life approached its paradoxical climax: to be honored as God's Royal Son, He must suffer and be shamed by people.

2. CRUCIFIXION OF JESUS 15:21–32

It might be worthwhile to survey the larger context, from arrest to crucifixion, by asking a pertinent question: "How might Mark's readers be affected by the presentation of the crucifixion narrative as a whole?" Surprisingly, they may be carefully protected from much of the physical violence of the crucifixion. Notice how it was almost unanimously performed by individuals who are represented by unnamed, third-person pronouns. Interestingly, Mark gave more attention to the time (15:25, 33, 35) and the place (15:22) of the crucifixion than to the actual event itself. As a matter of fact, the only two direct references to the actual pain-searing act are minimized into a few nondescript words: **And they crucified him** (15:24; see Matt. 27:35; Luke 23:33; and John 19:18 for equally brief descriptions). No information is given about the nail placement, the position of feet, the style of cross, or Jesus' writhing in agony. There is not even a word or comment made about Jesus' blood.[2] Mark provided little commentary that might emotionally charge his audience beyond the bland description.[3]

Assuming that Mark purposely adopted this minimalist approach in which to report the crucifixion and death of Christ, what does it accomplish for his readers? First, from a negative perspective, it prevents the reader from being overwhelmed by the pain inflected by the Jewish leaders or the Romans soldiers. Though each of them was complicit in corporately convicting Jesus, the text does not primarily focus on the pain they inflicted on His body. Next, from a positive perspective, the text calls the reader's attention to focus squarely on the shame and humiliation Jesus received.[4] Any historical understanding of Jesus' flagellation and crucifixion must by its definition assume excruciating pain. Nevertheless, the bulk of the text that describes Jesus' death centers on the verbal insults that were heaped upon Him during this ordeal. Moreover, the description of the physical abuse of Jesus by the Roman soldiers is toned down as the mocking and pseudo-coronation becomes the central core of Jesus' agony (15:16–20).

The verbal injuries escalated. There were three groups of people who mocked Jesus while He was on the cross. First, **those who passed by hurled insults** (15:29). The literal reading of the text is that they were "blaspheming Him." Mark's carefully chosen word "blaspheme" must not be overlooked as he condemned Jesus' accusers of no less than mocking the divine Son of God. The word is used almost exclusively in Greek literature and in other biblical texts of speaking evil against God. Thus, the ridicule being hurled by the passersby was the charge for which Jesus was earlier condemned by the Sanhedrin (14:64). Further, this word sets the tone for the reader as each subsequent mocking is encountered. Humanity once again was blind to the nature of Jesus. As a precursor to the full contents of the insults themselves, Mark described the mockers' body language: **shaking their heads and saying.** This is a short quotation from Psalm 22:7–8[5] and makes another prophetic connection with reference to the suffering of Jesus. This messianic psalm, first mentioned in 15:24, continued to overshadow the following events as the writer returned to it again in 15:31 and in the final cry of Jesus in 15:34. The insult of the passersby was then quoted by Mark: **"So! You who are going to destroy the temple and build it in three days, come down from the cross and save yourself!"** (15:29–30). It should not surprise the reader that this mocking is another unproven charge brought against Jesus in His earlier trial before the Sanhedrin. It was there that witnesses brought an almost identical testimony against Him, but the text makes clear, "even then their testimony did not agree" (14:59). Hidden behind this blasphemy was a declaration of innocence.

The second set of taunts against Jesus came from the chief priests and the scribes who are introduced with the adverbial phrase, **in the same**

KEY IDEAS

Psalm 22	Mark
22:1–21— Sufferings	15:20–27—Crucifixion
22:18— Dividing clothes and casting lots	15:24— Psalm 22:18 quoted
	15:29— Psalm 22:7 quoted
22:7— Insults hurled	15:39— Centurion's confession
22:27— Gentiles' worship	15:43— Joseph looking for the kingdom of God
22:28— The Kingdom of God	
22:29–30— Resurrection	16:6— Jesus' resurrection
22:30–31— Proclamation to God's people	16:7— Command to tell disciples

way (15:31). Mark was making a connection between their words and their immediate predecessors. **"He saved others," they said, "but he can't save himself!"** (15:31). Ironically, this may be the first time that the words of Jesus' accusers were in perfect agreement, yet they were theologically wrong. Being other-centered as He is precluded Jesus from saving himself. But then the mocking went in a new direction from the scribes: **"Let this Christ, this King of Israel, come down now from the cross, that we may see and believe"** (15:32). These words are reminiscent of the demands for a sign (miracle) by the Pharisees in 8:11. Thus, the chief priests and the scribes were demonstrating their ignorance with reference to the nature of faith. Belief is in no way tied to a miracle. The passion narrative of chapters 14–16 demands a faith that is deeply rooted in a man who hung dying on a cross. Most people today would prefer to follow a Messiah who looks more like the Jesus of the first half of Mark. But the death of Jesus will have nothing to do with a Messiah who is not clothed with shame and suffering. It is He who we are called to trust in and faith in whom the Jewish leaders reject outright.

The threefold series of mocking is complete when **those crucified with him also heaped insults on him** (15:32). One wonders what must have been on their minds as even these fellow sufferers spoke ill of Him.[6] Jesus was isolated from even the hint of a supporter, and He was encircled by enemies. As one can see, Mark shaped the crucifixion scene with an overwhelming attention on the mocking from the onlookers and the shame the innocent Jesus endured. Rather, Jesus' death is portrayed by Mark as foretold in Scripture (14:49), in submission to the will of the Father (14:36) and housed in the language of corporate rejection and personal shame. All the while, Jesus was effectively silent and passive.

3. DEATH OF JESUS 15:33–39

At the sixth hour darkness came over the whole land until the ninth hour (15:33). The readers have now been carefully informed of the temporal aspect of the crucifixion above all other elements, darkness from 12 noon until 3 p.m. The paragraph begins with "darkness," and immediately the reader must determine if this is meant literally and in a metaphorical sense. The obvious irony found in the three previous mocking passages is keenly set off by the subtlety of the paradoxical employment within 15:33–39. Is this darkness theme also to be seen as a commentary on the characters' inability to perceive the reality stored in the deeper meaning of these events?[7] Then, following Jesus' heart-wrenching cry, **"My God, My God, why have you forsaken me"** (15:34), the reader encounters another cold act of misunderstanding on the part of the characters. As Jesus cried out to God, the onlookers merely heard Him calling out a human name, Elijah.

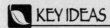

KEY IDEAS

ELIJAH AND THE MESSIAH

Elijah's significance within the Jewish tradition stems from two facts: first, he did not experience death (2 Kings 2:11), and second, Malachi spoke of him as a precursor to the Day of the Lord (Mal. 4:5–6), causing the Jews to see him as the herald of Messiah. In today's Passover celebration, the front door is opened as families await the arrival of Elijah to usher in the messianic age.

The reference to Elijah by the crowd during Jesus' crucifixion (15:35) apparently came from their misunderstanding of the Aramaic word *Eloi* (Jesus' call to God in 15:34).

Mark focused his readers' attention on several other events surrounding the death. First, the actual Aramaic cry of Jesus, ***Eloi, Eloi, lama sabachthani?*** followed by Mark's insertion of a translation of Jesus' words into Greek. The importance of the translation should not be minimized. On one level, it serves as an aid to cross ancient language barriers. For it is quite probable that members of Mark's original audience would not have been conversant in Aramaic. Additionally, it is one of only a few places in the Gospel where the words of Jesus in their original Aramaic are preserved (see also 5:41; 7:34; 14:36), adding an air of authenticity to His final statement (15:34). Yet, modern readers must remember that the original audience would have heard the text of Mark read aloud (see introduction), and they also encountered the Aramaic cry aurally, just as the onlookers at the cross. They could just as easily have misunderstood these words as they were depicted by a passionate gospel reader. But, Mark's addition of the translation prevented the first-century listening audience from making the same aural mistake as the bystanders at the cross. In Jesus' day, Elijah was the one who would come as an agent of God to relieve the suffering of the helpless. The onlookers at the cross had yet to incorporate Jesus' suffering and death as an integral part of the divine plan. They waited for a miraculous deliverance on their own terms. The miracle came in the form of Jesus' death, but since it did not fit their criteria, they failed to recognize it. They assumed Jesus was crying out for deliverance and for the arrival of Elijah, the redeemer of the righteous sufferer.

Moreover, only Mark's audience has the interpretive key of Psalm 22 against which to hear the death cry. They know it to be a poetic story of personal humiliation and suffering, all the while containing a hope of future vindication. As a whole, Psalm 22 is a psalm of victory. The eyewitnesses of the crucifixion misunderstood the last words of Jesus, for those caught inside the world of Mark did not *hear* or *see* correctly. Then, they fashioned His cry of dereliction into their own humanly interpreted appeal. Yet the framework of Psalm 22 will help all future generations into understanding.

Next, Mark interjected an eschatological event; **the curtain of the temple was torn in two from top to bottom** (15:38). The juxtaposition of the tearing of the curtain with Jesus' death allows the reader to view two spatially separate events as intimately connected. From the place of the crucifixion, an onlooker could not see the inside of the Temple. Thus, Mark's readers understand the connection of Jesus' death with the Temple veil tearing; access to God has been made available through Jesus' death, surprisingly spoken in advance of His resurrection (see also Heb. 10:19–21). Also, a subtle yet profound sense of vindication arises. Since Jesus' entrance into Jerusalem in chapter 11, His actions and teaching had forcefully addressed the inadequacy of the Temple as it stood. This began with His Temple-cleansing action in chapter 11 and culminated with His prophetic words regarding the Temple destruction in chapter 13. Now, anyone can find God because the veil is torn.

The tearing of the veil forms a kind of a bookend with an earlier cosmic event in the Gospel. The last time the word "tear" (Greek *schizō*; English "schism") was used by Mark was in Jesus' baptismal scene. When He came up out of the water, He saw heaven "being torn open and the Spirit descending on him like a dove" (1:10). It was at that point in Jesus' life that He was filled and empowered by the Holy Spirit. One wonders if the tearing of the curtain at the death of Jesus meant that now God would soon turn loose on the world the same empowering and purifying Spirit.

Finally, Mark's audience encounters the confession of the centurion, which placed him in the same location as the previous mockers. With that in mind, Mark connected the sensory perception of the centurion with Jesus' death when he ***heard* his cry and *saw* how he died** (15:39, italics added). This is certainly an overt contrast with earlier misperception of the previous bystanders at the cross (15:35). For throughout the Gospel, it has been the sensory mistakes of humanity that have caused the recurring messianic misunderstanding. They have seen but not truly perceived; they have heard but not truly understood (4:12). Now the centurion, based on his hearing his cry and seeing how Jesus died, said, **"Surely this man was the Son of God!"** He was the first human to confess Jesus' true identity.[8]

The person at the cross who probably had the least background to grasp the truth of the event was the Roman centurion. He may have been the only man present without a personal agenda. He was simply acting in obedience to his superior, Pontius Pilate. Ironically, he was a Gentile and the person most directly involved in Jesus' death, for he undoubtedly carried out Pilate's order to crucify Jesus. Surprisingly, it was not Jesus' wonder-inducing miracles or His authoritative teaching that conquered human blindness to His identity. Rather, it was the witnessing of Jesus' suffering and death. The goal throughout the entire book has been to have people confess what God the Father has spoken (1:11; 9:7) and what the demons realize (1:24, 34; 3:11; 5:7): Jesus is the Son of God.

Mark helped his readers see that the crux of the atonement was not only to deal with issues such as human injustice and its outworking of human suffering, important as they may be. Rather, the core problem is that humanity is incapable of grasping the mind of God, and this is due to the fact that humanity is under bondage to Satan. The climax of Mark's story is not that suffering is relieved because of the cross. For just the opposite is called for by Jesus (compare 8:34–35; 13:9–13). True discipleship is a call to share in suffering, shame, and death. Mark carefully reduced the display of physical suffering in order to reveal a worldview so radical that it caused "those who follow Christ to embrace that cruel and shameful death which anyone in his right mind would do anything to avoid."[9]

With a loud cry, Jesus breathed his last (15:37). Jesus relinquished His breath and ultimately His life in utter obedience to the divine will and according to the Scriptures. One might assign blame to Judas for the death of Jesus, or the frightened disciples for failing to protect their master, or the envious Jewish leaders who conspired to put Him to death, or Pilate for issuing the fateful order. But in the end, the text of Mark does not allow that conclusion. It has been clear from the outset that the suffering and death of Jesus has been the central core of the gospel message (8:31–32; 9:30–31; 10:32–34), both scripturally (14:27, 49) and from the will of the Father (14:36). The cross may appear on the surface to be evil triumphant over good, but that is nothing but a false perception. God is in sovereign control, even in the face of the worst of human situations.

Thus, it is within the ironic shaping of the material that Mark chose to reveal Jesus' person and the heart of the gospel. The *titulus* affixed above Jesus' cross read "King of the Jews," yet Mark has conveyed to his readers that His coronation was as no other previous king. His throne was a cross and He died as a king without an apparent kingdom or subjects. The first servant to metaphorically bow at His feet was the Gentile centurion who stood with a bloody hammer in one hand and Jesus' robe in another. The truth of the cross is profound: unless one fully embraces his or her own responsibility for the death of Jesus, there is not a full understanding of the person and work of Jesus.

4. BURIAL OF JESUS 15:40–47

It is difficult to tell if the verses describing the women witnessing the events fit best with the death of Jesus or with the burial. It may be more appropriate to describe them as transitional, for in the end they prepare the reader for the resurrection. Moreover, the women are the only human witnesses to the resurrection account in the Gospel of Mark; thus their presence at Golgotha and at the tomb assure that there have been no mistakes. The tomb of Resurrection Sunday is the same location as the place of burial.

Some women were watching from a distance (15:40). All the disciples had fled from Jesus (14:50) and were absent in Mark's account of Jesus' crucifixion and death (however, see John 19:26). These women are distinguished from the other mockers with a subtle location marker as they were surveying the events **from a distance. Among them were Mary Magdalene, Mary the mother of James the younger and of Joses, and Salome** (15:40). Mark's use of names in the gospel is sparse, so it is significant that they are mentioned here for the first time. Mary Magdalene is well known for her demonic deliverance (Luke 8:2) but also as an eyewitness to the resurrection in all four Gospels. Mary, the mother of James the younger and Joses, has often been identified as Mary, the mother of Jesus, who we heard introduced in similar fashion in 6:3 (Joses is an alternative spelling of the name Joseph), so the precedent has been set to identify her as the mother of Jesus' younger brothers without naming her as His mother. Moreover, what we have heard about Jesus' mother and family earlier in the Gospel (3:21, 31–35) does not indicate that she had been "following" and "serving" from their time in Galilee. Mary, James, and Joses are all quite common names in first-century Palestine, making identification uncertain at best. Salome will reappear with Mary in 16:1. Matthew, in his parallel account identified one of the women at the crucifixion as "the mother of Zebedee's sons" (Matt. 27:56).

Possibly Salome and the mother of James and John are the same woman.

Up to this point in Mark, "following" Jesus appeared to be a male-only group. Mark did not interject the general supporting role women played in Jesus' ministry (Luke 8:1–3) nor the specific ministry of Mary and Martha (Luke 10:38–42; John 11–12). But the description of the women here is interesting: they **followed him and cared for his needs** (literally, "serving" 1:13; 10:45) (15:41). Both of these terms are laced with discipleship language. And these women were only part of a larger following that had been with Jesus since He was in Galilee, maybe even from the inception of His ministry.

It was Preparation Day (that is, the day before the Sabbath). So as evening approached (15:42). As mentioned previously, the time elements of Mark in the last chapter are tightly measured, almost in equal, three-hour increments. Jesus was officially charged by the Sanhedrin at dawn (15:1); at the third hour (9 a.m.) He was crucified (15:25); from the sixth to the ninth hour darkness reigned (15:33). Now, dusk was fast approaching. Additionally, this is the first clear reference in Mark that the day was Friday.

Joseph of Arimathea [was] **a prominent member of the Council** (15:43), which is most likely the Sanhedrin (15:1). He would have needed such a position to approach Pilate.[10] Mark further described Joseph as **waiting for the kingdom of God.** This phrase certainly hints at discipleship language, at least in a subversive way, as did Matthew (27:57) and John (19:38). Roman custom was for the body to remain on the cross, without a burial, as a lingering warning to others. Thus, it must have taken boldness to ask for Pilate to honor the Jewish request for a burial before nightfall (Deut. 21:23).

Pilate was surprised to hear that he was already dead (15:44). The surprise was not the fact of Jesus' death, but that the death had been so speedy. Most crucifixions lasted for many hours if not for days. One must carefully balance the fact of Jesus' suffering with the length and severity of His agony. The passion of the Christ was not based on the quantity of inflicted pain, but on the injustice that the perfect Son of God should suffer *at all*. Thus, Pilate called to the centurion to verify the death itself. **When he learned from the centurion that it was so, he gave the body to Joseph** (15:45). There is an interesting word play in this verse with the preceding one. Joseph asked for the "body" (*sōma*) of Jesus. The word *sōma* can have many meanings, often a living body, even in later New Testament language, the body of Christ, the Church. But Pilate granted Joseph the body (*ptōma*) of Jesus. This word means exclusively "corpse." The resuscitation of a *ptōma* is not possible; He was dead and only fit for burial. Not surprisingly, the only other time Mark used this word is when John the Baptist's disciples came and claimed his *ptōma* after his beheading by Herod.

The hurry of the event is understood, for timing meant everything on this day. Yet the reverence and the respect Joseph had for Jesus stands out. The **linen cloth** was a formal part of the burial process, as was washing and perfume or spices (15:46). Yet the latter may have had to wait until after the Sabbath was over.

Joseph **rolled a stone against the entrance of the tomb. Mary Magdalene and Mary the mother of Joses saw where he was laid** (15:46–47). The only people on earth who had the key to the proclamation of the Gospel were women, for they were the sole witnesses to Jesus' death, burial, and the first to hear about His resurrection. Their witness is central to validating the contents of the gospel message.

<h3 style="text-align:center">ENDNOTES</h3>

Key Ideas Sidebar: Joel Marcus, *The Way of the Lord* (London: T & T Clark Publishers, Ltd., 2004), p. 182.

1. The soldiers under Pilate's control may not have been pure Roman troops but "auxiliaries drawn from non-Jewish inhabitants of neighboring areas" (France, *Mark*, 637).

2. With all the violence (explicit and implied), it should be pointed out that prior to the passion narrative, the word "blood" is only used in Mark with reference to the woman in 5:25, 29. Its only reference in the passion narrative is found in 14:24, with Jesus' words, "This is my blood of the covenant, which is poured out for many." It is at this vital point in the Gospel's closing passages that Jesus expressed the full extent of His mission. The surprising reference to blood in 14:24 and its absence at the crucifixion should alert the audience to this paradox. It also allows the audience to focus on the importance of the Last Supper words of Christ. This may prevent the blood reference from being subject to interpretation based only on the physical death on the cross. Rather, Mark forces the reader to define "blood" by its usage in the Last Supper passage in its metaphorical

and symbolic salvific use.

3. This certainly is not the only explanation for not lingering over the actual crucifixion in graphic details. The first-century literary world did not document the act of crucifixion because of its horrific nature. This observation has become the accepted answer to explain the sparseness of crucifixion accounts in extant literature. However, other compelling factors might just as adequately explain this historical absence.

First, this form of death sentence was almost exclusively carried out on people of no historical importance, namely slaves and rebels. Historians, therefore, should not expect to find documents transcribed and preserved for unimportant individuals.

Second, crucifixion, as barbarous as it was, was employed by Rome exactly for its abhorrent nature—to discourage slaves and rebels from seditious acts. Crucifixion's restraining value upon the lower classes was found in its visual effect upon eyewitnesses and in the ensuing story's graphic oral transmission.

4. For a recent reappraisal of "shame" being the core of the crucifixion, see Joel B. Green and Mark D. Baker, *Recovering the Scandal of the Cross: Atonement in New Testament & Contemporary Contexts* (Downers Grove, Ill.: InterVarsity Press, 2000).

5. This is also a well-established ancient gesture of contempt (2 Kings 19:21; Job 16:4; Ps. 109:25; Isa. 37:22).

6. There is certainly a different "feel" in Mark since he does not include Luke's repentant robber (Luke 23:40–43).

7. Precisely, as a fulfillment of Christ's prophetic words in 13:24, "But in those days, after that tribulation, the sun will be darkened, and the moon will not give its light." Possibly a reference to Amos 8:9 (RSV): "'And on that day,' says the Lord God, 'I will make the sun go down at noon, and darken the earth in broad daylight.'"

8. One must remember that earlier in the Gospel, Peter proclaimed, "You are the Christ" (8:29). But at that time Peter was proclaiming Jesus to be the coming agent of God who would heroically vanquish the pagan Romans who possessed the land of Israel. For Peter, the term "Christ" and the mission of the Christ that Jesus would fulfill could not include suffering and death (8:31–21). Three time Jesus attempted to correct His disciples' distorted misperception of who He was (8:31–32; 9:30–32; 10:32–34), and each time they ignored His corrective. To use Mark's words to describe this perception dilemma, the disciples were blind and deaf. The centurion who "*heard* his cry and *saw* how he died" was the one who finally comprehended Jesus to be the "Son of God."

9. Morna Hooker, *Not Ashamed of the Gospel* (Grand Rapids, Mich.: Eerdmans, 1995), p. 52.

10. The Gospel of John reports that Joseph went to Pilate with Nicodemus (19:39), also a member of the ruling council (John 7:50).

24

THE EMPTY TOMB

Mark 16:1–8

Since the best textual evidence today points scholars in the direction of 16:8 being the true end of Mark, this commentary will put aside the text's critical problems of the Markan ending and follow the caution of T. A. Burkill, who concisely addresses the interpreter's responsibility to the text: "The primary duty of the exegete is to elucidate the gospel as it stands, not as he thinks it ought to be."[1]

The best place to begin is with some initial observations about the effect of 16:1–8 as the ending. First, the story completes without resolution. This has been driven in part by the theme of prophecy and fulfillment. The story ends with three unresolved prophecies[2]: (1) the post-resurrection meeting in Galilee (14:28), (2) the disciples' proclamation of the gospel and their corresponding suffering for Jesus (13:9–13), and (3) Jesus' baptizing with the Holy Spirit (1:8).[3] How does the recurring role of women in the close of Mark impact its resolution? Throughout the narrative, minor characters have provided an immense amount of data to the audience regarding a proper response to the person of Jesus. Once the disciples left the story—as a group in 14:50, and finally Peter in 14:72—the story's hopeful resolution of Jesus' true identity and a corresponding pure faith commitment is grounded in the minor characters of Simon of Cyrene, the centurion, the women, and Joseph of Arimathea. Furthermore, throughout Mark, many of the minor characters were women. Thus, Mark may be summarizing all of these previously faithful characters into these women and then placing the hopes of the readers on their sole response to the resurrection news.

Second, the material in 16:1–8 may have a diverse effect upon Mark's readers. For example the women who were called by name three times

(15:40, 47; 16:1) were portrayed favorably at the crucifixion.[4] Mark used words that equated the actions of the women with the characteristics of a disciple: "served" (translated by NIV as "cared for," 15:41; see usage with reference to the angels in 1:13, Peter's mother-in-law in 1:31, and the disciples in 10:45) and "followed" (15:41; compare 1:18; 2:14; 8:34; 10:52). Also in 15:47, Mark has told his readers that "Mary Magdalene and Mary the mother of Joses saw where [the body of Jesus] was laid," thus making them the only eyewitnesses to Jesus' death (compare 15:40), to His burial (15:47), and to the resurrection announcement (16:6–7).

However, in 16:8 Mark included a series of somewhat ambiguous comments beginning with **trembling and bewildered** (16:8). How did Mark intend his audience to react to this insider information? This ambiguity continues as Mark described the women's distress and that **they were alarmed** (16:5), used previously to describe the turmoil of Jesus in Gethsemane in 14:34. The response of the young man, depicted in angelic fashion in the tomb, begins with a negation of the same intense verb: **"Don't be alarmed"** (16:6).[5] The women's immediate response is they **went out and fled from the tomb** (16:8). Though it could be argued that fear is a natural response to supernatural figures, the response is reminiscent of the disciples' desertion in Gethsemane (14:50) and of the flight of the unidentified naked man (14:52). In neither of these cases was the flight warranted or seen as faithful behavior. Next, via the force of a double negative, the women are depicted as speechless: **they said nothing to anyone** [literally no one]. And this silence was on the heels of the first real command to go and tell the message of Jesus. Finally, Mark explained their silence: **because they were afraid**. The comments in 16:8 give the reasons for the women's actions in two consecutive clauses, first fleeing and then remaining silent. Yet as the story ends, it gives rise to several unanswered questions: did the women ever tell the disciples, did Jesus appear to the disciples in Galilee, and why were the women afraid?

The only way to understand the impact of 16:1–8 properly is to expand beyond the individual verses and to seek answers in the gospel of Mark as a whole. Yet one real difficulty is that the data can move readers easily from one position to another, without a sense of certainty. This may be best illustrated from the writings of Larry Hurtado, who changed his stance regarding 16:8. He wrote,

> [S]ince early Christian tradition (e.g., 1 Cor. 15:5) views the Twelve as influential witnesses to Jesus' resurrection and as leaders in the early church, it is difficult to imagine how Mark could have expected the first-century readers to see 16:8 as indicating that the Twelve were never informed of Jesus' resurrection [by the women].[6]

Hurtado added parenthetically, "This amounts to a change in my own understanding of 16:8 from that reflected in my commentary where I took the verse as indicating that the women temporarily disobeyed what the 'young man' commanded."[7]

Historically, defining the role or function of the women in the narrative has been problematic for commentators. Two schools of thought emerge from the debate. On one side we find scholars who have determined that the text of Mark describes the disciples and the women in a negative light.[8] On the other side of the debate are their critics who say that they have exaggerated the negative portrayals in the second Gospel.[9] They contend that the passages are much more gray, not a pure black and white. For example, the argument can be made that "the disciples [and women] are not simply the 'bad guys,' rather they are fallible followers of Jesus."[10] Is it possible that "the composition of Mark strongly suggests that the author, by the way in which he tells the disciples' story, intended to awaken his readers to their failures as disciples and call them to repentance?"[11] This Gospel is a word of warning directed to each subsequent generation, right down to our present day. No one should trust that simply being in close proximity to Jesus will have salvific merit on its own. Moreover, the book of Mark teaches that even the disciples who were privately instructed in the secret of the kingdom of God (4:11) could not get beyond their own hard hearts (6:52; 8:17–18) without personal repentance and acknowledging the work of the cross and the empty tomb.

Even if we cannot be absolutely certain as to how Mark wanted us to understand the women in the end of the story, one thing is true: stories and events often affect us in advance of our fully understanding their logic or meaning. If that is true, maybe one way out is to realize that "too much attention has been paid to the silence [of the women] and too little attention to the awe. The silence is a function of wonder, subordinate to it, and not the main feature of the narrative."[12] If so, then possibly readers of Mark are asking some of the wrong questions, or at least demanding more of a resolution from the text than Mark was willing to give. And, if Mark's ending is more focused on "reader awe" than on delineating a precise literary meaning, maybe we would be better off identifying what clues are present that would help us understand the historically unsettling passage: **They said nothing to anyone, because they were afraid.**[13]

First, how might Mark be directing his readers? A starting point would be to examine the function of the two *for* clauses in 16:8. The New American Standard translation more clearly translates the explanatory clauses: "*for* trembling and astonishment had gripped them . . . *for* they were afraid" (italics added). Comments in Mark introduced by the word "for" are almost always used to explain confusing or surprising events that have been reported in the previous sentence.[14] Even though it might be unusual to find the "for" clause at the end of the story, there is another instance where Mark's comment comes at the end of his story: Jesus' walking on the water (6:45–52). In this case, the "for" clause of 6:52 does give some insight into the disciples' amazement that is described in the preceding verse. Initially we know that "they did not understand the significance of the loaves," and then we are informed the reason: "for their hearts were hardened." Thus, Mark was giving insider information regarding the real issue, sin.

Next, three emotional responses are reported in 16:8: fear, astonishment, and trembling. Grasping Mark's intent can be troubling, so the best way to unlock the meaning of 16:8 is to examine its closest verbal parallel that comes in the response of the woman with the flow of blood who came to Jesus (5:33). The parallel is both in word usage and in the source of her fear. First, immediately following her healing, she knew that the blood in her had dried up (5:29), and "she fell at his feet trembling with fear." At the same time, once Jesus realized that power left Him, He looked for the one who did this (5:28, 32–33). An astute reader may be asking, "Is the woman fearful of the healing or does her fear arise as a response from the words and searching of Jesus?"[15] Returning to our passage in 16:8, the fear of the women may be similarly linked to the words of the young man in the tomb, especially with the emphasis he places on the promise of Jesus: **"He is going ahead of you into Galilee. There you will see him, just as he told you"** (16:7). R. H. Lightfoot purposed that the purpose of the Markan ending was to emphasize the appropriateness of holy fear in response to God's revelation in the resurrection. He went on to say, "I desire to suggest . . . that it may be exceptionally difficult for the present generation to sympathize with St. Mark's insistence on fear and amazement as the first and inevitable and, up to a point, the right result of revelation."[16]

Mark wanted to establish a connection of faith, human emotion, and the lasting effect of an encounter with a Holy God. How is one to (re)act when his or her life has been impacted by a divine visitation? Many of us would be just as the women, asking ourselves, "What is the nature of the world now that its most frightening force, death, has been defeated?" On one hand one might rejoice, since all things really are possible. Yet, if Jesus was right about defeating death, He most certainly must be right about everything else. All the enemies of the coming Kingdom have (or ultimately will be) defeated. All the unfulfilled prophecies of the Gospel are now not only possible, they seem assured. However, another question may arise in our minds: "What about the nature of my relationship to Him? Where do I stand with Him?" This question makes it easy to see how "fear and trembling" can quickly grip a human heart. If He has risen from the grave, then He is exactly who He says He is—the Lord of the universe. Now that He is back, what will He do to us? This, of course, was Mark's entire agenda addressing the question, "Who is this man and what will He do with a wayward people?" Suppose that the disciples do go to meet Him in Galilee; will they be judged guilty and destroyed? Or will they discover something even more powerful about the Son of God—that He came to earth to make available the forgiveness of sins and the cleansing of our hard hearts?

The real irony of the ending of Mark is that Jesus' resurrection confronted humanity in a new and unsettling way. Throughout the Gospel, the disciples were fearful and faithless because they could not (or would not) grasp the truth regarding Jesus' teaching of His *death*. The women, then, seem unable to have come to grips with His *life*. Life as they knew it just a few moments before appeared quite predictable: the power of the pagan oppressors wins out over the god-fearing meek; hope is again dashed against the rocks of faith; finally, brutal force stays the tide of change. But in the resurrection, life has taken on a whole new dimension. A life of faith with Jesus may not always be visibly victorious and confusion can easily overshadow joy. Moreover, one should not be surprised that failure, if only temporary, is a part of the human experience, even inside the Church. Yet in the midst of darkness, the young man at the tomb shouted out for all future generations to hear, "He has risen; he is not here." These are the words that disarm the power of the evil one and begin our journey to wholeness. Thus, as Donald Juel says, "the successful conclusion of the story cannot be dependent upon human performance,"[17] but upon the in-breaking of the world by the power of God.

ENDNOTES

1. T. A. Burkill, *Mysterious Revelation: An Examination of the Philosophy of St. Mark's Gospel* (Ithaca, NY: Cornell University Press, 1963), p. 5.

2. There is a fourth, the coming of the Son of Man, but that one was never intended to take place within the narrative time of the story (13:24–27).

3. These last two prophecies may be linked, since there are only two times in the Gospel where the phrase Holy Spirit occurs (though different in form, 1:8; 13:11). This may imply that in part, Markan baptism with the Holy Spirit may involve standing faithful when one is delivered up to councils.

Of course, other theological tensions are left unresolved at the end of the story, such as how can the Church's mission go forward without a resurrection appearance? This tension in the early church may have been a prime motivator in giving rise to additional endings to the Gospel as a whole. Persecuted people were being asked to believe and to suffer for Jesus' sake, not based on believing by seeing, but by believing without seeing the risen Savior. Another tension may lie in the Markan interpretation of what will constitute the vindication of Christ.

4. Essentially all women in Mark are presented in a positive light: Simon's mother-in-law (1:29–31), the woman with issue of blood (5:25–34), the Syrophoenician woman (7:24–30), the widow (12:41–44), and the woman with the alabaster jar (14:3–9). The only other named woman is the notorious Herodias (6:19, 22).

5. It is also reminiscent of comfort given to one experiencing a theophany (6:50).

6. Larry Hurtado, "Following Jesus in the Gospel of Mark—and Beyond," in *Patterns of Discipleship in the New Testament*, ed. R. Longenecker (Grand Rapids, Mich.: Eerdmans, 1996), p. 23.

7. Hurtado, p. 23. Reference also can be found in Larry Hurtado, *Mark, New International Biblical Commentary* (Peabody, Mass.: Hendrickson, 1989), p. 283.

8. Theodore J. Weeden, *Mark: Traditions in Conflict* (Philadelphia: Fortress Press, 1971). Werner Kelber, *Mark's Story of Jesus* (Philadelphia: Fortress Press, 1979). Joseph B. Tyson, "The Blindness of the Disciples in Mark," *Journal of Biblical Literature* 80 (1961), pp. 261–68. David J. Hawkin, "The Incomprehension of the Disciples in the Marcan Redaction," *Journal of Biblical Literature* (1972), pp. 491–500.

9. Robert C. Tannehill, "The Disciples in Mark" and Joanna Dewey, "Point of View and the Disciples in Mark," *Society of Biblical Literature Seminar Papers* (1982), pp. 97–106.

10. Elizabeth Struthers Malbon, "Fallible Followers: Women and Men in the Gospel of Mark," Semeia 28 (1983), 33.

11. Tannehill, "The Disciples in Mark: The Function of a Narrative Role." *Journal of Religion* 57 (1977), 393. Malbon slips into the same reading scheme when she says, "I read the data Kelber collects for 'discipleship failure' as evidence of Markan pastoral concern for the difficulty of true discipleship" (*Narrative Space*, p. 179, n. 26). Notice her methodological shift from story level to effect level.

12. Timothy Dwyer, *The Motif of Wonder in the Gospel of Mark* (Sheffield, England: Sheffield Press, 1996), p. 192.

13. The best contributions to understanding the end of Mark's Gospel are J. Lee Magness, *Sense and Absence* (Atlanta: Scholars Press, 1986); Thomas Boomershine and Gilbert Bartholomew, "The Narrative Technique of Mark 16:8," *Journal of Biblical Literature* 100 (1981), 213–223; Thomas Boomershine, "Mark 16:8 and the Apostolic Commission," *Journal of Biblical Literature* 100 (1981), 225–239; Norman Peterson, "When Is the End Not the End? Literary Reflections on the Ending of Mark's Narrative," *Interpretation* 34 (1980), 151–66.

14. See 1:16, 22; 2:15; 3:21; 5:8, 28, 42; 6:17, 18, 20, 31, 48; 9:6, 34; 10:22; 11:13; 14:2, 40, 56; 15:10; 16:4.

15. This is not the only occurrence of fear based upon the words of Jesus. See the following passages: 9:32; 10:32; 11:18; 12:12.

16. R. H. Lightfoot, *The Gospel Message of St. Mark* (London: Oxford University, 1962), p. 97.

17. Donald Juel, *The Ending of Mark and the Ends of God* (Philadelphia: Westminster John Knox Press, 2005), p. 234.

25

THE LATER ENDING(S)

Mark 16:9–20

There is significant manuscript evidence that suggests Mark ended at the conclusion of 16:8. However, this type of conclusion leaves the disciples with an undesirable characterization. A better tactic is to read the closing of Matthew, Luke, and John if one desires a more comfortable sense of closure to the narrative, for Mark has no real "sense of an ending."[1] In light of this characterization, there are two variant endings proposed. The first proposal occurs only in a fourth-century manuscript, "And all that had been commanded them, they told briefly to those around Peter. And afterward, Jesus himself sent out through them, from east to west, the sacred imperishable proclamation of eternal salvation" (NRSV). The second proposal is presented in verses 9–20, shown in the NIV translation.

So what does all this mean? It is the opinion of most scholars that Mark did not end as shown in the NIV, but rather it ended after verse 8. Therefore, in order to bring a more desirable conclusion to this narrative, the gospel of Mark has been concluded and come to modern Christians as the text now has it. Mark does not end with the fear and silence of the disciples, but the narrative concludes with significant events: first, a resurrection appearance (16:9–13), second, a commission given by Jesus (16:14–18), and third, an ascension account (16:19–20). The effects of these three events produce a picture of obedient followers, not dull and faithless followers.

Detailing the arguments for each of the textual possibilities is outside the scope of this commentary.[2] It should be noted that ending the gospel with "for they were afraid" is unusual, and the fact that several different endings were added by the early church shows that it was perhaps regarded as incomplete. The rationales for the variety of Markan endings are just as varied as the textual options: (1) the text was never finished, (2) the conclusion was lost or destroyed, or (3) the conclusion was deliberately suppressed.[3]

There are two main categories of data with which a reader should wrestle in coming to a conclusion about how to approach the ending of Mark—external textual evidence and internal literary matters. First, we will deal with the external issues. The earliest ancient manuscripts of Mark's gospel do not contain anything beyond 16:8. Eusebius of Cæsarea (the famous church historian, died A.D. 341) devised a means of categorizing similar sections of the gospels into a parallel reading (called the Eusebian canon). He was not aware of Mark's text extending beyond 16:8. Jerome, who translated the Greek text into Latin (*Vulgate* circa 400) was not aware of the traditional longer ending.[4] Finally, the longer ending is not found in the two most famous ancient manuscripts, *Sinaiticus* and *Vaticanus* (both mid fourth century A.D.)

Though the external evidence is most compelling, the internal characteristics of the longer reading convince most scholars that 16:9 does not belong to the original work of Mark. First, the content of the longer ending seems to be an amalgamation of resurrection stories from Matthew, Luke, and John. For example, Jesus' appearance to Mary Magdalene alone (Mark 16:9–11; John 20:14–18), the appearance to two other disciples (Mark 16:14–16; Luke 24:13–35), the Great Commission (Mark 16:14–16; Matt. 28:16–20), and the ascension of Jesus (Mark 16:19; Luke 24:50–53; Acts 1:9–11). Given that Mark is the earliest written Gospel, this most likely means that someone after Mark pieced together a resurrection narrative that gives proper closure to the story as a whole. Second, parts of the longer ending that do not parallel the other resurrection accounts may actually be drawn from other stories outside of Mark. Speaking in tongues (Mark 16:17; Acts 2:4–11, 10:46, 19:6) and the strange "snake-handling" language may arise from the similar story of Paul in Acts 28:3–6 and 16:19–20, sounding more like a summary of the book of Acts as a whole than like the material of the first sixteen chapters of Mark. Scholars as well have dealt with the vocabulary and stylistic variation that accents 16:9–20.

Finally, the transition from 16:8 to 16:9 is linguistically rough. In 16:8, the women are the subject, and in 16:9 Jesus becomes the subject. The NIV glosses over this problem by making Jesus the subject of the verb in 16:9, even though the name Jesus does not appear in the Greek text. The grammatical reason for the subject switch is that the phrase "arising early in the first day" demands a masculine noun. Literally, both the longer and shorter endings contradict the silence of the women in 16:8, for they immediately go and report to the disciples what they had seen and heard. In addition, when Jesus speaks, He does so only to Mary Magdalene, ignoring the other women. The writer of the longer ending also awkwardly adds "out of whom he had driven seven demons." This is the fourth mention of Mary in the Gospel by name, so why would the writer wait until now to include this information?

Biblical scholar Morna Hooker states that it would be "remarkable that an accidental break would have occurred at a point where a case can at least be made for arguing that Mark intended to stop."[5] It makes more sense to claim genius, or to use a more theologically grounded term, it was inspiration. This "ending without an ending" forces all readers to evaluate what they would do in a similar situation. Would fear keep them silent? Moreover, the reader has much more information about Jesus than any other participant in the story. The disciples were oblivious to the material in the introduction (1:1–13) and to the omniscient insider information that was made known to the readers by Mark. The readers have traversed the countryside of Galilee, the Decapolis, and Judea. They have heard the words of Jesus with interpretative insights far beyond that given to the disciples ("the secret of the kingdom of God," 4:10). They have even gone firsthand beyond the cosmic veil as they heard the voice of God from heaven (1:11; 9:7) and as the demons shuddered in fear at the presence of Jesus (1:24, 32–34; 5:7). Thus, the failure of a contemporary reader to tell the story would bring on immediate self-judgment and should cause a worse response than Peter's "breaking down and weeping" following his threefold denial. So, who do you say Jesus is?

ENDNOTES

1. Regarding the later ending of Mark, read Frank Kermode, *The Sense of an Ending: Studies in the Theory of Fiction* (Oxford: Oxford University Press, 2nd ed., 2000).

2. Bruce M. Metzger, *The Text of the New Testament: Its Transmission, Corruption, and Restoration* (New York: Oxford University Press, 1992), pp. 226–29; Bruce M. Metzger, *A Textual Commentary on the Greek New Testament* (New York: UBS, 1994), pp. 102–107.

3. These summaries are found in C. E. B. Cranfield, *The Gospel According to Mark* (Cambridge: Cambridge University Press, 1979), p. 470.

4. Jerome was aware of another ending, known as the Freer Logion, a portion of which has been made known through a Latin citation. See William Lane, *The Gospel of Mark* (Grand Rapids, Mich.: William B. Eerdmans, 1974), p. 606.

5. Morna Hooker, *The Gospel According to St. Mark* (Peabody, Mass.: Hendrickson, 1991), p. 383.